There are memoirs that are so inter⟨…⟩ joys spending time within the story they ⟨…⟩. There are others where the author has learned much, perhaps the hard way, and we are wise to listen in, absorbing her hard-won truths. And there are those that are sheer testimony, giving glory to God who seems the real actor in the story's drama. It is rare when a memoir is all three, and Margie Haack's *No Place* is thankfully one of these rare treats that is fun to read, offers profound wisdom, and through which we learn much about the God who is there.

    —BYRON BORGER, co-founder of Hearts & Minds Bookstore

Margie Haack invites us on a journey among the pueblos to find out if the God of her youth was all there was. Along the way she learns to be faithful in the moment, finding that God can be in the center of her life regardless of whether she is in Minnesota or New Mexico. In *No Place,* Margie writes authentically about young marriage, motherhood, and finding God in the everyday.

    —DAN KIRKBRIDE, rancher, politician, and poet

With honesty and courage, Margie Haack tells a story of leaving home, finding home, and making a home. As her story demonstrates, a life of faith is an all-encompassing work of creativity.

    —JONATHAN ROGERS, host of The Habit podcast

To my mind, memoir is a difficult genre, as one must not only share one's perspective but also invite the reader's evaluation of your life. In her first memoir, *The Exact Place,* Margie Haack wrote about her life as a child growing up in northern Minnesota and of leaving home to begin life as a young adult. Now, in this sequel, *No Place,* Margie writes about meeting her husband and of the early years of marriage—including the discovery of 'father issues,' navigating differences in parenting styles, and the difficultly of establishing healthy boundaries as marriage expands to encompass serving and caring for others. Most importantly, for those of us who know the Haacks, Margie also writes of learning to practice a rhythm of hospitality that has remained with her and Denis through all the stages of their life.

    As one scene gives way to another, we find ourselves not only reading about Margie's life but helped to reflect upon how we might live our own. In this sense Margie offers us a well-crafted memoir that is at points humorous, yet always honest and humane. This is a delightful work that I will return to and read portions of for discussion around my dinner table. Thank you, Margie, for sharing your story with us!

    —MARK RYAN, director of the Francis A. Schaeffer Institute

In *No Place,* Margie invites us along on a hard-fought journey of discovering how to be faithful in the ordinary routines of daily life; of applying a thoughtful Christian faith to the fears, doubts, and questions about all parts of life; of seeing and practicing creativity and beauty in serving and caring for others. As a receiver of Denis and Margie's generous, hospitable love over many years, I have learned so much from Margie about loving others simply and well. Her model of welcoming the stranger in for food and unhurried conversation has profoundly shaped our attitudes and practice of hospitality through the years.

—MARY GUTHRIE, Trinity International University

When I read Margie's first book, *The Exact Place,* I reveled in her Annie Dillard-caliber storytelling. I was moved by the unbelievable empathy, wit and clear-sightedness with which she regarded her younger self. It felt like greed to hope that she would plumb those depths again someday and share stories and insight for the station of life I am now in—marriage and parenting. Margie's courage, hilarity and honesty in *No Place* are a strong and gentle hand to hold for the rest of us who are stumbling along as we learn to walk by faith.

—KATY BOWSER, author of *Now I Lay me Down to Fight*

In *No Place,* Margie intimately recounts what we now call the emerging adult years of her life. It's the time in our lives when we investigate and then declare who we will be and what we will believe, for life. It's when we shift from believing whatever our parents said to professing whatever we've investigated and settled on ourselves. Pretty important time of life. Consistently surprised by God's timely farsightedness during these critical years, Margie gradually realizes that God's curriculum for life includes joy and art in addition to the Bible and prayer. This gradual eye-opener changes Margie's life, and Denis' too, as they grow into the mature servants many of us know and love.

—DONALD GUTHRIE, Trinity Evangelical Divinity School

In *No Place,* Margie tells her story of becoming. Weaving through joy and through pain, through periods of confidence and bewilderment, the story's persistent thread is Margie seeking Jesus while befriending others with compassion. Written with humility, humor, and the unique insight gained from a rare path taken, Margie invites us to join her as she finds her place of service "among the hippies and the stoners, the Jesus freaks and the dropouts," learns her rhythm of hospitality as an act of Christian faith, and grows into a profound wisdom.

—NANCY NORDENSON, author *Finding Livelihood:*
　　A Progress of Work and Leisure

NO PLACE

A Desert Pilgrimage

BOOK TWO OF
THE *PLACE* TRILOGY

No
PLACE

A Desert
Pilgrimage

BOOK TWO OF
THE *PLACE* TRILOGY

A Spiritual Memoir by
Margie Haack

FOREWORD BY Andi Ashworth

SQUARE HALO BOOKS

In Christian art, the square halo identified a living person
presumed to be a saint. Square Halo Books is devoted to
publishing works that present contextually sensitive biblical studies,
and practical instruction consistent with the Doctrines of the Reformation.
The goal of Square Halo Books is to provide materials useful
for encouraging and equipping the saints.

Cover painting by Abigail Clark

©2021 Square Halo Books, Inc.
P.O. Box 18954
Baltimore, MD 21206
www.SquareHaloBooks.com

ISBN 978-1-941106-19-8
Library of Congress Control Number: 2021936574

Printed in the United States of America

for Marsena, Jerem, and Sember

Wilderness

EMILY AWES ANDERSON

wilderness true
awakening space
would you draw me nearer
to a spiritual place?
would I be advised
by mountains atremble?
there, do the angels
prepare and assemble?
do deciduous trees
or pines with their needles
improve the acoustics
of praise from the people
to an alpha that's fearsome
omega, and all?
will the fear make me shudder
and marvel, and fall?
if I camp near the water
can I cool there each day
and fish with the fishers
of men by his grace?
and when I'm weary
will my tent prove its worth
with aluminum poles
and spikes in the earth?
if not, will the pillars
of fire and cloud
descend thru the darkness
and around my heart shroud
protection and mercy
despite my poor skills?
his fierce holy love
in the true wild hills.

contents

FOREWORD

I have a file in my computer titled "Letters With Margie." I began saving our correspondence in October 2003. In September that same year, I met Denis for the first time. He came to Nashville from Minnesota to speak for a Friday night gathering in our home, the Art House. Denis was traveling solo, but Margie came in spirit by sending along a card and a gift. I was touched by her thoughtfulness and sent a card back, thanking her for the unexpected kindness. Though I'd not yet met her, I was already a fan of Margie and her work. Her writing was so good and so relatable. I gobbled up every issue of her quarterly, *Notes from Toad Hall*. I was in awe of her ability to write about life in such an authentic, engaging way. She could take an argument with Denis, a crisis somewhere on the globe, and the gnocchi she prepared for dinner, and draw a thread of grace through it all.

A week or two after Denis left Nashville, I read the newest issue of *Notes* over lunch. When I finished my peanut butter sandwich, I went straight to my office and wrote an email to Margie. It is the first in my collection of our letters. I wanted her to know how much I loved her style, her wit, her honesty and sharp insights. I told her, "I breathe a quiet Amen of recognition every time I read your work."

We finally met in person at the Calvin Festival of Faith and Writing in April 2004. By then, we'd exchanged several email letters, each one more detailed and personal than the next. Meeting up in Grand Rapids sealed the deal. We were kindred spirits, friends for the long haul.

I've saved our letters because I treasure Margie's friendship. She's an honest soul and that frees me to be honest in return. We don't keep in touch constantly, but when we do, those words are worth holding on to. I value the history that lives in those letters. Besides, Margie is one of the finest writers I know. I would save a napkin if she'd written on it.

So it was with eager anticipation that I sat down to read *No Place*, the beautifully told story of Margie and Denis' early years together. I was riveted from the start. There is a literary magic running through the pages that makes this book a delicious read, so wonderfully captivating I could hardly wait to see what happened next!

I was a young girl growing up in California when Denis and Margie were starting their life together. I was still a few years away from grappling with the big questions of life. Fast-forward to young adulthood and I was married, hungry for meaning, and longing for a rightness that could only be found in Jesus. When I began to follow him in 1982, the Haacks were already into the flow of their long vocation, inviting people into the living rooms of their life. As I read this latest memoir, I was transported in time. With each story Margie told, I thought about what it would've been like to meet them back then.

I was so taken with the idea, I had to put the book down for a moment and write to Margie. I told her, "After Chuck and I were married in 1975, we spent the next years trying on an array of beliefs and lifestyles. We had no mentors or safe, hospitable places to help us figure things out. I can only imagine the difference it would have made if we had a Denis and Margie in our lives. Having said that, what makes your book so beautiful and believable is that you tell it all true. The struggles of self and of marriage, the realities of hospitality, the shaping effect of family, and the slow formation of faith and vocation in all its mess and pain and joy."

Margie and Denis have traveled many roads to find out if Christianity is worth living and dying for. She writes about this with a striking, emotional honesty. There's no skipping over the hard parts or the funny parts, which makes this book such a compelling and fascinating read. The story rings true.

Such is the beauty of memoir. We have the privilege of stepping into another person's shoes, learning about life through their experience, and along the way, finding the kinship of our shared humanity.

There's a quote attributed to C.S. Lewis that says: "We read to know we're not alone." In *No Place,* I felt that way. Sometimes I wrote in the margins, "I understand. I've experienced this, too."

It is Margie's gift to bring her readers to a time, a place, and a story we did not occupy with her, but somehow make us feel like we were there. We see the landscape, taste the food, and meet the people. We feel the frustrations and tenderness of a young marriage. We know what it is to wonder and wander, and ache to know grace more fully. With humor, humility, wise reflection, and rich detail, Margie has written a stunning book. In the huge dramas and the small moments of delight, she shows us that God is at work in the ordinary and the not so ordinary, drawing us ever more deeply into a love that will not let us go.

Andi Ashworth, author of *Real Love for Real Life: The Art and Work of Caring*

BOOK I

[1965–1968]

Mesas

Mesas are flat-top tables of rock that rise with steep escarpments from the desert floor. Thousands of years ago, some became places of sanctuary for the Pueblo Indians of the Southwest. One established in 1150 AD called Sky Village is still inhabited by the Acoma Indians. On the tops of these sun-drenched, wind-blown land formations, families built adobe homes complete with fire pits and round brick ovens. They collected rainwater in cisterns. From this height they could be warned of approaching visitors by the long feathers of dust in the distance that trailed behind those crossing the desert. A stealthy climb up the steep sides to the top would make the approach difficult if not treacherous for enemies.

Sometimes as a family, we camped at the base of a mesa where a small, cold brook bubbled past our tent and the cottonwoods shaded us from the sun. During the day, we carefully picked our way to the top where we found the remains of ancient adobe walls, blackened fire pit stones, and scattered pottery shards. We tried to imagine what life was like for the people who once lived there. Their mesa villages seemed impregnable, but did not protect them from the changes that were coming.

PROLOGUE

Slap. A blue-covered composition booklet landed on my desk as the professor moved down the aisle, returning our first assignments. It was my freshman year of my first class of my first quarter at the University of Minnesota. I congratulated myself on being the first one in my family to go to college. My test scores and scholarships all pointed toward success. Confidently, I opened the blue book and just as quickly snapped it shut. A red F slashed the title page like a wound.

F. Failed. Flunked. I composed my face to neutral and busied myself with pen and notebook. My geeky neighbor left his booklet open, pretending nonchalance as he glanced at the comments below the neon letter A. I wanted to slap *him*.

This composition class was open only to students who had tested out of freshman English. Simple, simple, simple. I'd been at the top of every English class since the middle of first grade where I learned that reading and writing were as easy as swallowing cooked noodles. Ninety-ninth percentile me.

I had agonized over the assignment: "Write a 1,000 word essay illustrating the use of jargon." *Jargon?* What the heck was that? Back in my room I had opened *Webster's College Dictionary* for the definition. It was the first time I had used this costly purchase since arriving at the university. *Special words or expressions used by a particular profession or group that are difficult for others to understand.* Where had I encountered jargon in all my seventeen years of life? I wasn't an insider to any particular profession or group. Jargon must presuppose a life infinitely more complex and urbane than mine. I was a farm girl pretending worldly experience, but this proved I was a not a player. With that admission, there arose a faint sound of shifting plates, earth tremors of something cataclysmic about to happen.

The only topic I could think of that *might* involve jargon was my knowledge of horses. I knew them better than most, I guessed. I hoped. I had grown up riding and training horses western style. Perhaps this instructor didn't know horses. The language used around barn and corral might work. I began scribbling. It was a long shot. I don't remember exactly what I wrote because I threw the essay away as soon as the quarter was over. I do recall the instructor struck out the words I thought were jargon, commenting that "in season," for example, was the correct and commonly used word for a mare in estrus. It wasn't jargon at all.

I had expected an A. The professor suggested if I rewrote the essay I might get a passing grade.

I faded from the classroom back to my room, where I gathered up the shamed pieces of my ego. My throat ached. My imagination was dry as a dead leaf, so how could I even begin to rewrite the assignment? When at last I turned in another paper, it only proved again I had no clue what I was doing. The professor returned it with a C-. I think he was being generous.

This marked the beginning of my destruction as a student. It has shamed me for many years, even though my seventeen-year-old self probably can't be blamed for not having understood jargon. But there were other signs of disintegration.

If I plan to write honestly about my years of life from college, to marriage, to motherhood, I must begin with another confession. What I've hidden for years may seem ridiculous, but I hope confession might lend some trustworthiness to my recollections recorded in this book, whatever it may cost my reputation.

Until recently, I avoided ever mentioning it. Few know about this because I skillfully dodge the issue and never correct misperceptions when they arise. Ask me where I went to college and I honestly answer the University of Minnesota. When asked what I majored in, I laugh as I answer pre-med. Blood and guts always intrigued me; they still do. Helping the sick and injured fed my quixotic desire to be a hero. With no pause after revealing my major, I quickly ask about my questioner's college and major. Most people eagerly tell you about their experience of higher education. No one thinks much about the details of my history after that. Fine with me!

So this is the Big Secret—I mean, *lie.* I never finished college. I do not have a degree. Not even a bachelor's. Not even an associate certificate. Nothing. I've been so ashamed to admit this that I lie on forms requesting my level of education. Like at the doctor's office or insurance forms or online surveys. Why should they care? Why do they need to know anyway? Sometimes I even fill in the little circle that says graduate degree, because maybe on that day I *feel* like I have a graduate degree.

But here's what's worse. When I entered university the fall after I graduated from high school, I expected to break the high-end barrier of class curves in any course I took—even the math classes I cursed and never understood. My self-confidence had been inflated by holding the top position in my rural high school class of twenty-five students. Knowing my IQ, because I worked in the principal's office and snuck into the files, further elevated my arrogance. National test scores gave me more confidence. I wouldn't have any trouble with college.

By the time I quit the university between my sophomore and junior year, I had dropped courses, failed courses, barely passed others and was on academic probation. I didn't know why I was such a miserable student. Was it moving from a backwater farm to a large city? The stress of working to support myself and pay for tuition? Was it coming from an environment where there was no academic competition? Had I never learned real study skills? Lots of students successfully coped with all these disadvantages and more. Had God arranged this exquisite failure knowing I harbored a kind of pride that, if nurtured, would be more toxic to my life and relationships than I could imagine? Or was he sparing me from a life in medicine that would never fulfill his purpose for my life?

It has taken me these many years to admit I failed as a student and it hurt. It challenged my perception of myself, but I have learned a thing or two. There are many ways to measure a person's intelligence. There are parts of you that cannot be measured by standardized testing or success in formal education. They are not the final litmus test for how smart you are. Another good lesson grew from this stickery thorn: I've tried to never judge a person's worth by her degree. I know someone's education, no matter how long or costly or prestigious, is not a predictor of merit or a measure of success. Nor should it be grounds for worship. When I meet some august, celebrated, degreed person, I want to treat them with the respect and dignity due to any human being who pulls on their pants one leg at a time just as I do.

As I sift through our years spent wandering in the desert, I am determined to be as truthful as memory allows, even if that honesty hurts.

In my first memoir, *The Exact Place,* I wrote about my life as a child growing up in far northern Minnesota on the Canadian border. It was there I struggled to understand the tangled experiences of my family and came to understand that God had no trouble finding me, even in that remote place. When I left home at seventeen to begin my life as an adult, I entered a lengthy stage of wondering whether the faith of my childhood was viable. Believable. Life-giving. They were years spent wandering in a kind of spiritual desert along with my husband, Denis. It was no place I expected to be.

FIRST IMPRESSIONS

Alone in a cold room on a gray December day, I wrapped myself in a blanket and arranged my notes and textbooks on the desk in front of me. It was the end of my first quarter at the University of Minnesota and I was studying for final exams. I was living in a room rented from friends of my parents'. Their home was far out in a western suburb of Minneapolis, two transfers and three long bus rides to class each day. As a commuter student, this isolated me even more from the possibility of friends and activities. No prospects of meeting up with friends at the end of the day because none were close by. No iPhone, no iPad, no nothing in a pre-social media era. And for sure, no boyfriend. The weight of loneliness was depressing; it seemed no one in the world cared about me. I had just turned eighteen and was beginning to think I would remain single and lonely all my life. I prayed God would help me get over that feeling. That he would somehow comfort me and tell me what to do. There was silence. Nothing but the wall heater ticking away.

After an hour of feeling the tragedy of being me, I indulged in something I had never done before. Some call it finger-dipping. It involves using the Bible as a kind of horoscope to predict the future. You close your eyes, open the book, place your finger on a verse, open your eyes, and that's your message from God. If it doesn't give an answer you like, keep repeating it until something pleasant turns up.

The very first verse I hit was Isaiah 54:5.

> For your Maker is your husband—the LORD Almighty is his name—the Holy One of Israel is your Redeemer; he is called the God of all the earth.

Somehow I knew God was speaking to me. I was crushed. I couldn't believe it! I didn't *want* to be God's wife, for heaven's sake. I didn't want to be single.

I tried again. Isaiah 55:8.

> "For my thoughts are not your thoughts, neither are your ways my
> ways," declares the LORD.

Crap.

I wanted a soul mate, a lover. As miserable as the prospect of singleness was, I tried to convince myself that God's plan for me, whatever it was, was best. But it wasn't working. I didn't want his plan. I wanted to serve God, but I was afraid it would include enduring impossible things and would result in everlasting unhappiness.

The desire for someone (other than God) didn't disappear just because I faced the possibility of remaining single. What I didn't understand at the time is that the human desire for love and companionship is good. It's natural. It's how God has made us.

There is a poignant moment in creation when God has Adam name all the creatures. I imagine them as they pass before him in all their original glory. Giraffe. Rabbit. Whitetail deer. Elephant. Lion. Star-nosed mole. Or even the red-lipped batfish. It is recorded that among all the animals, no one was found for Adam. He must have been looking, hoping to find his soul mate, but not even man's best friend, the dog, can fill that role. Then God said, "It is not good for man to be alone," and he created woman to walk beside him—so they could be part-ners, lovers, friends (Gen. 2:18). Together they would patch the hole of loneliness in their hearts. Sadly, because of the broken world we live in, there are no guaran-tees that everyone will find a partner. Following Jesus does not mean we will never be alone or lonely, and yet learning to live with grace and dignity is possible.

I've often wondered if God indulged me by allowing me to land on these verses, proving he controlled even random things like finger-dipping. Or was it a warning to not use inspired Scripture like a horoscope to predict my life? Whichever. It was a lesson I've never forgotten—don't mess around with chance predictors or God may really give you something to think about.

Committing myself to God was not an opening gambit in negotiating the life I wanted. We don't bargain for it. In the future I would learn I could not thwart his grace in my life and that he truly wanted the best for me, but at the time I could only sit with my fears and inner conflicts.

Farther along in that same section of Isaiah where my finger landed on the devastating verse, there is a promise and a comforting message I had not noticed.

"...yet my unfailing love for you will not be shaken nor my covenant
of peace be removed," says the LORD, who has compassion on you.
(Isaiah 54:10)

About four weeks after this incident, at the beginning of the next school quarter,
I moved into a dorm on campus. It was a relief not to juggle my campus job,
classes, and bus schedules. It was then I had my first conversation—if you can
call it that—with Denis Haack, the man who eventually became my husband.
Yes. I know. The irony of the timing.

The first time I saw Denis, a friend pointed him out across a crowded church
fellowship hall. This person mentioned Denis was going to be a freshman at
the university just like me and we should get to know one another. We were
both attending the same Bible conference—a combined group of the Plymouth
Brethren Assemblies in the Twin Cities. The Brethren are a small group of fundamentalist Christians following J.N. Darby, an Anglo-Irish clergyman who in
the 1800s broke with the Anglican church because he believed he had uncov-
ered biblical truths that had been lost since the first century. Whenever someone asked what religion I was, I found it difficult to explain: we were insular,
independent sectarians who considered ourselves to be the only True New
Testament Church by taking no name at all, only calling ourselves *believers
gathered together in the name of Jesus Christ*. No clergy was allowed because we
were all equally together saints, none better than the other. I often suggested we
were sort of like Baptists in order to forestall questions that would need more
complicated explanations. It usually did the trick.

Denis and I didn't personally meet that day, but his image stuck—tall, thin,
dark-haired, soft brown eyes, glasses. He was attractive in a brainy sort of way. I
didn't spot him again on campus until four months later—no surprise, because
I wasn't looking. In the fall of 1965 there were 26,000 incoming freshmen, so
random sightings of anyone you knew were rare. When I did finally see him, we
were registering for the beginning of second quarter.

Before computers were available, scheduling classes was a nightmare. At a
large university like U of M you could accidentally be assigned a class scheduled at the same time as another course you were taking. The English department had so many sections and so many hundreds of students trying to switch
class hours after picking up their schedule that a lottery system was invented to
sort us out. You stopped by an administration window and picked up a random
number that gave you a place in the drop/change class line. When you finally
reached the row of desks at the front, you were able to swap for a section that
didn't conflict with other classes.

I had drawn a number in the three hundreds and standing right ahead of me was someone who looked familiar. It took a minute to place him, but when I realized it was Denis Haack, I wondered why he hadn't acknowledged me. When he paid no attention I thought, *What a jerk.*

As the line inched forward, a new thought occurred: perhaps he is shy. I scolded myself. *As a Christian maybe you shouldn't be so concerned about who speaks first. Perhaps* you *are the one who should learn to show a little kindness and reach out to others.*

Guilt was a well-oiled machine in my soul, but it didn't help me think of how to begin a conversation. Reaching out to him felt risky. Even hello sounded awkward, but finally I blurted, "Don't I know you?" Which is probably one of the stupidest pick-up lines often used by men. And there I was, using it as a girl, and I wasn't even trying to pick him up.

He turned, looked at me solemnly, blinked, and said, "No, you don't," and turned back. Typical. I had guilt-tripped myself into something that wasn't working out. My eyes narrowed as I bored white-hot stink holes in the back of his head and thought of punching him in his little kidneys.

The next day was the first day of classes. I arrived late to chemistry and had to take a seat in the front row of an auditorium that held about 250 students. Sitting just down the row from me was Denis. What were the odds? There must have been at least 10,000 students taking freshman chemistry. This time, I determined, reaching out was not going to come from me. But as the days passed we began to nod in acknowledgement and sit next to one another. The following week I ran into him at the library; he happened to be sitting in the same reference room where I always studied between classes. Was this merely coincidence or did God have a purpose in these improbable meetings? I wondered.

We began to make small talk, sharing insignificant details about one another. Like me, he was also on the work/study program. We were among students who needed financial help and were hired to work on campus in various departments. My job was in a greenhouse on the St. Paul Campus in the Department of Agronomy and Plant Genetics. I cross-pollinated alfalfa plants for research projects hour after hour, alone. Denis was a chemistry lab attendant, working a window where students lined up to check out test tubes and Bunsen burners. At least he got to see live human beings.

Several weeks into the quarter, Denis approached me after class to ask if I would like to go to the youth group that met at his Assembly on Saturday night. I didn't want to seem too eager. The memory of his rudeness in the admin line still smarted so I archly replied, "I'll let you know tomorrow." As if I needed to check my busy calendar. Making him wait would be good for him. The following day I demurely announced I would go. His response was quick and warm, "Good,

I'll let Jim Upton know so he can pick you up from your dorm." Jim was an elder who worked with the youth group.

I grossly misunderstood his invitation. Jim would pick me up? I assumed he was asking for a date. How could he have been such an insensitive idiot to not know this? Although he was socially clueless, he did have a reason for asking. Later I learned he was vice president of the youth group and in charge of recruiting warm bodies. *Bah!* Smoking with humiliation, I told him to forget it, and stormed off, leaving him with a What-have-I-done? look on his face.

That night I reconsidered my response and asked myself, *What do you really want from life?* And then, *What should I want?* I longed to find a special person with whom I could share life, not that I necessarily expected this boy to be The One. My quick temper and hostility seemed to seriously handicap chances of finding anyone who would stick around long enough to learn I had one or two appealing qualities. This could easily become a poison that killed any friendship. At the same time, I wished I could love and follow God closely enough so all these silly distractions could be avoided.

As I examined my reaction to Denis' invitation to the youth group, my response seemed to underscore a certain churlishness of character. I thought about needing a more generous attitude toward people, even toward those who offend me. I seemed disproportionately more hostile and angry than the situation called for. However humiliating, I determined to apologize for being a bitch and promise to attend the study. The next day I told him I changed my mind and would go after all. It's a good thing God is patient toward us, because even as I agreed to go, I was still annoyed enough to look for a way to publicly shame him.

When I climbed into Jim Upton's car to go to the meeting, Denis was in the front seat chatting up another girl. He was obviously interested in this art student from Philadelphia as they animatedly compared the classes they were taking. As I sat in the back seat with two high school girls, I felt invisible. At the meeting, I was pleased to find others I had known from my years of attending Bible Camp. At the end of the evening, I walked out with another boy who offered me a ride back to the dorm. By then, the art student had left Denis' side and moved on to more promising prospects. He suddenly took an interest in me again. "Hey, where are you going? You came with us," he demanded as Keith and I walked out the door. That was my moment. I paused and stared him down, "What's that to you? Just because I came with Jim Upton doesn't mean I need to leave with him." Everyone around laughed, and so did I, knowing with that little exchange I had paid him back in full.

The following Monday, as I studied in the library he walked in with an armload of books and sat down next to me. I smiled. It appeared he was willing to overlook what I had done on Saturday night, and I was willing to overlook his

inept invitation. Despite a rocky beginning, our hearts began to thaw and seeds
of friendship grew. Our shared classes and study times at the library became
something I looked forward to. We studied chemistry together. I began attending the same Assembly he did. Growing up with the same fundamentalist background lent an important understanding of one another and we grew closer.
Looking up to see him walk up the steps of the library to meet me did something
to me I wasn't expecting. This happiness. This talking when we should have
been studying. This reluctance to part at the bus stop.

What attracted me to him were characteristics that have remained over the
years. His approach to life is more linear and objective than mine—this com-
plements my more intuitive nature and love of risk. It pleased me that he was
intelligent and actually enjoyed conversations about things that mattered. We
agreed that making Christianity vital and even radical was important, but we
had no idea how or where that was happening or even if it could make a difference to anything. We just wished the Christian faith was more relevant to all of
life, not only to the privatized spheres of religious practice and morality. We had
no idea we were beginning a journey into spiritual shakedown together.

Denis and I spent the following summer together. We were like otters,
children on endless play dates. On weekends when it rained, we rolled down
the hills of the park and rose sopping wet and crazy. When it was sunny and
hot, we ate picnics on the beach and swam in Lake Bde Maka Ska. We rented
bikes and chased one another down trails. We read together on the couch,
and went to church on Sundays. That winter we kissed at the bus stop and
didn't care who saw.

One special Sunday, I decided it was time to impress this boy with my ability
to cook. He would be so amazed, I knew he would love me forever. I had heard
that the way to a man's heart is through his stomach. Ridiculous. But I sorta believed it. Sundays were a great eating day in my family and I planned to carry on
that tradition. Our family would arrive home from a long morning of worship
wild with hunger. The moment the door to the kitchen opened, a delicious wall
of roasting meat and garlic savory enough to put Julia Child on her knees would
greet us. Mom was always a blur as she appointed tasks; we rushed to heat rolls,
set out butter and jam, toss the salad, slice the roast beef, stir the gravy, mash the
potatoes, and plate the blueberry pie. I would be the same.

That's what I planned for this boy. I would produce a feasting experience
like he'd never known, which was a pretty low bar to jump since his mother was
a disinterested cook. I thought all women cooked with gladness and skill, but his
mother never stood in the kitchen with confidence. Her food was sad and gray
compared to my mother's gorgeous feasts. Years later, I would hear his father
sarcastically tell his mother to get the recipe as he chowed down at another

woman's table. For Denis, I would introduce a new level of cuisine like it was the easiest thing on earth.

In my mother's kitchen, I learned to do many things well under her supervision, but I had no idea how much her presence stabilized my execution. Away from her, my experience wasn't nearly enough to match my conceit as I planned our little Sunday menu. For one thing, I failed to consider that my mother was cooking for a crowd while I was attempting to cook for two. When my family left the house on Sunday morning there would be a seven-pound roast in the oven. All morning it sizzled away and by noon it was perfectly rare in the middle, tender and glazed on the outside. The drippings made at least a quart of delicious brown gravy.

The roast I put in the oven on Impressing Denis Day was the size of my fist. It was all I could afford. When we arrived back from church and opened the door we were engulfed by the smell of charred meat. I ran to the oven and pulled out a shrunken hockey puck. Not one to give up, I cut it in half to find any bits of the tough gray strands in the middle that were somewhat edible. I scraped the burned fond off the bottom of the pan to deglaze and make a little gravy. After it thickened, I poured it into a dish and set it aside while I mashed the potatoes. I asked Denis for help in carrying the dishes to the table. He lifted the plastic gravy bowl from the electric burner where I had placed it, having forgotten the burner was still on. The bottom of the bowl stuck to the surface as the sides pulled up in long strings, and gravy flowed through them in a river and disappeared into the middle of the stove. Toxic fumes filled the air.

I gasped and yelled, "NOOOO!" Denis anxiously raised his eyebrows in a question of what I would do next. I burst out laughing and, relieved, he joined me. There was no gravy to salvage, but we polished off the mashed potatoes and gnawed the meat.

We spent the afternoon together scraping melted plastic off the burner and cleaning out the mess beneath it.

A disaster, but it didn't take long to rectify that first impression and seduce him with my cookies, pies, breads, and roast beef dinners.

THE LONG ENGAGEMENT

The apartment door clicked shut and Denis' footsteps faded down the hall. From behind the drapes, I peeked out as he made his way down the icy steps and across the snowbank piled high between the sidewalk and his car. *You're coming back. You're coming back,* I whispered.

He opened his car door, the headlights flashed on and the car slowly disappeared down the street into the night. *What?! You can't be throwing me away.*

It's past midnight. This is despicable. I'm not going to cry. I'll never beg a boy for anything.

The phone rang and rang. *Where was my mother?* No answer. I needed someone. I threw myself on the bed and covered my head with a pillow. Twenty minutes later I sat up. This was insane.

I was insane.

Against every instinct that made me one tough woman, I picked up the phone again, but this time I didn't call Mom. Before the second ring, Denis picked up. "Margie? Margie?" I couldn't speak. I could only choke. "Calm down. Go to the window and watch, I'm coming back."

Nothing I had experienced was stockpiled against a day of rejection and loss. Who is prepared, anyway, to lose someone you planned to keep forever?

Early in life, I concluded that losing was synonymous with weakness or doing something wrong. You hadn't tried hard enough. You weren't in the right spot to catch the pass. You hadn't read the right book or prayed the right prayer. The possibility of loss inspired me to keep on practicing and winning. Grades. Sports. Horse races. Games. Friends. Even knowing the shortest distance to your destination was important. Being right and righteous about the smallest thing confirmed you were strong and you were a winner.

I never intended to fall in love with this boy, not at the beginning anyway. He wasn't my type. I wanted an athlete, a hockey player, a big man of few words who rescued people in trouble, more like a Marvel comic book hero. But here he was, slender, fine-boned, brilliant, and far wittier than me. He was someone who knew God and wanted to talk about life and meaning, not just make out in the back seat of a car.

Leaving home and beginning college began to eat away at the idea I was always going to be a strong winner. Life was subtly shifting to the losing side of the ledger and it was making me apprehensive. It was bad enough to have almost flunked out of school. That most certainly would have happened, except before it did, I quit. But here, in love? I never expected to get beat up by life like a country western song where you lose everything and then your dog gets hit by a car. What was I doing calling a boy who had just cut me loose, begging him to come back? Lord have mercy.

One year earlier. Evening. Things were still not going well for me academically. I had dropped out of advanced calculus and was falling behind in political science. I couldn't seem to keep up and my grades were suffering. I knew I'd be in trouble if I didn't pull them up.

Denis and I were studying together side by side when he reached for my hand. Out of the corner of my eye, I knew he was watching me. It was making it hard to concentrate. "I have something important to tell you." I knew exactly what he was going to say and couldn't help grinning, but I wouldn't look at him and pretended to be engrossed in my book. Finally he blurted, "I love you." I grinned more widely. I may have even laughed. It was exactly what I hoped he would say, and it amused me that he was afraid to say it.

I had already fallen in love so hard I began to worry I had made him an idol. He was far more important to me than anyone else in the universe, and guilt kicked in. He was everything I wanted in a lover after all. I couldn't think of living without him, so it was hard to tell whether he was God's blessing or a colossal temptation. I kept thinking about that Scripture my finger landed on: *your Maker is your husband.* I prayed obsessively about our relationship. I even asked God to take Denis away if it was not his will for us to be together. I told God I was too far gone. I couldn't break it off myself. He would need to do it for me. As we steadily grew in commitment to one another, there was no sign we should break it off.

I had a dream of becoming a medical doctor. I knew I would love treating illnesses and injuries. I was fascinated with the way the human body functioned. I even loved the smells of doctors' offices and hospitals. That was why my declared major was pre-med. However, when Denis told me he could not stand to even think about blood or see me take up *any* vocation related to medicine, I was willing to give up the dream. I know later it became a moot issue, but it was something I had to think about. If he felt that way, for him, I was willing to give it up.

There was one thing in my life that made me believe if anyone knew about it, they would never be able to love me. For the sake of full disclosure I felt compelled to tell him my secret. As a child I had been diagnosed with psoriasis. It wasn't nearly as severe as some experience, but it did cause patches of rough, scaling skin on my arms and legs. I hated it and I hated the commercials advertising medications and calling it "the heartbreak of psoriasis."

As I told him his eyes widened in disbelief. "How," he asked, "could you think that would ever make a difference in my love for you?" That did it. I knew then I wanted to be with him forever. Who else on earth could love me like this?

My mother, of course. She did love me. Not my stepfather. He clearly did not like me. He often called me *straight hair and curly teeth*, which had some truth in it. I did not look like my beautiful mother with her full head of auburn hair. And indeed, my teeth did not fit properly in my small mouth. When I became an adolescent, it hurt more when he mocked my curves and called my developing breasts *peas in a harness*. On the outside, I had to laugh it off, but such things have a lasting effect on a person's perception of themselves. It caused me to doubt myself in the wrong places at the wrong times. But perhaps the most surprising thing for me was how easy it was to be with Denis. We had grown to trust one another and it gave us a sense of safety.

Denis proposed during final exam week that spring. Again, I sensed it was coming—I guess it wasn't difficult to figure out. After our initial struggles, it had not taken long to realize we were meant for one another. We had talked about marriage but were not formally engaged because the timing of the wedding was an issue. We wanted to wait until his missionary parents could attend, but they were not due back from the Philippines for almost two years. We were sitting in the student center where I was studying for a biology test, cramming genus and species. Flash-carding myself. He kept pestering me to come outside to the patio, saying he needed to tell me something important. When I reluctantly walked out to a bench and sat down, he knelt in front of me, took my hand, and asked me to be his wife. The setting for such a decision wasn't romantic but I didn't care. He beamed as I threw my arms around him and said, "Yes. Always and forever."

I was already on academic probation while I waited for my third quarter grades to come out. When they arrived, I was not surprised at how bad they were, but it hurt deeply. Somehow I still couldn't make education work and I didn't really understand why. Rather than waiting to be kicked out, I decided not to go back. I kept my reason for dropping out a secret from everyone except Denis. Since we were now publicly engaged, it was more acceptable for me to quit school, get a job, and save money for our marriage. I was fortunate to find a job at the press office on campus. It allowed us to see each other more often as Denis continued his studies.

It was a long time before his parents would return. There was no chance they would come back earlier, since Denis' father had always made it clear that his missionary work took precedence over family. We wanted to include them in the wedding, so we waited, longing for the day when as evening came we would not need to part. As the months slowly passed we began experiencing more tension, including sexual. Everything was on hold. Then Denis began having doubts. He was no longer certain of marriage.

Eighteen months had passed since we first met, knew we were going to marry, and became formally engaged. On a beautiful fall day Denis stopped by the office where I worked. This was not unusual. He would surprise me and I loved stepping into the hall to chat for a few minutes. On that day, he began our conversation, saying, "I'd like us to take a break from seeing one another." This was so stunning it was like falling through a rotted bridge into flood waters. It was difficult to even comprehend what he was saying. "Not seeing?" Did that mean no phone calls, no attending church together on Sunday? No contact? Nothing? Yes. When I asked, "But why?" he couldn't give an explanation. By the time he left, I agreed not to see him for two months while he thought things over.

The work day was not finished and I had to get a grip on myself. I returned to my desk and tried to keep typing as the pages blurred in front of me. That day as I rode the bus home in a fog of confusion and grief, I forgot to get off at my stop and rode it to the end of the line. When I looked up I was the only one on board and the driver was saying, "Miss? Miss? This is the end. Are you okay? You need to get off." Bewildered, having no idea where we were, I asked if he was returning on the same route. He kindly let me ride back.

During our time of separation I prayed, cried a lot, and choked every impulse to contact him. I worried he might not be thinking about us at all, but was having fun with his friends, glad to be free of me. At least my roommates were sympathetic. They thought he was nuts. I began attending another small Assembly, but people were so closely connected everyone knew we were a couple and there were questions. "Where's Denis?" people asked. They knew something was wrong, but I didn't know how to answer. I was angry at myself for hurting so much, for being so emotional. I especially hated this vulnerability because I saw it as one of my weaknesses. I pleaded with God to take away my love for Denis. I pleaded with him to dial back the hurt. I promised I didn't want to marry at all, not even Denis, if God had not blessed it.

We had set a date, an evening when we would see one another and reevaluate. We planned dinner and a movie. I bought a seductive mini dress. Soft brown velvet with a white lace collar—hardly Victorian, as the hem crept up my thighs. We chatted through dinner and left for the movie. We returned late to my apartment and sat on the couch. I bit my tongue, determined *not* to ask about his decision. Silence. Was he *never* going to bring it up? Finally I could stand it no longer. All I said was *"Well?"* He knew exactly what I meant, but sat for the longest time. At last he admitted he still wasn't sure and didn't think we should continue our engagement.

Hoping to shock him with the finality of this decision, I removed the ring from my finger and laid it in his hand. "Here. Take this back, then." He put it in his pocket and stood up. "Good night," was all he said, and left.

That's when, contrary to everything I believed I was—a strong woman able to shake off disaster, fight back, and even endure rebuff from a man I loved—I called him back.

I watched him park outside my apartment building. I waited for the knock on the door. He came in, took me in his arms. Held me quiet and close. "Let's see where we go from here. I'm still not sure about the future, but I'm hopeful."

Two days later, I left for a work conference in Chicago and he offered to drive me to the airport and walk me to the gate. This was in the time before TSA and security. We passed a magazine kiosk and he suggested, "Why don't you buy a *Bride's* magazine?" My heart clenched. This was either really cruel, or…? I replied, "And why would I need one of those?" I hoped I sounded playful, but a little sarcastic. His reply was exactly what I hoped. "You may need one to plan a wedding."

Five months later, on June 15, 1968, we married.

The doubts Denis had experienced were mainly rooted in something he had been taught by his father: if you live right, you don't ever need to make a mistake. Mistakes and accidents can be avoided if you pay attention and obey the rules. In his house there were no exceptions. No excuses for failure of any kind. Failure merely proved that you were negligent, irresponsible, stupid, and worst of all, you were disobeying God. Years later, Denis explained, "I was paralyzed by the fear that in marrying you I could be making a mistake. I knew there would be no turning back from it."

At the time I didn't know much about the way our family histories influenced our responses to life. During our engagement, we were between the ages of eighteen and twenty, and really, what young person knows or cares much about how their family of origin has shaped them? I didn't. Nor did Denis. Gathering insight into family dynamics and learning how to navigate them has been a life-long journey. At that time, we were just beginning to discern connections we didn't fully understand.

FIRST DAYS OF MARRIAGE

August, 1968. Two months post-wedding. "If I was a boy, I'd beat you up!" The door slammed behind me. I was running away into the night. Not a clever plan when all you are wearing is a sheer nightgown.

In a few short weeks, we had established a home of our very own in a tiny attic apartment with a bathroom so small we had to bend under the sloped ceiling to use the toilet. Our queen bed fit in the bedroom with barely room to walk on one side and keep a dresser at the foot. We squished our clothes into a tiny closet. The kitchen was all mine. For the first time, I was sole proprietor of the spices, the pots, and the pans. Soft light spilled over the couch we shared for napping and a soft chair for reading. We even had a Siamese kitten named Anastasia who made us laugh every day in spite of her naughtiness. She galloped through the rooms with fake ferociousness, leaping onto the bed with her back arched and her tail spiked. She hid behind the stove and attacked our feet as we walked past. Somehow she wrestled our socks to the floor and bit large chunks from the heels as they dried on the rack. When I made cream puffs that did not puff (an art I've never mastered), they hardened into little hockey pucks that she shot across the floor into hidey holes throughout the apartment.

Our days took on a familiar routine. Denis had made the difficult decision to quit school himself. He had become unhappy with his major in the sciences but wasn't sure what to do next. Moving into the arts was tempting, but that was so frowned upon by our community and especially his father, we thought it better to wait and figure it out later. As young as we were, we thought we had all the time in the world. For the moment, we were content to drive together to our campus jobs in the morning and enjoy our domestic life in the evening.

Between moments of sheer joy and the beginning of ordinary, everyday life, something sweet grew up between us. It was a sense of rootedness related to the geography of Minnesota, which is part of my DNA but quickly burrowed into Denis' heart too. For the first time in his life, *place* became a part of his identity.

As we drove north to visit my family, we passed through familiar landscapes of forest, marsh and fields. Lakes sparkled through the trees and beckoned us to stop and picnic by their shores. I couldn't imagine living anywhere else. Despite our differences in temperament, we found a place of safety in one another. As I write, it makes me anxious I'm painting an incomplete picture of our relationship. It was a rocky mix of trouble one day and pleasure the next. There was a slow growth we barely perceived and couldn't have precisely identified back then, but as the years passed, we understood that both commitment and love were becoming a solid foundation to our relationship.

At the same time, each day, married life revealed new conflicts. On one occasion we were driving down the freeway arguing about something and, in a moment of outrage, I slapped Denis on the face. Without missing a beat or driving off the road, he slapped me back. I settled back in my seat, stunned, thinking: *Well. This isn't the plan I had in mind.* He was bigger and not afraid of me. Another strategy, perhaps? I reached over and turned off the ignition (note: cars were different back then) and the car rolled to a stop. We coasted to the shoulder, avoiding the traffic. After shouting at one another we eventually made up, but clearly not all of marriage was going according to my expectations.

No one prepared us for the raw frustration we sometimes felt towards one another. It would have been reassuring if someone had mentioned this was pretty normal. It might have helped if they had also punched a few holes in my Hallmark-card love notions and also suggested Denis stop passive-aggressively icing me out with silence when we had a conflict.

It looked to me like most of the married couples we knew weren't experiencing significant hardships of any kind. Did they really live in perfect harmony? Martin Luther, a father of the Reformation, would have questioned that impression. In his marriage to Katherine, he understood they would face difficulties in their relationship as we all do, and he saw "the hardships and opportunities of marriage as one of God's primary ways of making disciples."[1]

There have been many cherished moments in our marriage. Times of sweetness and comfort, smooth as a Mexican flan. But I had no idea that far from continuous blue skies and sunny beaches of love, marriage would take us on a long, sometimes painful, always hard-fought journey to a place of maturity, understanding, and forgiveness. We regularly misunderstood, angered and wounded one another. If thwacking the daylights out of him sounds abusive, my only regret was I hadn't the strength to actually do it.

During those early days, we were still part of the same fundamentalist church we grew up in. Garrison Keillor, humorist and creator of *A Prairie Home Companion,* was raised in one of these congregations and in the "News from Lake Wobegon," he often referred to them as the "Sanctified Brethren."

Wedding Day, June 1968. The honeymoon begins.

Elders were not ordained in the Brethren Assemblies, but we were assured we would know who they were because of the prompting of the Holy Spirit. Our premarital counseling consisted of several sessions with one of those leaders, the man who would perform our ceremony. He was a kindly person, a successful banker, and someone who cared about us. We liked him very much.

We were the first wedding this man performed and on the day, he was as nervous as the bride and groom. Apparently he forgot to send our marriage certificate to the county clerk's office, because only last year, when I went to the license bureau in 2019 to get an enhanced driver's license, the copy of the marriage certificate I presented was not official. My name had changed from Margie Sorenson to Margie Haack, but it had never been recorded. For more than fifty years, we assumed our marriage was legal and now our children wonder who they really are. One of them suggested we were pretty hypocritical teaching them about morality when all these years we had been living in sin. Given the number of official forms where I've lied about my level of education, I can hardly blame him.

During premarital counseling, on the cusp of marriage, I was radiant. I was going to live with the man I loved, and nothing compared to this dream come true. We eagerly listened as the elder read passages from Ephesians on Christian marriage. I had heard those verses all my life. They bored me, but now they took on brilliant new meaning because this was going to be *my* life. It would be *our* life together.

The man was to love his wife as Christ loved the church. The woman was to submit. This would please God. Every day my husband would lead and I would follow. We were going to pray together and read the Bible regularly. The elder warned us about "not forsaking the assembling of ourselves together . . . and so much the more as you see the day approaching" (Heb. 10:25 NKJV), which meant no skipping church on Sundays because if Jesus returned and found you in a coffee shop eating bagels and cream cheese and reading the *New York Times,* well, let's just say that wouldn't win you a crown in heaven. We would attend the Assembly Sunday morning, Sunday night, and midweek prayer meetings, too. Denis and I needed to live as though Christ could return any second and we needed to be found doing spiritual things like praying, reading the Bible, and witnessing in order to be prepared for his coming again.

We received little practical advice about daily living. How should we navigate differences of opinion? Finances? Who decides what to save or what to spend where? What about how to forgive one another when one of you has seriously wronged the other? How do we handle mistakes like forgetting to pay a bill, or double scheduling, or any of the many details that are required to coordinate two people living together? How were we to decide our proper vocations? Our premarital counseling didn't address any of this. In the minds of most men we knew, these questions would be a non-issue if the wife was submitting to her husband in all things as she should.

We were taught as followers of Christ that we must not be worldly, even in our choices of vocation. Accordingly, the best choice was to become a missionary or a full-time Christian worker. The next best would be some vocation that was valued, like medicine, dentistry, education, engineering, or even working with your hands. Witnessing as much as possible during the day would justify your work and make it pleasing to God. Some vocations were considered too worldly, ones involving such things as art or literature or mental health. At the end of the age, everything would be burned in God's refining furnace and only what was was spiritual would remain.

This was why on the day a plumber was repairing a plugged sink in our apartment, a friend who happened to be there spoke to the plumber about his soul. As the plumber knelt on the floor with his head and wrenches under the sink and black gunk dropping into a bucket, our friend knelt beside him and began to aggressively preach that his life was like this plugged pipe, filled with all kinds of sin that defiled his heart. The only way his life could be cleaned to function properly was if he confessed he was a sinner and asked Jesus into his heart.

Then all his pipes would be flushed clean and replaced by clear living water. I was impressed by our friend's boldness. At the same time, I felt stricken for the plumber who had been caught like a caged animal and forced to listen, whether he wanted to or not. Many evangelicals have a lovely desire to introduce people to Jesus; many, however, like our friend, have never reflected on how evangelism can be perverted into verbal bullying, as this was.

The beliefs we were taught began setting off tremors of doubt. We wondered if it was possible to follow this dictum and remain happy or even human. If I thought about the physical love between a man and a woman, for example, I wondered, *is it possible to serve this high calling when my heart and body wants nothing more than to be possessed by earthly ecstasy?* I had no answers. My doubts were dialed down and plowed under.

When I recall the first days of marriage, it was going to bed together I loved most. My whole desire was to be with Denis and now here he was, my partner for life. My friend. My lover. He was taking off my clothes and climbing into bed beside me. Joy of joys. No more leaving before dawn, closing the door to my apartment, entering the frozen winter night to start a car and sit shivering in darkness. No sneaking back into his basement room after midnight. All night long, I couldn't get enough of him by my side.

In my fantasy of what marriage ought to be, I imagined walking together into whatever life threw at us. We would do everything together. We would laugh at our poverty. When there were no groceries until payday, I would conjure food from my magic kitchen. I did. But that was more my mother's legacy than my own giftedness. She had taught me to make comfort food from almost nothing. A dish of mac and cheese soothed our worries. A small tart could be made with one apple, brown sugar, and a sprinkle of cinnamon. When there was no money for the Laundromat, I washed clothes in the bathtub.

> I can wash out forty-four pairs of socks
>   and have 'em hangin out on the line
> I can starch and iron two dozens shirts
>   'fore you can count from one to nine
> I can scoop up a great big dipper full of lard
>   from the drippins can
> Throw it in the skillet, go out and do my shopping,
>   be back before it melts in the pan
> 'Cause I'm a woman! W-O-M-A-N,
>   I'll say it again . . . I'm a woman.[2]

Yeah, I loved this song. I was a WOMAN whose hands were were a mess on laundry day—raw and blistered from hot water and bleach. But I didn't mind.

I expected we would each slip into our preordained roles—Denis as spiritual leader and me happily standing beside him as his helper, even though my own birth order predisposed me to be the responsible, bossy, oldest child in charge. My five siblings can confirm this. You don't shed that predisposition as easily as a snake sheds its skin. But I was naively ready to relinquish my position and become Mrs. Compliant Housewife. We would pray, read, talk, and go to bed together every day.

Reality was more like this:

> We prayed together—when I initiated.

> We read together from a daily devotional calendar called *Choice Gleanings*—when I asked.

> He made decisions about our spiritual life—when I pushed.

I began to question him on how I was supposed to do my part if he didn't fulfill his. It didn't take long to abandon my sanctimony and start nagging until we were both exasperated. I was afraid of becoming the nag who was the butt of scornful man-jokes. My stepfather used to tell one: A man and his new wife were headed down the road in his carriage when the horse stumbled. "That's once," the man said. It stumbled a second time and the man said, "That's twice." The third time the horse stumbled, he said, "That's three times," got out of the carriage, and shot the horse dead. Shocked, the wife said, "Honey, why did you do that?" The man replied, "That's once."

After I had asked Denis to pray with me, I don't remember how many times, he finally admitted, "I don't like praying with you because you use a fake voice with talking to God."

Boom.

That hurt. Deeply. I blamed my pious cadences on the public prayers I'd heard growing up in the Assemblies. Men prayed with affectation, repeating the same phrases time after time, from table grace to communion prayers. There was nothing inherently wrong with what they said, it was more about the lack of feeling or real connections to life. It was all I knew. I rarely heard women pray because we were not allowed to pray in public unless we were in a group of women only. I didn't *want* to sound or be insincere. But how?

But wait. Why wouldn't *Denis* lead us in prayer? "The way I pray is not an excuse for you not to pray," I told him. He was failing as my spiritual leader. I wanted to bosh him. Trying to discuss this problem about prayer didn't help, so I gave up. Apparently it was going to be just me and God. I'd make my spiritual path without Denis, lonely and alone, thank you very much.

When we were calm and able to discuss such things, Denis admitted he was having a lot of doubts about Christianity. This scared me, but it explained a little more about his lack of leadership. Neither of us was ready to abandon it—at least I wasn't. Our faith was characteristic of a lot of the Christians we knew back then. Os Guiness labeled it as "socially irrevelant, even if privately engaging."[3] What that meant was, yes, I could love God and find comfort in the Bible. I could have my devotions, and sing and pray. It made me feel good. As far as the world outside the church was concerned, we did not engage it. We did not go to movies or museums or concerts. Many of us did not vote. We were not involved with helping the poor or working for justice. We had nothing significant to say to the world except: *Repent*. Although we were living in the world, its beauty shouldn't tempt us, and its problems shouldn't concern us.

At university, we didn't have answers for the questions our classes raised. What is the origin of humankind? How did the universe begin? Does life have meaning and purpose? Is there life after death? What is truth? Can you prove the existence of God? Of course, we couldn't. Religion, one professor told us, is a psychological crutch for the weak. But if you need it, and it makes you feel good that's okay. On and on. I couldn't defend my beliefs, but I stubbornly refused to give up on God or the Bible. In my heart it didn't matter what anyone said, I had loved Jesus since I was four years old. Jesus loved me and I wasn't giving him up. My way of coping had been to accept the dichotomy between private and public, sacred and secular, and to try not to think about the inconsistencies too much. Denis could not accept this dichotomy even though he was afraid his doubts might slide into unbelief. The more we talked about the problems our faith posed and the inadequate response from older Christians, the more I came to agree with Denis.

Now we both wished there was a seamless connection between what we believed and how to live faithfully in the real world. I joined Denis in asking questions that were barely disguised accusations. We wanted authenticity and answers. It seemed as if people in our Assembly didn't live as if their beliefs touched everyday life—their business, their vocation, views of politics and justice, art and beauty, the daily struggles of living with and loving one another. It was rare when a conversation outside of Sunday services included anything about spiritual matters of consequence. What, then, was the point of living a holy life? If Christianity applied only to personal morality and eternal salvation, then it had almost nothing to say about ordinary reality. This didn't seem sufficient. Hedonism sounded a lot more attractive than no dancing, no drinking, no going to movies. Was there nothing in life that was of eternal significance except Bible reading, prayer, and witnessing?

In addition to our questions about the faith, we didn't know of a place or a person where we could safely air the struggles we faced in our relationship. We watched married couples and witnessed public demonstrations of affection as they sat together in their pews on Sunday morning, the husband's arm around his wife. No one ever admitted having trouble, or that life could be thorny and complicated. Marriage looked easy for everyone except us.

Navigating relationships can be among the most torturous passages in life and none of us are exempt from this struggle. As we matured, I realized we could offer support or the possibility of hope by telling our story. That admission alone might cause people to feel less lost and isolated. It would have made a world of difference to us back then.

Some of what complicated Denis' life as he finished up high school and began college was the living arrangement his father made for him during his senior year of high school. His parents returned to the Philippine Islands, and Denis was placed in the home of an Assembly family who had been the first to offer to host him. His father had been quietly warned by other church elders not to leave his son with this family. They made it clear it was not a good choice and there were other families more suitable who would be happy to keep Denis. Milton refused to listen to that advice because one of the principles he lived by was avoiding conflict at all costs. In this case, it was easier to go with the first offer because it could never cause anyone to take offense. He considered this an essential part of living a blameless life and key to having a "good testimony."

His concern was not for his son, but his own reputation.

It soon became clear that the family was severely broken, much of it due to mental illness. Among the symptoms was a phobia about germs which meant all surfaces needed to be covered in heavy plastic. Paranoia about health meant monitoring in excruciating detail all the food you ate and every bodily function. Denis also discovered that the parents of the family were secretly reading his mail and going through his papers and grades. He set up a test by leaving an envelope from his parents on his desk pad and making tiny unnoticeable marks at the corners with a nasty note on snooping inside. When he came home and saw it had been carefully returned to the wrong place it confirmed what he already suspected. This also explained how they had learned of things they had no way of knowing unless he told them.

These problems eventually led to a crisis and the mother needing to be hospitalized with what was termed a nervous breakdown several years after Denis moved out. At the time we had little sympathy for them or for the suffering mental illness brings to a family. Later as our understanding broadened it led us to grieve for them and all their troubles.

Denis felt lonely and completely trapped, with no way out and no one to speak to about it. At the time he did not know his father had been warned about this family because such things were not spoken of openly, and no one ever approached him to ask how he was doing. There were uncomfortable similarities to his own family and his childhood experiences. The circumstances were different, but the unhappiness was familiar. Secrets were whispered but never spoken or explained. Landmines exploded if you asked the wrong question or brought up a forbidden topic.

Milton made it clear if Denis complained to anyone about his living situation he would be disobeying an express order. Denis would be considered rebellious, he might be accused of being a gossip, or of being ungrateful toward a family who sacrificed to host him. And it would certainly reflect on Milton's ability to control his son.

When our dating relationship became serious, Denis had been living with this family for nearly two years. It was causing daily stress for him. As life grew more miserable, I urged Denis to move out. I argued it wasn't rebellion against his parents because there was at least one couple who understood his difficulty in living there. Without ever mentioning anything about the problems the family had, a lovely older couple from another Assembly took Denis aside one day and told him if he should he *ever* want to move, for any reason, they would be delighted to give him a room rent-free in their basement. He only had to say the word. They were exceptionally kind, honest, plain-spoken people. They did not fearfully tiptoe around, whispering secrets. They were like angels to us. It was such relief to have an option and a perfect spot for him, but Denis was sure his father would never support such a decision.

One weekend when the family was out of town, I encouraged Denis to pack up and move. He felt a little cowardly springing this on them, but having finally agreed to do it, Denis was ecstatic. It was a right and brave thing to do. Together we threw his few belongings in his car and drove to the new home where he was welcomed as if he was their own son. We were delirious with happiness for a new start in a stress-free home where he was treated as a responsible adult able to make his own decisions.

Denis' father was furious when he learned what Denis had done. In his letters he called Denis a disobedient son. Milton was convinced I was fanning the flames of rebellion in him. And yet, I observed that Denis was one of the most outwardly compliant people I knew. His father was certain the host family would be offended—which was true, they were. I hardly cared or needed any justification for the decision. It was his father's fault and he shouldn't have been living there in the first place. Denis struggled with guilt for a while and would have loved his father's support, but he agreed the move was liberating.

I was learning his father's response was consistent with who he was. What others thought of him was always more important than the well-being of his family. No matter how difficult or painful it might be, the opinion of others came first. If you did anything that anyone at any time might consider sin, even if it wasn't, you might cause someone to "stumble" or think of less of you. You were to avoid even the appearance of sin at all cost.

The first indication that I observed of problems between Denis and his father came in letters written from the Philippines. When he left Denis in the States to complete high school and begin college, his father reminded him of the rule he had repeated over and over: *You must never do anything to ruin your Testimony.*

I admit it must be difficult to leave your teenager in the care of others and live half a world away, especially a teenager who has not been taught to make any choices on his own. Denis was not prepared to make any of the countless small decisions people make every day just to get by. For example, he was not taught how to take care of his finances. While living at home he was not even allowed to decide what clothing to wear. To me, this was staggering. In an effort to continue controlling him, Milton had friends in the Assembly report regularly on what Denis was doing, what he wore, how he styled his hair, and who he was hanging with to ensure that he was complying with all the rules and not ruining his testimony.

"Testimony" was a term from our Assembly life, and familiar to many who grew up in other fundamentalist churches. We understood it well. It was used in two ways. First, a Testimony was the story of your conversion. To have a genuine conversion the history of your life was divided into a *before* and *after* getting saved. Before conversion, you were a sinner on your way to hell because of all the nasty things you had done. When you came to understand this, you asked Jesus to forgive your sins and to come into your heart to be your Savior. That was conversion, and after that, you were on your way to heaven. This scenario played out in different degrees for different individuals. The best conversion stories included scandalous events from those whose prior lives included a lot of wickedness, cursing, carousing, and other forbidden acts. When these individuals gave their Testimonies, they usually mentioned their wrongdoings in very general terms, but it always left me curious about *what* those sins were. I wished they'd be more specific.

My Testimony was boring compared to most; it was even questionable by Assembly standards because I didn't have an actual *conversion*. I had simply loved Jesus since my first memories as a child. I don't know why. When my mother converted to Christianity, she taught us the Bible and the stories made sense to my five-year-old mind. When I heard them, I thought, *Yes, this is wonderful*. I knew God was amazing just by looking at the Northern Lights he had made, by watching a cow give birth to a calf, and by receiving answers to desperate prayers like *please don't let my brother die* after I told him to hit the rear end of a horse with a stick and the horse kicked him in the head. Jesus was one of us, he understood me, he loved kids, and was God besides.

In my small, somewhat isolated world in the countryside of Northern Minnesota, anyone in the Assembly who claimed to be a Christian was expected to confess her Testimony in public and get baptized. How did you come to know God and when? This was a traumatic problem during my teen years when I attended Bible camp and was questioned about whether I was truly a child of God because I couldn't remember ever having a conversion date. Denis fit the rules of Testimony-telling better because he was nine years old when he suddenly became convinced he was headed to hell and asked Jesus to save him.

The second use of the word Testimony prescribed the ongoing life of a Christian. This mainly focused on maintaining a flawless public reputation. Because Milton was a missionary, he believed his son's reputation directly reflected his own. How Denis dressed and wore his hair; the books he read, the music he listened to, where he went—his father considered all these things a measurement of his own success in the eyes of others. He insisted Denis scrutinize every detail of his life and ask, *Am I being spiritual?*

The question, at least for his father, was not so much about holy living before God or where your heart was at, but was more about spinning your public image to control what others thought of you.

You had a good Testimony if you conformed to the rules. The Bible commands us to "come out from among them and be separate from the world" (2 Cor. 6:17 HCSB), that is, be separate from the culture surrounding us. You ruined your Testimony if you were friends with someone who did any of the forbidden things. If they danced, smoked, went to movies, watched television, wore clothing that was popular (especially for women)—any or all of these could place you in the dreaded ruined-Testimony category.

Milton so emphasized this in his family life and public preaching that both Denis and his sister thought in such terms as well. In anxious and loving letters, she urged Denis to keep a "good Testimony" for the sake of his parents. It was interesting how she considered this being for the sake of his parents, not for Jesus.

Being told to have a good Testimony was a weaponized way of controlling everything you did. We must be careful to never break a rule because that could stumble someone who witnessed it. Stumbling was defined as anything that could cause an immature Christian or a non-Christian to turn away from the faith. "Do not cause anyone to stumble, whether Jews, Greeks or the church of God" (1 Cor. 10:32).

The list of forbidden things was overwhelming: reading the wrong books, wearing a hairstyle similar to the Beatles, dressing in loud colors and short dresses, listening to popular music, having a glass of wine, or even being seen with friends who were not Christians. The problem was we never met a non-Christian or immature believer who left the faith because they saw someone doing any of these things. In reality, those who were stumbled by someone breaking a rule were actually not stumbled at all. They were just older Christians who simply didn't like what you were doing. It wasn't something that affected their faith. This observation was another reason I began to question what I was hearing.

Denis and I had been married about six months when we began attending special meetings led by a traveling evangelist who worked among the Assemblies. We were struggling to find our way spiritually and had a sincere desire to give Christianity a chance even if it meant participating in "Gospel Meetings" and going door-to-door, inviting people to come to this series of weeknight preaching services. After work, we gathered with a few other members of our community, and during the week before the meetings were scheduled, we went block by block around the chapel, knocking on doors and asking people to join us. It wasn't that either Denis or I enjoyed this, but we thought, well, maybe this is a way to draw nearer to God.

It did seem fruitless. I never saw a single stranger come through the door, wondering what these Gospel Meetings were about. Still, night after night, this man thundered and preached to our little choir about heaven and hell and sin and rebellion and the need to be saved. Denis and I sat attentively in the front row. I was determined that if this was the way to prove to God that I loved him, that I wanted him, I would endure it. I didn't know any other way. On one of those evenings I was wearing a pair of earrings with a pearl hanging on the end of a small gold chain. In the middle of his sermon, the preacher began to attack women, accusing them of sinful worldliness, declaring they were following the path of Jezebel, that cursed queen. As he spoke, he looked directly at me and described the Jezebels of this world as women with pierced ears who wore dangling rings. There was no other person in that small gathering of Christians wearing earrings. Only me.

My soul turned a violent shade of red—I'm not the cheek blushing type—and I felt a deep, deep surge of anger toward this man who was condemning me without having any idea who I was or where my heart lived. I knew then this was not the kind of Christianity I wanted any part of. I was sitting there, not because I couldn't think of a lot more pleasant things to do, but because I loved Jesus. At the time I thought loving him meant practicing an aggressive kind of evangelism that enabled you to accost anyone anywhere. You had to be brave. You had to expect rejection. I was willing to do it. But I wasn't willing to be called Jezebel and be rejected by a preacher like this small man.

While we were still students, another confusing experience confronted us at university. We met people from other denominations who loved God and wanted to serve him as much or more than we did. We weren't the only ones? We had been told that was impossible! And we met students who claimed no faith at all and yet were often kinder, more loving and patient, more thoughtful than many Christians we knew. How could this be?

More confusion sprang from our textbooks and university lectures. In our little sectarian corner of Christendom, academics who taught the theory of evolution, for example, were not just opposed, they were treated with contempt. They were depicted as idiots rejecting truth that ought to be evident to everyone: "No wonder they think we came from monkeys," some preachers said, "they are monkeys themselves." We expected our university professors to be ridiculous, arrogant, and predatory toward any who disagreed with them. It was disturbing and astonishing to find many were thoughtful, kind, and even respectful of the Christian faith they personally rejected.

Consequently, we began asking our Assembly leaders more questions. What we really wanted were thoughtful answers and counter arguments to what we were learning. We wanted them to apologize for misrepresenting people who they thought held beliefs contrary to biblical truth. Our professors were not monkeys. In several conversations where Denis tried to express this, he was told that his problem was unconfessed sin in his life and that he needed to deal with it. In the end, we were told we needed to simply have faith, simple faith. We should trust in God and not become involved in philosophizing, which was sinful. Among those we spoke to, there were exceptions—some were kinder toward us than others, but they were often reluctant to discuss these matters.

This was neither satisfying nor comforting. It forced us to begin examining our beliefs even more rigorously. Assemblies were proud of following the New Testament and being different from others who merely thought they were Christians because they belonged to some church denomination and had been baptized. Again, there were exceptions, but the inconsistencies we saw in the daily lives of those around us caused us to point this out to our Sunday School teacher. For example, Peter wrote in his epistle that Christians had "joy unspeakable and full of glory" (1 Pet. 1:8 KJV). Where was that joy evident, we wondered?

Give an example. It wasn't obvious in our congregation. Even if we were reserved Minnesotans, wouldn't some kind of emotion break out once in a while if it really existed? Why didn't anyone ever speak about the difference their faith made in their everyday lives? People hardly mentioned God apart from Sunday worship, perfunctory Bible readings, and saying grace before meals. Where were answers to prayer? Answers not only about pregnant women being safely delivered of a baby or this or that person who was sick. Physical illness and pregnancy were popular topics for public prayer but what about all the other parts of life? Aren't they important? Problems at work, problems with relationships, family matters, mental health, finances? In this Denis and I agreed: we *wanted* faith to be passionate and full of life. We *wanted* Christianity to be vital—to require everything we had—as it seemed to have done in the first century church.

No one gave us satisfying answers, so we felt more justified in our criticisms. We were taken aside again and warned about our attitude—we were in danger of heresy. "Beware lest any man spoil you through philosophy and vain deceit, after the tradition of men, after the rudiments of the world, and not after Christ" (Col. 2:8 KJV). We reached a point where we no longer cared what they said. We were dissatisfied truth-seekers and, in our youthful idealism, we were becoming more vexed.

At university, Denis took a course on the History of Art where more questions surfaced. It was a poorly-run class, but it was a required credit for a bachelor's degree. The class was crowded with hundreds of students fulfilling their obligations. In a darkened auditorium with 500–600 students, many of them napping, a bored teaching assistant stood on stage, his back to the students and clicked through slides of classical art. Denis learned there were Christians from the past who created amazing art. Rembrandt. Dürer. Vermeer. Denis was spellbound and yet confused. How could such compelling truth and beauty come through work that was thought at its best to be without spiritual significance? All of it would simply burn up on Judgment Day at the return of Christ. Denis invited me to sit in on some of the classes so I could understand more of what he was thinking about. It was all new to me, too. The beauty, the tragedies, the lively depiction of who we are as men and women in love, at war, at rest—the grandeur of creation could not be hidden, however inept the teaching assistant.

The confusion continued at work where Denis was a lab assistant. He loved his boss, Ernie, who was head of the University's Department of Chemistry labs. Ernie demonstrated a lively faith. He was a kind man; he listened and engaged in dialogue about spiritual matters with anyone who was interested. He didn't hide his faults, he chain-smoked, he was divorced. He sometimes cussed, but he believed that Christianity was true and worthy of consideration. He blew up every belief Denis had been taught about what a Christian should look like.

Our marriage fledged into a strange union where Denis actively doubted Christianity and I was willing to make trouble, but wasn't experiencing doubt in the same way. I didn't question God's existence or his love, not just for me, but for everyone. It was something I could not deny. When Denis talked about leaving the church I couldn't imagine it, even with all my criticisms. It seemed important to remain in the community and hope for reform. Though how that was going to happen, I had no idea.

Over the years, as Denis has reflected on this time, he maintains he was in crisis and about to give up faith altogether. He quit reading the Bible, which in our church was practically the same as gambling away your paycheck and having sex with a prostitute. There didn't seem to be anyone in our church who had questions quite like his. Discouraged and confused, we kept on with the pretense of attending Sunday meetings. It seemed like we were destined to become the very hypocrites we despised.

As we struggled to navigate these intense spiritual issues and how to resolve them, we also struggled with mundane, everyday issues. Who should take out the garbage? Who keeps the cash and how much? Who has to take a bag lunch while the other buys lunch at work? Marriage became an unexpected arena for conflict. The reality of two intense personalities trying to get along in daily life wasn't getting any easier. We clashed over the most mundane issues. Dietrich Bonhoeffer's words from a wedding sermon were unknown to us at the time: "It is not your love that sustains the marriage, but from now on, the marriage that sustains your love." More than anything I'd encountered in life, marriage revealed how deeply hostile I could become when opposed by anyone, even the man I loved. I longed to be serene and demure and beautiful and a lot of other impossibilities. The falseness of my piety depressed me. Our fights depressed me, but it wasn't enough to stop me warring with Denis.

Our ways of handling disagreements were polar opposite. After a head-on collision where I exploded, after some reflection I was ready to apologize, work out a deal and restore our relationship. Not Denis. He disappeared into the Arctic for hours, sometimes days. I accused him of cutting me out, of not talking about what really mattered. His retort was that a simple hug and a kiss is not going to fix it. He claimed I didn't respect his privacy and it annoyed him. True, I didn't leave him any room for it. Privacy wasn't important to me, growing up as I did in a three-room house with eight people and no indoor bathroom. In fact, I liked being close with others. I couldn't understand why Denis had to close the bathroom door. Nothing should separate us. After all what the heck did it mean for two to become one? (Mark 10:8).

What I didn't understand then was that when he was growing up, the only safe place in the house was the bathroom. There wasn't a square inch of life where he was not sternly surveilled by his father. The smallest thing did not escape notice. Not even thoughts were allowed freedom—as if that were possible—and this made the bathroom a welcome escape into privacy.

We were only about two months into marriage when we fought over something—I don't remember what exactly—possibly it was his habit of dropping clothes on the floor as he was getting ready for bed and leaving them there until I picked them up. Of the many things I admired about him during our courtship, his tidiness made me happy. His room was neat and organized, even though I could write D + M in the dust of his dresser. Mine was a family where boys didn't do anything related to indoor home-keeping. Not that they didn't have responsibilities, but there was a gender division of labor. Once my brothers were old enough they helped Dad milk the cows and feed the livestock and do other farm chores. My mother and us girls cooked, picked up the clothes, and made all the beds. But here in the city, where I imagined sharing everything, leaving clothes on the floor was definitely unfair. "I'm not your slave," I told him. I remember saying, with brittle sarcasm, "It won't kill you to put your clothes in the laundry basket that is sitting right there in front of you!"

It seemed obvious that with the two of us working, no farm to keep, no outside chores to do, the least he could do was pick up his clothes. We hadn't yet understood that our expectations of one another were informed by our different childhood experiences, and we didn't have anyone in our life who could help us explore these issues in a healthy way. So, after an exchange of boiling whispers—we had to be quiet because the elderly Czech couple who rented to us lived on the first floor and kept a constant watch on us—that was the night I stormed out of the apartment in my nightgown. I'd show him.

It was summer and if the mosquitoes hadn't been massively aware of me as I crouched under the lilac bushes in the dark, I may have run away. Forever. I waited and waited. I wanted him to search for me, take me in his arms, say he was sorry and that he'd never do it again—whatever it was—and oh, how he loved me.

Finally the door opened and I eagerly watched his silhouette in the dark as he stepped onto the landing. He hoarsely whispered, "Margie, GET IN HERE. Now." I silently begged, *Come get me.* But he didn't. He didn't even come down the steps. Eventually he went back inside. In my flimsy bridal negligee *he* had given me, hiding under the bushes, I became an insect smorgasbord. At last, I went back inside, covered with bites. I don't remember a happy ending. I don't remember an ending at all. My romantic dream—of being pursued by my lover into the dark night and taken into his arms, as he begged forgiveness—did not happen.

BOOK II

[1968-1969]

The Saguaro Cactus

In the continental United States, the saguaro cactus grows only
in the state of Arizona where the hot, dry, Sonoran desert reaches
north from the Mexican border. It quickly became the iconic symbol
of the Wild West, and Hollywood seized the image for background
shots of the desert. Long ago it was named by the Indians and
pronounced "sah-*wah*-ro." On our journey from Flagstaff to Phoenix,
we saw saguaros for the first time and were impressed by their
forbidding beauty. There is something majestic and alien about this
cactus, which at first glance appears utterly unfriendly to life. It is
a patient plant, standing solitary and unmovable, waiting for up to
seventy-five years before it grows an arm that points to heaven.
Within the next 150 years, it may send up fifty more arms of
supplication or, as some do, none at all. In maturity, a saguaro may
reach a height of forty-five feet and live to be 200 years old.
Although it may look inhospitable, many inhabitants of the desert
call it home. Among them is the desert elf owl, a tiny bird that
nests in holes drilled by the Gila woodpecker. There, in a
hostile environment, the owl finds a protected home
among the spines of the giant saguaro.

JOURNEY AWAY

Denis walked into the kitchen with a smile on his face. Whole wheat bread fresh out of the oven was cooling on the counter. Hamburger gravy simmered on the stove. I was preparing supper. He was just home from work at a medical research lab at the university. "I've been reading my Bible during lunch," he told me.

My heart went on alert. This was new. I had been praying he would resolve his doubts because I knew he was slipping away from faith. I still measured a person's spiritual health by whether or not they read their Bible daily. A "Quiet Time," we called it—a time set apart to read, contemplate, and pray. Doing this regularly, I thought, would help prevent disaster and gain favor with God. Earlier that year I made a decision to stop taking his spiritual temperature every second. Instead I impatiently waited and fussed at God, wondering if he was ever going to answer me. Now, here was Denis saying, "I've found this verse and I want us to do what it says." Wow. This was good. A sign that God was at work in him. My heart lunged forward, ready to join him. I couldn't wait to hear what verse he was referring to.

Denis turned to the words of Jesus telling a rich man what he needed to do to become his disciple: "Go, sell your possessions and give to the poor, and you will have treasure in heaven. Then come, follow me" (Matt. 19:21).

About this time, we had come under the influence of two young men who belonged to the Brethren Assemblies and had been part of a movement in Europe called Operation Mobilisation, a Christian mission involved in evangelism. Its founder, George Verwer, had established radical guidelines for those who joined. He asked them to give up everything for the sake of the Gospel and take up a lifestyle that was austere and simple. Members spread literature through door-to-door campaigns and open-air preaching services. These two men brought the movement to the United States.

We were ripe for being radicalized. Denis was making a last ditch effort to give Christianity a try and I was ready to try something new and more meaningful. Among the sermons, audio tapes, and testimonies that swirled around us through the influence of these two, a pamphlet titled "The Chocolate Soldier" by C.T. Studd[1] struck a deep chord:

> EVERY TRUE CHRISTIAN IS A SOLDIER—of Christ—
> a hero "par excellence"! Braver than the bravest—scorning
> the soft seductions of peace and her oft-repeated warnings
> against hardship, disease, danger, and death, whom he
> counts among his bosom friends.
> THE OTHERWISE CHRISTIAN IS A CHOCOLATE
> CHRISTIAN! Dissolving in water and melting at the smell
> of fire. "Sweeties" they are! Bonbons, lollipops! Living their lives
> on a glass dish or in a cardboard box, each clad in his
> soft clothing...
> GOD NEVER WAS A CHOCOLATE MANUFACTURER,
> AND NEVER WILL BE. God's men are always heroes.
> In Scripture you can trace their giant foot-tracks down
> the sands of time.
> Difficulties, dangers, disease, death, or divisions don't deter
> any but Chocolates from executing God's Will. When someone
> says there's a lion in the way, the real Christian promptly replies,
> "That's hardly enough inducement for me; I want a bear or
> two besides to make it worth my while to go."

When you joined Operation Mobilisation, you were expected to live the life of an ascetic. Only necessities were allowed. You lived in a tent if necessary, with all your belongings stored in a cardboard box, in order to spread the Gospel to those who didn't know or believe. Food should be nourishing, nothing fancy, as cheap as possible, and served on plastic plates. Clothing was merely to keep you dry or warm. Fashionistas were reprogrammed for simplicity's sake. Art, holidays, and novels were among the expendables. These were the frills of life.

This was going to cost.

The two men dubbed their organization Team Outreach and committed to going to inner cities to work with churches, where they would do door-to-door evangelism, handing out literature and issuing invitations to evangelistic meetings. Originally from Milwaukee, they visited the Twin Cities to recruit young people for Team Outreach. They were viewed with some suspicion by the older generation, but were legitimized because they came from Brethren Assemblies. Both Denis and I listened with growing interest to their messages and wondered if they were speaking to us. Or was this *God* speaking to us through them, saying,

"Take the challenge"? There was a rising sense of anticipation in our hearts.

Denis stood in our kitchen that day and declared, "We need to sell everything we own if we want to follow Jesus. Let's join Team Outreach this summer." It was springtime and we were living in St. Paul. I don't remember my exact reply to this announcement. But it felt like God had just kicked me in the stomach. It was an unfair test of my sincerity. Did we need to be this revolutionary just because we wanted to follow God? Was getting rid of everything we owned really required? I liked our house and small collection of belongings. Suddenly the reality of this message was not so welcome after all. I wanted Denis to settle his doubts but wasn't quite ready to adopt asceticism and become a sell-all evangelist.

We had been married ten months. We were barely past our honeymoon. We had received many wedding gifts and friends had helped us furnish an apartment. I loved our soft linens and my dishes. Setting up housekeeping had been delicious and playful and now I was supposed to give it all up? I tried to hide my disappointment from Denis. It was strange to have wanted him to be a spiritual leader and now that he was showing some initiative, I was the one saying, yes, but not this.

That night I turned away from Denis and hid my face in my pillow and cried. *Yes, God, I want you to reach into Denis' heart, but does it need to be like this? Surely not.* I argued with God and prayed long into the night.

By morning, calm had descended and I had changed. Sometimes God counsels us even as we sleep and the Holy Spirit works to change our hearts. This was one of those times. When I look back on that night, I still see it as a small miracle. Scripture scrolled across my mind, words of comfort, and it was plain: "surely I am with you always even to the end of the age" (Matt. 28:20). I knew I could do it. We could do it together. I wasn't acting the role of martyr, I was simply on board.

The next day, I planned the yard sale. I made signs. We priced items and placed them on tables in the front yard. Buyers sifted through our belongings and gradually our furniture and furnishings disappeared. Stereo and records. Towels and bedding. Pots and pans. All the big items: our bed, chairs, table, and couch. Among the few things that remained unsold were some kitchen items and the English bone china tea set Denis' grandparents had given us as a wedding gift. Eventually, the leftovers were boxed up and went into storage. We gave notice at our jobs and in two weeks we were done and ready to move on.

When a twinge of regret arose, when moments of doubt and sadness came with a longing to hold onto the gifts that represented the beginning of our married life, I pushed them down, reminding myself I wasn't going to be one of those chocolate soldiers. We gave away the money from the sale and two months later we gave our car to a friend who needed one. All that remained was a little clothing, a few personal items, and two new sleeping bags that would become our marriage bed from then on. My one comfort was that the bags zipped together to make one large cocoon and we slept side by side under the soft flannel lining.

Several years later, I rescued the leftovers still in their original boxes where they had been stored. The cardboard was water-stained, smelling of must, and falling apart. I unwrapped the china tea set like treasure redeemed from a pawn shop. I understood then that God knew one day I would wish I still owned those delicate plates and teacups; I would cherish them and delight in sharing their beauty with others on special occasions. It was a sign of his love—unnecessary, unexpected, profligate.

But now it was mid-June of 1969 and Team Outreach had gone into operation. Ten of us recruits moved into an old run-down house that belonged to a man from one of the Assemblies. The house was across from a downtown mission and we used it to make our meals and host the people we hoped would come to evening meetings. Our goal was to spread literature throughout one of the poorest neighborhoods of Minneapolis. Our team leader assigned us to a partner and explained which blocks would be on our route. We were dropped off with a handful of little booklets titled *Steps to Peace with God*[2] put out by the Billy Graham Association. Following these four simple steps with a prayer, anyone could be assured of eternal life. Two by two we trudged up and down the streets, knocking on every door with a message: Come to Jesus.

Door after door remained closed. I didn't understand. No one wanted to come to Jesus? No one wanted to hear a message from a white girl without the slightest idea of what it was like to live in this neighborhood? When a rare door opened a crack and dark eyes peered out, before it closed we urgently asked, "Do you know where you would go if you died today?" We urged anyone who showed the slightest shred of interest to join us for the gospel meetings held in the run-down mission each evening. Doggedly, we kept on, day after day, calling sinners to repentance, bolstering our resolve with evening songs and prayers. After all, we were committed to Pressing On. We were Faithful. No Chocolate Soldiers, we. Beneath this resolve was Denis' last crack at remaining in the faith. Would God, would Christianity rise to life and give new meaning if we gave it everything we had?

In the mornings, after early Bible readings and prayers, we ate a simple breakfast, crowded into the van, and headed out. By mid-July, the streets were hot and steamy as we moved block by block through crumbling neighborhoods, hoping to find a single soul interested in God's message. Around lunchtime, our leader picked us up at rendezvous points—a playground or a park—and drove us back to where our team was staying. The owner of the house next door had a bathroom and shower he generously allowed us to use. We took turns preparing our meals using the kitchen at the mission, and after we had eaten, we began our afternoon treks door-to-door. After supper, the mission was opened for the evening preaching service. Except for a few regulars—the homeless and the addicted—who strayed in off the street for a cup of coffee, no one else showed up. When it was over, we gathered again for more Bible study, prayer, and sharing the fruitless day. Like tired monks retiring after evensong, we climbed the stairs and crawled into our sleeping bags on the floor near the cardboard box that held what we'd kept of our former life.

One morning, I tramped down the street alone. Doing this solo was not the Team's normal arrangement, and I can't remember why I was alone. Perhaps my partner was sick? As I walked down the block, I began to feel a warmth spreading between my legs.

Instantly, I felt the panic every woman has experienced—*I'm in public and unprepared.* I rarely had the cramps associated with this periodic feminine inconvenience, but this time was different. Waves of pain clamped my stomach and I felt faint.

It's easy to forget that before the dawn of cell phones, there was no easy way to contact help if you had an emergency. *Get a grip,* I told myself. Desperate and unsure of what to do I finally knocked on a door. *God, please, please let someone answer and please let it be a woman.*

Of all the doorbells I rang that summer with no answer, this time a woman opened the door and I choked, "I'm so sorry to ask, but may I use your bathroom?"

"Come in, child," was her warm answer. She led me to her bathroom and I closed the door. Nothing was normal about what was happening. Not the pain, not the hemorrhaging. My insides were slipping out and I sat there until she tapped at the door. "Are you okay?" she asked.

"I'm fine, be out in a minute," I cheerfully lied. These were things one just didn't talk about. I tried to clean up and stuffed my panties with wads of toilet paper. Thanking God for the angel who'd let me in, I stumbled across the street and into a park where I sat under a tree as the ache spread through my middle.

I didn't know where Denis was. I didn't know what direction the mission was. I waited, convinced this was the most wretched thing I'd ever done for Jesus and hoped he noticed the sacrifice I was making.

The van picked me up at noon. I hoped nothing was showing. I was too embarrassed to tell anyone what was happening, except Denis, who didn't know what to do for me. That night I curled up under our zipped-together sleeping bag and hugged my stomach. Pain throbbed like fire and nothing staunched the flow. Luckily there was a commode in the old bathroom that still functioned.

Much later, I realized it was a miscarriage. Our first child. Gone before I knew she existed. Being with Team Outreach was not the victory-studded life I had imagined. My resolve began melting.

I don't recall a single conversion or even anyone who attended our evening meetings other than the grizzled men who habitually came to the mission for free coffee and cookies. In spite of the dismal results, companionship kept us going as a team. Together we laughed and sang and somehow made it through the month of July. If any lasting good came out of our stay in the poorest neighborhood of Minneapolis, only God knows.

In August, we left for Detroit, arriving the summer after the worst riots any American city had ever experienced. Center city neighborhoods had been burned and looted. The smell of acrid smoke lingered among the ashes of blackened businesses and homes. Many of the blocks we walked hung in a fog of hopelessness. People were suspicious and angry. In this city, like most, the poorest neighborhoods were black—the result of systemic racism and redlining that kept them separate from white neighborhoods.

To be clear, I was completely naïve and unacquainted with the African American experience. I had no idea how much privilege I inherited simply because I was white. Denis and I had no idea how the impact of poverty, racism, and injustice had devastated the families and culture of these neighborhoods. Sadly, we were only focused on one thing: pass out the literature and talk about sin and death and hell and repentance. The Gospel, the Evangel of the Lord Christ, with its richer, deeper, broader call to all of life was as yet unknown to us.

By then our team had dwindled to eight young people and we were housed in a central church that had survived the fires. The pastor of this white church had invited us to do door-to-door evangelism and hold a vacation Bible school for children. The weather was still hot and humid, but the basement Sunday School rooms where we slept on the floors were cool and damp, and I felt the comfort of my husband as I nestled beside him. As we slept, I released anxieties about our future and questions about the value of what we were doing. It was just me and Denis and God, who was somewhere up there orchestrating the events of our lives, I hoped.

There were only a few children who came to the vacation Bible school. They liked the Bible stories we told and were sweetly cooperative, but I think they came more for the snacks and drinks. We had little to offer and they seemed so hungry.

When we finished our stay in Detroit, Denis and I headed to Massachusetts in the car we planned to give away after we rejoined the team back in Minnesota. We had gratefully received some anonymous gifts of money that allowed us to pay for gas and other necessities along the way. It would be a long time before we would take another vacation together. Denis was eager to introduce me for the first time to his east coast aunts and uncles, especially his Aunt Ruth. We crossed the international bridge in Detroit and headed across Ontario—our first long road trip together—just the two of us. Married fourteen months. As we breezed along the Trans-Canada Highway, the heat of late August made us so thirsty we were ready to drink from a stagnant pond. We had nothing in the car and in that part of Ontario there didn't seem to be towns or gas stations where travelers could stop for water.

We passed dozens of apple orchards, trees with their branches bent to the ground, loaded with rosy fruit, and everywhere the honeyed scent of cider filled the air. Each orchard had a roadside stand advertising "Cold Apple Cider" scrawled on homemade signs. Finally, unable to resist, we pulled off the road at the next stand, and ordered a tall, fizzing glass of the most fragrant, ice-cold, thirst-quenching drink we ever had in our lives. In seconds we tossed it back and exclaimed, *Let's have another*, unaware that in Canada, apple cider was a naturally fermented alcoholic drink. Feeling happy and delicious we drove all the way to Niagara Falls in high spirits. Denis had never been so witty. Never had we laughed so much.

Until that day, the only alcohol that ever touched our lips was a sip of Mogen David wine from the communion cup on Sunday mornings. Except. I admit to those little sips of Molson's Canadian my Grandpa Frolander left in the bottom of his beer bottle on hot summer afternoons. To this day I can't open a bottle of Molson's without remembering what a gift he was—the only man of my child-hood who loved me with a constant, unremitting love. No strings attached.

On arriving in Massachusetts, we stayed with Aunt Ruth, Denis' favorite of his mother's four sisters, a woman who loved *him* with a constant, unremitting love. She was glad to have us, even though she was still raw from the death of her husband who had died from colon cancer the previous year. Often she turned her head away from us. I think it was the pain of seeing Denis and I to-gether, our young bodies, our affection for one another—all reminders of what she had lost.

I didn't know this at the time, but throughout the rest of her life she would be the bearer and interpreter of Denis' place in the family, and the story of Denis' mother and father, who by then had returned to the Philippines. Through her, we learned more about his mother's history and her family. It was often a story of sadness and confusion created by a man who claimed to know and act on be-half of God, allowed no disagreement, and was righteous in all he did and said. Aunt Ruth was a front line witness of the way Denis was treated by his father even before he was old enough to understand. The story was nearly inconceiv-able. It influenced us to the core of our being, our marriage, and our children. Over time, grace and mercy helped us face our own histories and it brought with it a measure of healing to our hearts.

Although Minnesota has more than 10,000 lakes, and even though one of them, Lake Superior, has the honor of being the largest fresh-water body in the world, I was in no way prepared for the vastness of an ocean. That first week of our visit, Aunt Ruth took us to Horseneck Beach where I had my first look at the Atlantic Ocean. The experience was so intense, I still recall the details.

It was late morning when Aunt Ruth drove east toward the coast and the land began to flatten and change. Pine trees became smaller and stunted until they disappeared altogether, replaced by masses of low-growing junipers and marshes filled with tall reeds. Along the road, eastern asters in full bloom created a haze of soft purples. The air felt baby-soft and hung with the tangy scent of salty tide as we pulled into the parking lot at the end of a gravel road. The sea was still hidden behind sand dunes, but as we climbed up the wooden steps through sandy soil lined with rafts of fragrant wild roses and beach grass, the sea loomed like an enormous presence. I stopped for a moment in the breeze to listen to the gulls as they wheeled and screeched above us and to hear the gigantic murmur of an ocean breathing against the shore.

When it finally came into view, the vast expanse of rollers stretching for a thousand miles fell off the horizon where sky and sea blended in blue haze. I felt like I was seeing God for the first time. Or something from him. About him. I couldn't name it. I stood by the shore, my feet in the flowing, sandy foam, my face stinging with spray and wet with tears. The unrelenting breakers turning over and over and over reminded me of something I had hoped existed and always longed for: evidence of God's patient, unchanging, relentless, unstoppable love. As the oceans roll, so is he, forever and ever.

Not before or since have I experienced the stabbing awe of creation, of recognizing in quite the same way: *this is my God.* Sublime, Unknowable, Frightening, Ever Present, and Powerful.

FAR FROM HOME

Summer was nearing its end when we returned to Minneapolis from Massachusetts and rejoined the Team. In preparation for the next leg of our journey, Denis and I completed the last step in getting rid of everything we owned in order to be a disciple of Jesus. We gave our car to a friend who needed one. We did our laundry and repacked for our next stop, which was going to be a rural Assembly in southwestern Minnesota where the elders had asked us to come and do a two-week evangelistic series. Then we would travel on to Phoenix where we would stay for a month.

Families from this little Minnesota Assembly kindly opened their homes to the Team, and Denis and I were sent to an old farmhouse where an elderly couple gave us a room on the second floor that smelled of mothballs and lavender powder.

We smiled and said thank you, this will be wonderful, but the moment the bedroom door closed, in the privacy of our room I created a fuss about the sleeping arrangement. I took one look at the two single beds and announced there was no way I was sleeping alone. What was this couple thinking? We were newly married and could not be expected to sleep apart in twin beds. I was feeling more worn out than normal and had been looking forward to sharing a comfy bed. Denis was shaking his head and I could tell my complaints were stressing him out. "It won't hurt us. This is only temporary. What are we supposed to do? Refuse to sleep here?" he said, in an effort to reason with me.

Finally, we compromised. I agreed to stop complaining if he would help me move the mattresses to the floor each night so we could sleep side by side. Reluctantly, he agreed. In the morning we replaced them, hoping our hosts would never know.

I did not understand how traumatic it was for Denis to navigate staying in a stranger's home. Later I learned more about how his past had affected him. The daily vigilance he had grown up with became more intense when his parents traveled across the country, raising support for their mission work. Night after night, they stayed in the homes of people they didn't know. After arriving at a host's home and being conducted to a guest bedroom, his father often sat Denis, his sister, and mother on the bed, and in impassioned whispers, lectured them on their behavior and how important it was to never let an unguarded comment slip. They must appear frugal and be careful to receive offers of anything from used clothing to food you didn't like. Denis detested green peas, but when a hostess served peas for supper, not only was he expected to eat them, but his father would announce how Denis loved peas, knowing he hated them. Then he would place an extra-large serving on Denis' plate.

Sleeping in Sunday School classrooms with Team Outreach.

The farmer and his wife probably heard unusual bumps and thumps coming from our bedroom, though we tried to be very quiet. Perhaps they recalled the distant past when they were young and in love, and perhaps they excused us for the passion they may have imagined. Or maybe we simply annoyed them. I'll never know, but I was a much happier partner for the nights we spent there before making our way to the southwestern United States.

Our Team was headed to Phoenix where another Assembly had asked us to come for a month and head up an evangelism campaign. Once we arrived, we'd do our usual door-to-door passing out literature during the week and inviting people to special gospel meetings on the weekends. There wasn't a central location for all of us to stay, so we were going to split up and stay in the homes of various volunteer hosts.

When we reached Flagstaff, an unexpected situation arose. It had taken a while for Denis and I to figure it out. We thought travel was making me feel exhausted and sick to my stomach. Every day I was experiencing overwhelming nausea. Then it dawned on us. It had been more than seven weeks since my last cycle. I was pregnant. For the previous two weeks, as we traveled to the Southwest, we'd been living mostly on peanut butter and jelly or tuna fish sandwiches slapped together at rest stops. The scent of tuna was so revolting, most of my meals became ditch fertilizer as we careened to the side of the road and I jumped out of the car holding my hair back and bent over the weeds. I quit eating. It was easier. My breasts were on fire. My head ached. I most assuredly did not want anyone touching me. I lost every ounce of humor. All I wanted was to go home and sleep, but we no longer had a home.

We were ignorant of what pregnancy can do to a woman's body, and since I wasn't doing very well, our Team leader reasoned that getting Margie to Phoenix and moved in with the people who were hosting us might help. Surely, there, I would settle down and feel better.

Sadly, we parted company as the Team went off to visit The Grand Canyon, Denis and I headed down Interstate 17 in one of our team member's cars. Mirages shimmered in the late September sun along the desert highway as we drove south with the windows down and the hot wind blowing through the car while my body roasted in the heat. Being pregnant explained so much of what I was experiencing. Bringing a child into the lifestyle we had adopted was beyond what we had imagined, so we were repressing questions about the future. It held so many notes of uncertainty, I thought it was best to not think about it for now.

Denis had wanted children and was ecstatic about the prospect. I wasn't. I'd had enough of them as the oldest of six. Too much babysitting. Too many dirty diapers and mashed vegetables. Now children were apparently inevitable, but it didn't stop me longing for freedom. Freedom from Team Outreach. From my body. From the crazy ascetic life we had chosen.

I had a habit of reading billboards aloud when we took car trips. At times this was funny to Denis. Other times it drove him crazy and he had found a way to quiet me and make us both happy at the same time: a bag of unshelled, salted sunflower seeds. He handed me a bag, but on that day I wasn't spitting husks and chewing seeds, or even talking, because I couldn't without crying.

I had never seen the Grand Canyon and that was just one of the disappointments I felt for both of us. Hoping to amuse me, Denis began reading billboards as they floated past the window—many advertised food. He was anxious about my not being able to keep food down and thought I should eat something, but nothing sounded appetizing.

It made some kind of sense that if we were going to live in the Southwest for awhile, we should learn to appreciate the local food. Before the globalization of ethnic foods, Mexican cuisine was far from my Minnesota Scandinavian-trained palate. I had *no* idea what an enchilada was or even that there was such a thing as green chile. There was just one exception to this: my mother made something we called Indian Tacos. Years earlier, she had learned a very mild, hybrid version of tacos from a missionary to the Navajos in New Mexico.

I sat up and tried to focus as Denis read advertisements for Mexican restaurants. Coyote Café. La Torta Gorda. Rosa's Cantina. All of them shouted *Authentic Mexican Food!* I was willing to try. We pulled in at Rosa's Cantina next to a truck stop, not knowing a cantina was a bar that may or may not serve food. We were in luck. As we walked through the door, a wall of cooking odors hit us. Tortilla chips frying in hot fat and the pungent smell of red chili sauce swirled us to our table. The scent of garlic and onions caused my stomach to lurch. We looked at the menu and decided to order a combination plate that included the most popular dishes: enchiladas, a taco, and a tamale. We didn't want to be the kind of people who complained about dishes that weren't like the ones our mothers cooked.

Our food came on large oval platters drowned in a reddish-brown sauce. The sizzling plates were dropped in front of us with a warning not to touch the hot rim. We paused, wondering where to begin. We could not identify anything except what looked like a pile of rice on the border. We didn't even recognize refried beans, the second-most ubiquitous dish that accompanies every Mexican plate on earth. I poked at the mass with a fork and tentatively extracted a lump from beneath the sauce. In one second I realized I had just placed a flame thrower in my mouth. I drank a full glass of water trying to extinguish the spicy heat of red chile. When the throbbing did not subside, I forced down a few tortilla chips and a little Spanish rice. I was mollified when Denis couldn't eat his food either, and he didn't have the excuse of being pregnant. We left most of it untouched. At the car, I leaned over and left what I had eaten on the pavement in a stinking puddle. We both vowed never to eat Mexican food ever again. We didn't care how godly it was for missionary-types in Arizona to learn to eat Latino food. We would need to find other ways to please God and love people because it was no enchiladas for these gringos, por favor.

It wouldn't always be like this. The transition into loving Mexican food was altogether unexpected. Slowly and gradually, our tastes shifted until one year later, red and green chile, the spicy combination of cumin, garlic, and onion contrasted with the mild nuttiness of corn tortillas wrapped around pulled pork and cheese, the lift and sweetness of honey-filled sopapillas gave us such pleasure we began craving Mexican food. Chile added to anything made it better. Eggs. Burgers. Even chocolate.

We owed the shift to Don Pancho's Buffet in Albuquerque. I'm not saying it represented gourmet Mexican food or even quality dining. It was the equivalent of a midwestern all-you-can-eat buffet where mountains of mashed potatoes, soggy green beans, and Jell-O fill the tables, and whatever is lacking in quality is made up in quantity. With an endless supply of fresh tortilla chips on every table, you could choose salsa according to the degree of heat you could tolerate, from mild to the fires of hell—your choice. Tacos, tamales, enchiladas that set your mouth afire were carried to the table—as many as you could eat. The best thing about Pancho's was the endless supply of sopapillas. Each table had a little pole with a Mexican flag; raising the flag was the signal for the server to bring you more of whatever you wanted. We always wanted more sopapillas. Those hollow little Mexican pillows of dough came out of the deep fryer hot and perfectly puffed, soft on the inside, crispy on the outside. You bit off a corner and as the steam escaped, you drizzled honey into the hole and ate them as they collapsed. There cannot be a sweeter, more perfect foil to the spicy heat of chile rellenos.

This change held a note of incredulity for us. It seemed to represent hope that one day I might miraculously learn to love many more things I thought I had disliked or even hated. Could living in a place so far from home—so lacking in familiarity and permanence be the place God wanted us to be? Here in the high desert, this *no place* we thought was empty of pleasure and even empty of meaningful nutrition, might it become the place we needed to be?

In Phoenix, our new hostess welcomed us and led us to the bedroom where we would be staying for the next month. She closed the door and left us to settle in. A double bed greeted us. There was a handy bookshelf layered with dust next to the bed. Insects trailed across the cloudy window and over the sill. I shuddered as a cockroach scuttled under the dresser. Baskets of stained sports clothes and old tennis shoes were stuffed into the corners of the room. It smelled faintly of sweat and locker rooms. A poster of Simon and Garfunkle's *Bridge Over Troubled Water* was taped to the wall above the bed. Obviously the bedroom had belonged to their son who was away at college. In spite of the dust and bugs, I was determined to make it work and be the best guest ever. I spread our belongings on the bed and began to reorganize the disarray from our days of travel.

Soon we were called out to join the couple for our first dinner together. We made small talk and I sternly told myself, *eat.* I swallowed as many bites as I could, then had to excuse myself to the bathroom. When I returned I apologized profusely and Denis explained I was pregnant and having trouble with nausea. I sensed some disapproval in the air and felt embarrassed, but didn't know what to do about it. On successive days I learned her go-to menus were all-American spicy, tomato-y, garlic-y dishes. Nothing wrong with that. Normally, I love pizza, spaghetti, and sloppy joes, but at the time they were about as appealing as boiled calf brains.

As the week began, Denis left to be with the Team, and the couple we stayed with went off to work for the day. Since I was having so much trouble keeping food down, I remained at the house. It made sense. I couldn't be vomiting on someone's doorstep while trying to tell them they needed to get saved.

It was lonely being in a stranger's home with little to do and no one to talk to. It made the hours creep past. I read a book. Walked around the walled-in backyard. Sat on the bed. The next day I had an idea. I would go to work cleaning up the house. Our hostess had a day job and when she returned from work, late in the afternoon and needed to make dinner for her husband and two visitors, I felt compassion for her. She must be exhausted, I reasoned. She didn't have time for herself or the energy to keep up with things around the house, which was why it was so dirty. I had been raised to help. I was a helper. My mother taught me when you spot something that needs to be done, don't wait for an invitation, get off your behind and help. That was her motto. I also thought it was a good way to win approval and affection from those around you.

I found the vacuum cleaner and sucked up the sand and dust on every carpet in the house. In the kitchen I found soap and scrubbers and tackled not only the cook stove and counter tops, but the dirty, grease-splattered tiles on the wall behind them. I swept and mopped the floors and wiped down the appliances. Pleased with how great everything looked, I expected our hostess would *love* this. It did a lot for me, too. After several days of this, I didn't feel so useless doing nothing.

A gorgeous, old orange tree in the backyard became my gift, a reward for the work I did. It was loaded with sweet, ripe fruit. I had never experienced such deliciousness, ready to drop straight into my open hands. Every day, picking a warm sunny globe, peeling the rind as it burst fresh citrus oil over my skin and eating it was like walking in the Garden with God.

When our hostess found out I was eating them, she made it clear they were being saved for someone else. It was my mistake. I felt like I had been stealing and I apologized.

Sitting across the dinner table from her was growing more uncomfortable by the day, and her disapproval of me seemed to increase. She watched with a cold eye when I left for the bathroom and glared at me when I returned to dabble at my food. She rarely spoke to me, and it wasn't difficult to tell something was wrong, but I didn't know what.

Only a few days into our stay, on a late afternoon, Denis returned to the house and called me into the bedroom. We sat on the bed and he put his arm around me. "I learned there was a special meeting called with the elders of the chapel and it's been decided we are to be moved to another couple's home for the rest of our stay in Phoenix."

"But, why?" I asked, puzzled. Why did it take a special meeting of the elders to make this change?

At first it was all secretive and I was left wondering what had happened. It was clear it had something to do with me, but no one told us specifically what I had done to get us kicked out. Eventually, it leaked out bit by bit—whispered to us by other team members and finally stated openly by our new hosts. After hearing what I was accused of, it was a wonder anyone would want to have us.

She accused me of criticizing her. She said I was ungrateful and impossible to please. I laid around all day and then refused to eat anything she cooked. I did not like the home provided for us at some cost and inconvenience to her. During the meeting she apparently broke down crying and said she couldn't stand to have us in her home anymore. When Denis and I heard this, we looked at each other incredulously. Life had come to this? He reached out to me to comfort, "You are not the person she described. She just doesn't get it."

Slowly, I began to understand what had happened. It wasn't only that I ate her oranges without asking and had trouble eating her food. I committed a more serious breach of etiquette thinking I could make myself useful by helping out. While she was gone, and I was alone in the house with nothing to do, without an invitation, I cleaned her house. Nothing could have been more insulting to her. I might as well have written her a message in the dust that said *you are a useless, incompetent slob.* That was not what I intended. Well. To be scrupulously honest, maybe I did think she was a tiny bit challenged in the housekeeping department.

I didn't know whether to feel guilty for being the world's most offensive houseguest or enjoy the gush of relief for getting out of there. I had inherited enough Minnesota-nice genes that complaining about what someone cooked or censuring the way one kept house might be enough to at least get a sharp scolding from my mother. She didn't allow her children to criticize others for such things.

There was a familiar pattern to this failure on my part. Once again, I was working hard to win approval and favor by being helpful. By doing everything I could think of to be pleasant and acceptable. It hadn't worked in the past with my stepfather. I had stripped cedar fence posts, cleaned the barn without being told, and restacked the wood pile in an effort to win his love. Apparently this was another case where it wasn't succeeding.

It became a lesson painfully branded on my heart. To this day, if I'm invited to help wash dishes at someone else's house, I am careful *not* to do what is obvious to me—wipe drips off the coffee maker, shine the faucet, and wipe the oven door handles.

The experience of trying to cope with a difficult pregnancy and the humiliation of being accused of being an ungrateful brat was devastating at the time. But as I reflected on the situation I had been in, it became clear that whatever problems this woman had were not altogether my fault. She was not someone who reached out with kindness or understanding to a young woman living with strangers who was sick, isolated during the day, and yet who wanted to be helpful in the ways she had been taught.

An unexpected gift followed this struggle. I soon realized it wasn't accidental that we had landed on a new doorstep. It was evidence that God cared for me and could rescue me from a difficult situation even if the difficulty was of my own making.

It was instantly obvious the next place was a home of shelter and safety, even if it was temporary. I was taken into the arms of a woman whose name I can't even remember, but what she did was like removing thorns from the pads of my feet and coating them with balm. She was the sweetest gift straight out of God's pocket and became my mother for the few weeks I spent under her care.

While we stayed with them, Denis kept up the pace of going out with the Team each day and returning in the evening when we joined the family for supper and relaxed together. I think he was so relieved by the kindness of this new host and hostess and that I was doing much better, we didn't talk about how he was feeling or what he was thinking.

This woman was perfectly equipped for taking me in hand and beginning my education as an expectant mother. From her own years of experience, she took one look at me and said, "You need B vitamins, especially vitamin B6, which is going to help your nausea. When you wake up in the morning, first thing, do not get up—here, take these soda crackers, eat one or two along with B6 before you even get out of bed."

After weeks of misery, I was ripe for anything to change my life, but it was especially sweet coming from this experienced older woman who did almost everything except tuck me into bed at night. She tackled my diet with supplements, healthy food, and more tips for controlling nausea. Then she handed me two books and insisted I read them immediately.

The first was *Let's Get Well*, by Adelle Davis.[3] She was one of the first nutritionists to criticize the American diet for being too full of processed foods and empty calories. She encouraged people to stick to naturally-grown vegetables when possible. This made complete sense to me, having grown up in a home where the deliciousness of garden vegetables and homemade food was part of our everyday diet. Davis emphasized that when you were pregnant, you needed to eat carefully and well to benefit the baby you were carrying. If she had insisted on a strict diet of raw eggs and lemon peels I probably would have jumped on that train.

Although not everything she wrote was something I put into practice, her book changed the way I thought about diet. The basic education I received from her became foundational to my belief that the food we eat, its source, and the way it is prepared, is important to our health and wellbeing. Many of the choices I made over the years could be traced back to Davis, who first inspired me to question a diet of highly-prepared, super-market products and American fast food.

Both Denis and I came from solid working-class people, surrounded by mainstream middle-class families. In the comfortable community of our church life, we were isolated from people not like us. We knew that in the world "out there," subcultures existed, but they didn't impact us in any significant way. Anti-Vietnam war protesters, the drug culture, most of the rock music scene, and even the civil rights movement remained in the background of our lives. The implicit and sometimes explicit belief was that Christians like us would not be associating with such people. Adelle Davis suddenly made me eager to associate with a nutrition subculture I didn't know existed. It helped in subconscious ways to prepare me for the next step in our spiritual journey, which would take us not only into the world of hippies and drugs, but would lead us to live in a commune.

As I followed my mentor's advice, I gradually began to feel better. This included the psychological comfort of being cared for by a kind woman in a clean home where I felt safe. Learning more about pregnancy was giving me the hope that I could do this after all.

The second book was *The Womanly Art of Breastfeeding* put out by the La Leche League.[4] I knew nothing at all about this practice that had been a part of motherhood since the beginning of time. Here was an entire book educating and advocating a return to this centuries-old way of feeding your baby. Breastfeeding had become a lost tradition among modern women until the end of the 60s, when the practice resurged as women rebelled against bottle-feeding. I became pregnant just as this practice was beginning to slowly shift the minds of young mothers.

In the years before the 1960s, babies were fed formula. One of the major reasons breast milk had fallen out of favor was due to aggressive marketing by companies like Carnation who advertised their canned milk as *helping babies to put on precious pounds and inches, helping arms and legs to grow straight and strong*.[5] What mother doesn't want that? Doctors and midwives routinely supported the practice of bottle-feeding and encouraged mothers to accept it. With more women in the workplace, formula became not just supplemental, but a primary solution and readily available. The practice spread to stay-at-home mothers. However, research gradually began to change this trend as scientific proof of the benefits of breastfeeding emerged. According to the American

Academy of Pediatrics,[6] breast milk gave a protection to the baby no formula could offer.

There were also strong social objections to breastfeeding. To Americans, it was considered unrefined because it involved bodily fluids and exposing the breast. I had seen men walk out of the room, disgusted and embarrassed, when a woman discretely nursed her baby beneath a blanket.

The terms used in the book were fascinating. *Latching on. Engorgement. Colostrum.* Being a farm girl, I knew it was important to allow cows to nurse their newborn calves because colostrum was an important benefit to their health. I didn't know women also had this amazing nutritional fix for their babies during the first few days after birth, which acted like a superfood and gave their immune systems a boost. Until then I hadn't thought much about the function of breasts. They were simply a part of anatomy men seemed fixated on. Now I was persuaded they had a preexisting role; they were useful and important. Breast milk was a beautiful source of health and nutrition. I wanted it to be the sole source of sustenance for my baby's life. I needed to make certain I knew *how* to nurse. I needed to be sure the quality of my milk would fulfill all her nutritional needs.

Furthermore, I was going to insist on a natural, drug-free childbirth, even though at the time few doctors supported or even allowed that to be a mother's choice. I didn't care how much childbirth was going to hurt or what anyone said—this was best for my baby and nothing would stop me from doing it my way. In a few months I would see to it that these decisions would be accomplished.

As if all this wasn't enough, our lovely host ushered me into an entirely new world of creativity: together we sewed maternity clothes that made me feel beautiful.

THE LAND OF ENCHANTMENT

Hot wind blew hair into my mouth and eyes as we stepped from the van onto a baked landscape of sand, boulders, and distant mountains hovering over the far curve of the earth. The air smelled like iron filings and copper rings. The sky burned turquoise. Watery mirages wavered far ahead on the highway. Grit clung to my lips. We rinsed our mouths and drank tepid water from the jug.

The only moving things as far as the eye could see were tumble weeds hissing across Route 66. An abandoned motel and a rusty gas station pocked the road beside us. Broken barbed wire and weathered gray fenceposts enclosed miles of mesquite and prickly pear, hinting of ghostly peoples who years ago failed to survive the land. Nothing grew in the sun-torched mesas and arroyos. Green was absent. The earth in shades of sand and dust was the floor of a brilliant sky.

We were passing through this incomprehensible landscape on our way from Phoenix to Albuquerque with the Team. Nothing called *stay and thrive* to one who grew up in verdant forests of pine and aspen, lush swamps, fields of wheat, and thousands of blue lakes in northern Minnesota. In travel guides, New Mexico, The Land of Enchantment was described as "a place of spectacular natural wonders from majestic 13,000 foot snow-covered mountains to beautiful desert vistas that defies imagination." Truly, they defied my imagination. Robert Sekuler writes, "In some instances the optical information reaching your eyes is too impoverished for context to be of help. You find yourself in a paradoxical situation, able to see but unable to tell what you're seeing."[7]

The Team had been invited to spend three weeks at the Garfield Gospel Chapel, a small Plymouth Brethren Assembly near the University of New Mexico in Albuquerque. They hoped our door-to-door evangelism would infuse new life into their small congregation. We arrived on a warm afternoon that didn't feel at all like November. Denis and I carried our boxes into a Sunday School room, pushed aside metal folding chairs, and unrolled our sleeping bags.

After staying in a real home for three weeks in Phoenix, the cold tile floor, the fluorescent lighting, and the asbestos ceiling made us feel chilled and homeless. I arranged our cardboard boxes, covered one with a scarf, and perched a candle on top as Denis echoed my thoughts exactly: "Why is asceticism killing us?"

I wandered through the rooms of the chapel trying to imagine a meaningful existence anywhere here in the high desert of New Mexico. The geography mirrored our lives. Barren. We had been married exactly one year and five months and this desert was no place I wanted to be. We were still looking for answers but finding few. I longed for Home, but didn't know where it was.

Percolating on the back roads of our life was a book by Francis Schaeffer, a strange little man who wore knickers, a theologian and philosopher who taught that historic Christianity rightly understood and applied could answer the questions raised by modern culture and give us a rich and dynamic hope for living life as God intended. We had included it among the few books we brought along with us. It wouldn't be long before *The God Who is There*[8] was destined to change our thinking and living. It would provide a theological structure for us to understand culture and reality and give us a worldview that would begin to shape our life, thinking, and work. It was a difficult book to understand. I eventually read it three times, in an effort to fully grasp his meaning. It would take time for us to wrestle with his intriguing ideas about the relevance of Christianity.

Meantime, our days at the chapel in Albuquerque began to take on a rhythm. Again, I stayed back at the chapel and cooked for the Team as they doggedly continued door-to-door canvassing with little success. The days were long and boring. We spent our evenings in Bible reading and prayer that failed to move me. I felt guilty. Physically, I was feeling better as my pregnancy progressed and nausea lessened, but at night we both felt discouraged and anxious. Denis and I talked about his dread of walking the streets, of ringing doorbells and trying to get people to listen to a canned speech. There was irony in inviting someone to read the *Steps to Peace with God* booklet when we had so little peace ourselves. If someone had expressed interest, it probably would have been so shocking we wouldn't have known how to respond. We hoped and prayed that the literature left inside screen doors might be picked up and read and taken seriously. In reality, it felt like we spoke a religious language no one understood. The pivotal question we asked, if we could ever get that far, was still, "Where would you go if you were to die today?" That often prompted a slammed door or an unprintable answer.

We whispered questions to one another. What was going to happen to us? I couldn't keep traveling from place to place or we'd end up like Joseph and Mary looking for a hotel in which to deliver a baby. Perhaps we needed to leave the Team. But to where? And for what? We had no money. No plan. No place to live.

We had sold everything we owned and joined Team Outreach as a last ditch effort to see whether Christianity had anything to offer life. This life we chose seemed to be a dead end.

The questions that prompted us to join the Team remained unanswered. We agreed there was some security in sticking it out where we were, but at what cost to our souls? Didn't pundits say "Better the problems you know than the ones you don't"? We were utterly disillusioned with evangelism and asceticism. From our sleeping bags on the floor, as we stared at the tile ceiling, our future looked bleak and uncertain.

Then, as if blown in by the desert wind, tiny seedlings of hope began to poke through the barren sand. A mystery began unfolding little by little around us.

The neighborhood near the chapel was full of rentals for university students, college dropouts, cohabiting couples, druggies, and a mixture of working class poor, along with a smattering of young people just out of high school looking for work. Hitchhikers and runaways moved through the city in droves that autumn, sleeping in parks, gathering in groups, buying a little marijuana, a hit of acid, looking for safe places to sleep and hoping to find a little something to eat.

The Vietnam war was at its peak in 1969 and it was blowing up the fabric of our nation. Across the country young people were holding mass protests over the bombing of Cambodia. The police and the National Guard turned out armed with tear gas, guns, and clubs. That year a tragedy unfolded at Kent State in Ohio when the National Guard fired on unarmed protesting students, killing four and wounding nine. Among the dead and wounded were students merely observing the demonstration from a distance. Following their deaths, four million students went on strike, forcing the temporary closing of hundreds of colleges and universities throughout the country.

Interstate highways were swollen with young people on the move, making their way from the East Coast to Haight-Ashbury in the West. Every person under the age of twenty-five knew the hit song "California Dreamin'" by the Mamas and the Papas.[9] At every interstate highway entrance and exit, young people gathered singly or in ragged groups, carrying back packs, leading dogs, holding cardboard signs that read "Need a ride to L.A." During the summer of 1967, 100,000 young people had converged on California, hoping, searching for a new life, a new way to live.

Albuquerque was a stopover on the southern route and hundreds walked or rode into town in sandals or bare feet. Young men with beards and long hair, wearing patched blue jeans and tie-dyed shirts, girls in long skirts and peasant blouses, hair tied back in bandanas and smelling of patchouli oil—all dreamt of a life that promised to be trouble-free, full of beautiful people making love not war while tripping out on acid. At first these people were as foreign to us as the native peoples of Irian Jaya.

As Denis and his partner Paul went door-to-door near the university, they began hearing a refrain from a few who were willing to talk for a minute on their front doorstep.

You sound like Richard and Terry.
Richard and Terry talk like that.
You should meet Terry and Richard.
Terry and Richard are really high on Jesus.
Richard and Terry are Jesus freaks.
They're pretty famous because they are Albuquerque's first dealers of psychedelics.

Denis stopped asking, "Where would you go after you die?" and replaced it with, "Where can I meet Richard and Terry?" A young man gave the address of a dilapidated rental house a few blocks from the chapel. Apparently, every night these two kept an open door where anyone was welcome to drop in. No reason was needed. You were offered a cup of coffee and invited to join or listen in on conversations and argue about whether or not Jesus existed, or whether getting high on Jesus was better than any blotter of Yellow Sunshine, and if the Bible might be true after all. Whether or not there was a spiritual dimension, whether good and evil existed—they discussed everything. Anyone who expressed more interest might be anointed with oil and prayed over. It sounded exotic and slightly dangerous.

That night, Denis and I told our Team leader we were going to visit them and walked through the dirt of their front yard and onto a porch hung with macramé planters and knocked on the door. There were old lawn chairs leaning against the house, Coca-Cola cans scattered on the porch floor and ashtrays full of cigarette butts. Lamps glowed through the paisley-curtained window and loud rock music pulsed through the walls. We knocked and someone opened the door. It was Terry. "Yes?" she asked.

We introduced ourselves as people who had heard about them from their neighbors, and Terry welcomed us into the foggy living room where we collided with a wall of sandalwood incense and cigarette smoke. The room was packed with young people sitting on the floor; some with guitars were singing, others in small groups were reading the Bible and intensely discussing it. Others looked like they were praying with their eyes closed as they held hands and rocked back and forth. Later, Denis learned that everyone who saw him enter the room dressed as he was, in a neat button-down shirt and close-cut hair, became extremely nervous. Some left the house. Denis was a dead ringer for a narcotics agent, come to spy on people like them.

Terry invited us into the kitchen and that began a series of startling conversations. In the few days following, Denis and I made our way back and heard
more of their story. As we listened, the air around us seemed to crackle with the
presence of God. Here was a demonstration of faith that seemed more authentic
than anything we'd experienced. Nothing had prepared us for this.

Or wait. We *were* prepared in a sense. All the doubts and questions that
surfaced in our lives had brought us to this point. We had stumbled across this
strange group of Christians that seemed to exhibit the very reality we were looking for. As they prayed together that night, we realized we had never experienced
prayer like this—filled with joy and passion. We had slogged door-to-door hour
after hour without any response, and yet here was a group of people so excited
to talk about their faith that their non-Christian friends couldn't stop asking
questions and wanting to know more about Jesus. We had a mysterious feeling
we were standing before a vast ocean and being told to step in. Urged to *swim.*

We had already concluded we needed to decide soon whether to stay with
the Team or leave. Could these new connections offer some possibilities? We
speculated and tried to be objective. This subculture of hippies where people
had dropped out of mainstream life seemed incredibly foreign and yet attractive. And hadn't we already defied the conventions we knew by selling our possessions, quitting university, and leaving our jobs in order to follow what we
thought was Jesus' call? That was already a pretty radical form of dropping out.

We thought about Luke's account of the disciples who were making their
way to Emmaus after Jesus was crucified. Everyone thought he was still dead,
when suddenly Jesus, freshly risen, joined them and began walking and talking
with them, explaining all the prophesies about himself. At first they had no idea
who this man was, but later they said of their encounter, "Didn't our hearts burn
within us?" (Luke 24:32 NLT). That's how it felt for us. As we heard Terry and
Richard's story, our hearts burned. Like moths attracted to light, we flew straight
into the flame.

Terry grew up in Albuquerque. Her father was a colonel in the Air Force; her
mother, a pueblo Indian converted to the Baptist church. Terry had a talent for
art that bordered on genius. In high school, that talent became her entry into an
artistic subculture where experimenting with new ideas, morals, and forms of
expression were encouraged. She was introduced to marijuana and became a
pothead.

Psychedelic drug use soon followed. At sixteen she became pregnant after
an affair with her art teacher. Horrified, her mother told her, "Either that thing
goes or you do." Her parents put her into the car, drove to Mexico, and forced
her to have an abortion. As soon as she could pull herself together, she ran
away to California with a terrible wound in her heart. There she met Richard.

They fell in love, married, and decided to move back to Albuquerque, where, they became the first dealers of the psychedelic drugs which were fast becoming popular across the United States. With their connections in California, they brought drugs back with them and soon became well-known on the street as sellers and users.

On one of their trips to California to resupply, they ran into an evangelist named Arthur Blessitt. When they met him, he was on the street preaching to the hippies on Sunset Strip.

Blessitt was a Baptist pastor who saw what was happening to the culture of young people in the late 60s. His heart ached for them. Established churches were distancing themselves from these threatening freaks. Churches, religious institutions, and Christian groups rejected not just the drugs, but the rock music, the dress, the long hair and sandals, the free love—they vigorously rejected the hippies themselves. Hippies were people to hate. God forbid one of your children should be seduced into joining this crazy movement that was destroying the nation. And yet everywhere, even young people from churches were listening to the music of bands like The Beatles and Led Zepplin and heading to Los Angeles and San Francisco with the hope of finding something they could barely name. They longed for some deeper meaning, something more demanding and beautiful than the predictable nine-to-five life of their parents, whose goals of personal peace and affluence hid an unbearable emptiness. Hippies were searching for love.

Blessitt built a large wooden cross, believing that in all its brown, splintered earthiness, it stood as a powerful symbol of Jesus and his love. The fact that Christ had suffered rejection, torture, and death was a way of connecting with an alienated generation searching for a life that held deeper meaning than that of their parents. Blessitt dragged this cross with him wherever he went. Sensing that hippies were looking for spiritual reasons to live, Blessitt also opened a space above a night club on Sunset Strip and called it His Place. He went onto the streets and invited runaways, stoners, drug dealers, anyone lost or hungry to come in off the street where he would tell them about Jesus and pray for them.

People listened to him because his authenticity shattered all the American religious stereotypes they had known. Love radiated from his whole being. When trippers stoned on acid saw and heard him preaching in his blue jeans with his long hair and beard, they associated him with Jesus himself. When Blessitt was evicted from His Place, he chained himself to his giant cross down on the street and fasted for twenty-eight days until another place opened up for him. Many listened; many were converted; and out of this the "Jesus People" movement was born. Among those converted were Richard and Terry. They stayed with Blessitt for several months to be taught and to grow in their new faith and commitment to Jesus.

When they returned to Albuquerque this time, they were changed. No longer using or selling drugs, they began reaching out to friends—opening their home and telling them about what had changed their lives. Sharing that real love, forgiveness, and meaning were found in knowing God and his son, Jesus. It was not to be found in all the places they had previously sought it. The influence of their lives reached deep into a throng of young people who had known them before their conversion.

Each evening, as Denis and I stepped through their door, it was into a world so foreign, so other, it made us gasp for air—and not just because of the incense and smoke. It was almost impossible to make sense of what we were seeing. What was being reported in the news all over the country and what was happening everywhere in the dark underground belly of our culture was happening right here a few blocks from the chapel where we slept at night. But that was only half the story. What wasn't being told was that here among the dropouts of society, in the most unlikely places one could imagine, we were discovering a faith so vibrantly alive that simply being near them set off indescribable longing in our hearts. Here were dozens, perhaps hundreds who wanted to know who Jesus was and what difference he could make to life. Groping through the fog, we were falling in love with the strangest people we'd ever met.

It was disquieting. If this spiritual reality was what we had hoped for in Christianity but hadn't found, the Holy Spirit had certainly revealed himself in a very surprising place. We hardly knew what to make of these strange phenomena. What we were discovering was going to require some difficult choices.

Meanwhile, the Team continued going door-to-door, inviting people to Bible studies and church meetings. No one ever showed up. When we were alone, Denis and I tried to imagine what our future might look like. We prayed; we begged God to help us know what to do. Where to go.

Then one day Denis and Paul met two young men who expressed an interest in discussing spiritual matters. They had questions about who God was. They didn't know much about the Bible or about church so Denis invited them to the Chapel's Sunday service. We were over the moon to at last meet someone with this much interest. It was unprecedented for our time with Team Outreach.

The Plymouth Brethren Assemblies typically have two morning services— the first is called "The Breaking of Bread," and is a simple communion service of prayer, singing, Scripture readings, and short exhortations. Non-Christians are welcome to observe, but are asked to sit in the back and not partake. The second hour is a teaching service open to anyone. That was the one Denis invited these two young men to attend. They were nervous, wondering how they should dress. "We don't have fancy clothes," they said. "We've never been to church." Denis promised, "How you dress doesn't matter, just come as you are and you'll be welcome."

On Sunday morning, we anxiously kept an eye on the door, hoping and praying that the two young men would show up. The second hour began and they still hadn't arrived. Then in the middle of a hymn, the door opened and two long-haired, disheveled, hung-over looking guys walked in and quietly sat down in the back row. One of them was barefoot. We could barely contain our joy and wanted to jump up and hug them. We didn't notice the consternation that rippled through the small congregation, a sucking in of air as members stared or furtively glanced back at this invasion. Then, without ceremony, two of the elders rose, walked to the back, took each by an arm, and escorted them out the door, firmly closing it behind them.

We sat stunned, unable to control the emotions that coursed through us. We were heartbroken. Disappointed. Angry. Terribly angry.

This was the only church we had known since childhood. The one all our family and friends belonged to. Now all we wanted was to get away. Away from the narrow legalism, the lack of love, the dead orthodoxy. We were done. We were ready to *drop out.*

Drop out, tune in, and turn on. The last referred to drug use, but when co-opted by the Jesus People movement, it suddenly sounded attractive. Dropping out of society and joining this movement of vibrant faith suddenly represented everything we wanted to do and be. Never mind that our anger made us seem uncharitable and unforgiving. Never mind that we had no plan, no money, and no place to go. We were just out. Period. Denis and I were dropping out and turning on to Jesus.

Could we be described as utopian? Immature? Romantic? Hungry? Heartbroken? Rebellious? Probably all those things. But in Albuquerque, at that moment, we had no doubt God had led us to this point. Bizarre as it was, we were ready for a massive change.

I don't remember all the details that flooded our lives in the following days as we made the monumental decision to leave both Team Outreach and Garfield Gospel Chapel. For some reason, during the short time we had known them Richard and Terry had grown to love us. We were filled with love for them, too. They were moving into a big old house in the middle of a city park. There would be plenty of space for everyone and an enormous living room large enough to hold the crowds that swarmed in for an evening of coffee and conversation. Terry and Richard wanted us to join them in this uncharted adventure. We didn't have a history of drug use like they did. Nor had we previously been exposed to the counter culture. What we did have was extensive Bible knowledge that gave us a presence and some authority among the young converts. From the time we were little children our knowledge had accrued through twenty years of Sunday School, sermons, Bible camp, and devotions.

I think back to this time and try to fathom why these young people were so eager to share their lives with us when we knew so little about their world. I'm not certain, but perhaps more than our Bible knowledge, it was because we loved them. We wanted to hear their stories, give them hope, heal their wounds, and carry them to Jesus. It didn't matter what they were high on, or what they believed, or how they looked; they became our obsession, our mission, our calling in life.

No longer homeless for the moment, we found our place among the hippies and the stoners, the Jesus freaks and the drop-outs, and all who believed we should make love not war. We shared everything we owned. His House. We were a Christian commune. A part of the Jesus People Movement.

This, at last, was ours: "joy unspeakable and full of glory." (1 Pet. 1:8 KJV).

We never expected to find it, least of all in such a place.

BOOK III

[1969–1971]

Hidden Rivers in the Desert

The Rio Chama is a tributary of the Rio Grande.
At 130 miles long, it's only one of many New Mexico rivers that
have nourished human populations for more than 13,000 years.[1]
The Rio Chama begins in Colorado and passes south through
northern New Mexico. Like all hidden rivers, the Rio Chama has
numerous beauties. The beauty I love most reveals itself against all
probability as you travel across a hot barren desert, passing massive
boulders, acres of prickly pear cactus, and twisted mesquite. As the
highway winds and drops, gradually each mile reveals the lush paradise of
a hidden valley. Green curtains open, revealing bubbling waters running
with trout. In the spring, a fog of cottonwood seed wafted by the wind
settles in white drifts along the banks of the river. Snow melt rushes
from the Rocky Mountains in little rills and ripples, providing water for
thirsty animals and pastures. Orchards emerge; fields of green chili and
pinto beans line up in long rows. Sheep graze on the hillsides.
A perfect place for a picnic of wine and bread.

HIS HOUSE

We topped the hill, turned into a circle drive in the middle of a small city park near the University of New Mexico, and climbed out of Richard's car. Perched on the crest was a log cabin. "Cabin" implies small, but this manor built of massive ponderosa pine logs with twenty-one rooms was a rustic mansion. And for the love of all things green, it was late-November, but the surrounding park still held patches of living grass. Perhaps spring would return one day, bringing trees and shrubs back to life; flowers would blossom and brown grass would come alive again, even in New Mexico.

We headed up the walk and climbed the steps to the large wraparound veranda. We paused, trying to grasp what we were entering. Terry and Richard had found this place available for rent and had already named it His House, acknowledging it was going to belong to God. We were there to inspect the rooms and claim a bedroom. Between us, we had pooled $500—enough to pay for the first month's rent.

The mansion had been built in 1903 by an architect who designed it after a Norwegian villa. It was originally meant to be an inn for people traveling through Albuquerque to California by train. When the railroad was finally completed, it ran too far west of the inn and was not convenient. Eventually the mansion became home to the family of the architect.

It passed from them to a new owner, who lived there for many years; then it was sold to a fraternity. Finally, it fell into the hands of the real estate company now willing to rent it to us. We were a rag-tag group of hippies, ex-druggies, and Jesus People without steady incomes or solid backgrounds. What business person in her right mind would lease such a place to us? That they were willing confirmed to us that God was clearing a path for us to walk.

The heavy wooden door, like none I'd ever seen, was hung with forged iron hinges and opened with a large wooden latch that lifted and slid to the side. Inside, a bolt could be dropped into place that made the door impregnable.

The cabin on the hill.

When the door opened, its hinges sounded a rich *screeee* and closed with a descending screech and a solid thunk as the latch fell into place. On the outside of the door were deep scars. We heard stories of First Nation people who shot it with arrows during uprisings early in the twentieth century. I don't know if the stories were true, but the marks were there.

There was a mystical aura about the place. We felt it in our bones and fell headlong into the charm of this old log cabin. The door opened into a grand living room with an imposing stone fireplace on the opposite wall. The scent of pine resin and the faint odor of wood smoke lingered in the air. Around the edges were built-in shelves with plenty of space for books. Even after we dragged in chairs and couches left behind by former tenants, we did not fill this spacious room. Furniture didn't matter much anyway because we were young and content to sit cross-legged on pillows or the floor for hours at a time. We constructed a huge cross of unfinished pine poles lashed together with rope and the guys suspended it above the fireplace. To all who entered, the cross marked us as followers of Jesus.

From the hard floors of Sunday School rooms to the warmth of a log cabin, this was going to be our home. For how long we didn't know. We tossed out the cardboard boxes, pitched the suitcase, and carried in our sleeping bags. Denis and I settled into a room at the top of the house. After six months of sleeping on the floor, sleeping on a double mattress someone donated was like finding morel mushrooms in the woods. Luxury upon luxury—a real bed! The sun, bright and warm, poured into the room through windows on three sides. An acquaintance dropped off huge sample books of outdated drapery fabrics, someone loaned a

His House Front Door

sewing machine, and I sewed squares together to make patchwork curtains that softened the room and filtered the light into warm rainbow colors.

Just off the living room was a small, dark room set aside for prayer and meditation. It was quiet and peaceful, with ancient wood paneling still fragrant with the soothing scent of pine trees. We covered a cedar chest with an embroidered cloth and leaned a small brass cross against the wall. In the middle of the chest we placed an open Bible flanked by a pair of candles. A cut glass cruet held

His House Living Room

aromatic oil used for anointing. The reassuring aroma of sandalwood incense
lingered in the air and reminded us that here in this simple place where we
knelt together before the cross, holding hands with one another as we prayed,
the Holy Spirit seemed to bless even the atmosphere itself.

This dedicated room especially caused me to reflect on our past. Candles?
Incense? Kneeling together? Altars and crosses? We had been taught that such
things were signs of Romanism or idolatry. Then, there was prayer itself. Men
and women, we all prayed together. Suddenly, at His House, I was free to join
in. I left behind my fake-sounding prayers and leaned into the chorus of voices
surrounding me.

Beyond the living room was a hallway with stairs leading up two floors to the
bedrooms. Leading down, the stairs passed rooms on other levels and ended in
a large dining room with a kitchen attached. The cabin, being built on a hillside,
placed the dining room at ground level where large windows looked out the
back onto stone gardens and walkways leading down to a small row of rented
apartments that at one time had been a horse stable.

Here in the dining room, we ate suppers together as a community, taking
turns preparing the meal, sitting down at a long harvest table with benches on
either side. Out of necessity, I began to tolerate Mexican food as long as it wasn't
too spicy. I learned to prepare our staple diet of pinto beans and corn tortillas,
with green chili added to nearly every dish we made. When we could afford
them, cheese, eggs, tomatoes, and avocado were welcome additions.

Having left behind my family of stolid Norwegians and Swedes, with their green pastures, harsh winters, and daily helpings of meat and potatoes, I found this new diet strange. Even the weather in New Mexico continued to feel alien. Compared to Minnesota, the months came and went with little more than the calendar to define seasons that left us hot, brown, and dry. It took at least a year of scrutiny to discern the subtle changes.

Like Alice in Wonderland, Denis and I gradually discovered we had emerged from a rabbit hole into a place and time in history when the Holy Spirit was at work reviving a generation that became known as the Jesus People. We joined them with the hope of bringing every hip-

Prayer Room at His House

pie from the coast of California to the boroughs of New York into the Kingdom of God. We were going to help reach a generation of searching, drugged-up, lost young people. We would let them in, we would love them and be glad even if all we did was lift a small corner of the darkness.

Captured by the compelling beauty of this vision and sheltered within the walls of His House, we did not pause to think about practicalities. None of our ten housemates held steady jobs or had a source of income. Denis and I didn't have regular support. We weren't even planning for the life and care of our coming child. We lived in the moment. We would trust God. That was all that was important.

Our stay in that log cabin would only be eight months. Eight tumultuous months. If I was a tree cross-cut to read the rings of my growth, it would witness the drought and fires of life that existed beside wide seasons of unprecedented flourishing. Those eight months in a Christian commune would leap from the rings of my history. It was a time when God exploded our indigenous religious beliefs—our pretentious knowledge of him and the legalistic works-righteousness that had shaped my life for years. It was like the waterbed Terry and Richard had kept in the living room of her parents' house when they were house-sitting. They had allowed a litter of puppies to sleep and play on the bed. One day while they were out, the puppies bit holes in it with their sharp little milk teeth. When they got back, and opened the front door—puppies and water gushed out of the house, down the steps, and into the street. Neither the bed nor the living room were the same again. We, too, were swept away by the power of the Holy Spirit and were never the same. Yet what remained of our past, what helped stabilize our community for a while, was our knowledge of the Bible. Like DNA, it was a good part of our heritage. We passed it on to our housemates who were newly converted, unchurched, and had only the barest understanding of what it meant to be a disciple.

Within a few weeks, more people joined us until we became fifteen house members altogether, including Pax the mutt and two cats—Bang-go and Boswell. We decided that was the limit and no more would be added. Except for Denis and me, nearly everyone had been heavy dopers. Richard and Terry had led all of them to faith in Christ, and those who were invited to join us were ones who seemed most committed to a new life. Except for the occasional blunder back into old habits, they had given up using drugs. At twenty-two, Denis, Richard, Terry, and I were the oldest by a few months. The rest ranged in age from eighteen to twenty-one. Along with Richard and Terry, we became leaders. That didn't mean much more than establishing a few rules and taking the lead in Bible study and conversations with visitors who were curious about what we believed.

We established a few rules:

- No drugs allowed in the house.
- No one allowed to stay overnight. *We're not a crash pad!* we told the many who wanted to move in or "just spend the night."
- No one who was not a house member was allowed past the dividing curtain that led to our living quarters and kitchen.

That was it. Nothing about dividing up responsibilities for shopping, meal prep, cleaning, or upkeep. We were going to let the Spirit lead. Uh-huh.

There were the guys—Michael, Manny, Bill and Al. All of them musicians who had formed a rock band together. They were such boys, like younger brothers to me, sweet and generally manageable. I loved them and felt they needed a mother. They were nearly always anxious or paranoid about something—partly a side effect from smoking too much weed and dropping too much acid.

There was Diane, a shy beauty who had been a rock star groupie. Apparently the signed posters in her room had been thanks enough for being a one night stand. Her search for love had led her into dangerous relationships that injured

My jamming housemates: LtoR Manny, Al, Michael, Bill.

her heart and body. In need of deep healing, she was drawn to God, finding in him a compassionate love that could not compare with her lovers. She found a measure of healing in Christ, and it made others want to know more about what had changed her.

David and Lisa were happy to be back from a military post in Germany. Giving up the image of stern, straight, and narrow, they, too, were ready to drop out of mainstream life. When they joined us, they were the most disciplined of all of us. They were determined to understand what it meant to be a Christian and put it into practice in their new life. They had a darling two-year-old boy who fit right in with the rest of us.

Bruce was the most weird, the most lost, most addicted, most articulate of all of us. And he was a dead ringer for Bob Dylan. He wore his hair in dreads before it was a meme. We often found him sitting on the floor, playing his guitar and harmonica, singing one of my favorite Dylan songs:

> Leave your stepping stones behind, something calls for you
> Forget the dead you've left, they will not follow you
> A vagabond who's rapping at your door
> Is standing in the clothes that you once wore
> Strike another match, go start anew
> And it's all over now, Baby Blue[2]

Bruce playing Bob Dylan

Bruce was also a speed freak who often disappeared for three weeks at a time in order to stay high, never sleeping day or night until he used heroine to bring himself down. I don't think he ever found stable ground, even though when sober he longed for it. We first met him outside the house where Richard and Terry used to live. He was kneeling in the dirt with a whip. He was repenting, he said, and whipping himself for punishment. He had had an argument with Terry about love. She claimed God loved him and so did she. He doubted that. "You would say you loved me as long as I didn't do anything to make you mad." She claimed he could do anything and she would still love him. So he picked up a kitchen chair and broke it to pieces. When she didn't become angry he said, "Okay, I believe." Bruce would return to the house after his bouts, looking thin, hollow-eyed, sick, and ready to try again.

Lauri was a young musician, an artist who played her guitar and sang like no one I'd heard before. She brought the songs of our generation to life with her honeyed voice; as she sang, her long blonde hair fell across her shoulders and hid her face. There was something strong but gentle about her that made people want to confide in her.

Before meeting Lauri, the collection of songs in my head was narrow, consisting mainly of old hymns and Bible choruses, like "Heavenly Sunshine" or "It

Only Takes a Spark." Even now, I repress them or they'll start a loop and play in my head for days. Sure, I had listened to popular music—mellow guys like Pat Boone and Frank Sinatra singing sentimental mush. *Fly me to the moon, let me play among the stars; let me know what spring is like on Jupiter or Mars. In other words, Baby, kiss meeee.* Embarrassing! I never imagined that many years later Sinatra would reemerge to fuel a modern taste for vintage sound. There were exceptions—I could sing along with The Doors' hit song "Light My Fire," though I had only a vague idea of what it meant.

I never grew tired of listening to Lauri. In the evenings when people came by, she often drew a crowd around her. People were mesmerized by her singing. When she sang, I held my breath. The plaintive quality of her voice fell like rain on dry ground and exploded into rich beauty. Where on earth did this music come from, the songs that sang my life? Even our life of wandering, searching, and longing were present in these songs. One in particular seemed to fit us at that moment and I still hear it in my mind.

> I pulled into Nazareth, feelin' about half past dead;
> I just need some place where I can lay my head.
> "Hey, mister, can you tell me where a man might find a bed?"
> He just grinned and shook my hand, and "No!" was all he said.
> Take a load off Fanny, take a load for free.[3]

The music of the era fell heavily into us. It was a staggering change for a young couple from a fundamentalist background, out of the conservative Midwest. In our isolation from culture, we had learned to ignore student protests against the Vietnam War, and even when Martin Luther King, Jr., came to the St. Paul campus to address a rally we did not attend. Psychedelic drugs were present among students, but remained quietly underground, and we steered clear of those who used. We were called "straight." But that soon changed: Denis and I were already looking like we fit in with this psychedelic subculture. My hair was long and my clothes were casual and colorful. Denis' hair no longer had that slicked-back look and his old blue jeans were now perfectly appropriate. The people, the colors, and music filled us with joy and made us want to dance. The longing we had to find a more meaningful, relevant faith was satisfied, and our faith grew deeper as each day passed.

Others came through the house whose names I don't remember. Some were drafted to Vietnam; others left for California seeking a better life; some simply disappeared and were not heard from again. All had made professions of faith and then some left it behind. Others stayed and eventually became leaders as they matured and dispersed into life, into the church, into the world.

No one among us was rich, powerful, or widely known. We were a poor, disorganized band of young people. We were shunned by most churches, belittled by the local press, and spied on by the police. We didn't canvass neighborhoods with invitations, or post ads in the newspaper. Social media hadn't been invented, and yet, spontaneously, word about His House spread like dandelion seeds blown on the wind. Hundreds walked through our door to learn what we were about.

By 1969, when we arrived in Albuquerque, hitchhikers with packs on their backs and sandals on their feet were still streaming across the land on the long road to California. Coming from the east on Interstate 40, travelers passed through Tijeras Canyon, between the Sandia Mountains on the north and the Manzanos to the south. The mouth of the canyon opened to a vast vista. From there you could see for miles and miles. Below lay the city of Albuquerque, spread out along the Rio Grande River and up into the Sandia foothills. Far across the valley the Western Mesa rose with its five ancient cone volcanoes and black lava beds. Hidden somewhere below them in the urban tangle around the university was His House. How did anyone ever find us?

The Jesus Movement still remains a mystery to me. Among the thousands of young people on the roads in the midst of this mass migration, hundreds came to Christ. This was happening not only where we lived, but in the underground all over the country. A fire hose of people were gushing into the Kingdom through small groups, through individuals like Arthur Blessitt, Christian coffeehouses and communes like His House.

Dozens who arrived on our doorstep reported they felt a "vibe" coming from our hill, a powerful attraction they couldn't identify. The vibe led them through the streets and up the driveway to His House. Again and again, as people came through our door the first questions they asked were: What is this place? Who are you? What happens here? These were their first words so many times, we came to believe it had to be the Holy Spirit leading them to us.

A number of arrival stories were more unusual. Some visitors opened the door and entered looking pale and alarmed as if they'd seen a ghost. More urgently they pressed us with the same questions. They were afraid, they told us, because as they approached the veranda, two men or beings—they didn't know which—stood on either side of the door, dressed in blazing white, watching as they approached. In spite of their fear, they edged past and rushed through the door. Could they have been hallucinating? Perhaps. However, many insisted they were not stoned. None of the members of His House ever saw them. We thought about these strange sightings and wondered, were they angels sent by God?

Some visitors arrived high on drugs and related a different story. *I was stoned on LSD and Jesus came to me and insisted I must come to this place.* We observed that for some, psychedelics seemed to lift a veil between what can be seen and touched in the physical realm, and another dimension where colors and objects were enhanced, where the true essence and beauty of things was revealed. A trip could also include strange experiences with mystical beings. Some were beautiful and good, while others embodied ugliness and frightening evil. None of this could be explained in a purely material universe.

Living in this subculture of kids on drugs who knew nothing at all about God or the Bible, but who experienced vibes and saw angels and demons, began to show us we knew even less about God than we thought. He was being revealed in ways that staggered our imagination. We were witnessing that God could declare his presence to anyone, anywhere, at any time. We had assumed God worked miracles during the lives of his Apostles, or in some country far away in place and time, but not here with us in 1969. What we witnessed raised the hair on our necks as the presence of the unseen—where the Holy Spirit, his angels, and demons dwelt—crossed over into the seen. It reminded us of Paul's words: "For our battle is not against flesh and blood, but against the rulers, against the authorities, against the powers of this dark world and against the spiritual forces of evil in the heavens" (Eph. 6:12).

Feeling incompetent and unqualified in many ways, Denis and I answered questions as best as we could: "You have come to the living God, to Jesus who truly exists, who wants to free us from the powers that imprison us, free us from evil, the evil we have done to ourselves, from the evil we have laid on others." I often shared Jesus' words of love, "Come to me, all you who are weary and are carrying heavy burdens, and I will give you rest" (Matt. 11:28 NRSV). We read Scripture to them, we invited them into the prayer room and knelt, our arms around them. Every night there were those who came, drawn by the kindness of God.

His House became that peculiar spot where anyone was welcome for coffee, conversation, and music. It was a safe place to gather and talk about anything or simply hang out until way past midnight. All around us in small groups, warming beside the fire, were murmured conversations with songs rising now and again. Bibles were opened and words examined, and people were welcomed no matter how screwed up their life. At least twice each night the fifty cup coffee pot was refilled and carried up the stairs from the kitchen, and the living room filled with the comforting burble and scent of coffee brewing.

DEEP HUNGER,
DEEP GLADNESS

There's somethin' happenin' here
What it is ain't exactly clear
There's a man with a gun over there
Tellin' me I got to beware ...
We better stop, hey, what's that sound?
Everybody look what's goin' down ... [4]

In 1966, Stephen Stills wrote this song, performing it with his band Buffalo Springfield. It stayed on the charts for months. Since then, many musicians have covered it, from Dave Matthews to Tom Petty, on down to the current generation. Even now, when I listen to the first few bars, I'm instantly transported to the up-heaval of the late 60s and early 70s. The song never grows old. I love it.

Like all good art that touches on universal human experience, that song moved us because we understood. We'd been there. The words and music spoke to our fears, questions, and deepest longings. We, too, had known fear, grief, and suffering as well as joy. Stills was only one of the musical voices of our genera-tion that helped us verbalize what we were experiencing.

Even though Stills was referring to the war in Vietnam, campus riots, and the National Guard, at His House the phrase *There's a man with a gun over there, telling me I got to beware* touched us. Police often pulled into our circle drive at night and surveilled the house. They were certain we ran a drug ring and could not be convinced otherwise. There were reports in the local newspaper that sup-ported these rumors about us. Sometimes the police entered our living room un-announced and conducted searches. They never found anything, but that didn't stop them. Free coffee and telling people about Jesus was too unbelievable.

Something *was* happening in our life and it wasn't exactly clear what. Stills follows the phrase with a command and a question: *We better stop, hey, what's that sound? Everybody look what's going down.* Since moving into His House, we were experiencing things we'd never seen or imagined before. What was happening to us? To our country? Our world? Our faith? Nothing in our sheltered, conservative, fundamentalist, Christian lives prepared us for this. As the Holy Spirit moved in strange, sometimes frightening ways, we realized there were battles between good and evil, similar to the ones J.R.R. Tolkien and C.S. Lewis described in their fantasy novels.

Of the many who came to us over those eight months, there are a few individuals I remember well. One young man stepped through the door in the middle of an ordinary day. The atmosphere in the house was quiet and calm. Two of the guys were in the living room, cleaning out the fireplace. Some of us had just awakened and come up from the kitchen with a mug of coffee. Terry and I were tidying up from the previous night when he walked in. He might have been nineteen or twenty. He had curly blond hair and intense blue eyes. I remember because he was staring at me as he approached. My belly had grown to the point where I was unmistakably pregnant and he reached out his hands as if to touch me.

By that time, I was used to the gesture. Something about carrying a baby drew attention. Even strangers who didn't know me were curious and gentle on seeing my condition. Perhaps I represented something universal about motherhood. Or maybe I stirred the longings they had for the tender love of a mother— for someone who would nurture and protect them through life's storms.

When this young man walked toward me, I wasn't expecting to hear him plead for help. His eyes were dark with pain and grief. "Mary," he said. "Please pray for me, I need help." I thought possibly that being high on some drug, he simply made a mistake calling me Mary. I corrected him: "My name is Margie." This was not the first time this happened. My pregnancy, for some, seemed to be a reminder that Mary was a real woman and underscored the mystery of how she became the mother of Jesus. I, too, wondered a lot about her during that time. So for whatever reason, people often drew near and wanted to place their hands on me.

But in that second, as he approached, there was a terrifying shift in his appearance and it seemed as if someone or something else looked at me through his eyes. In a rasping voice, he lunged for my throat and growled, "I see your halo, Mary. I'm going to kill you. I know you are the Mother of God." As he spoke those words, arms suddenly grabbed for him and held him back. He struggled fiercely to reach me. I hadn't known Richard and Michael had been watching him closely. Richard knew him from the past as someone who could be calm and rational one minute and wildly violent the next. They had prayed for him several times and believed he was demon-possessed but unwilling to trust that God could change his life. I was shaking as they propelled him out the door and told him not to come back.

There was one girl who must have been no older than fifteen when she came to His House with a friend. Her friend had heard of us and thought perhaps we could help. There were dark circles under her eyes; she was trembling and hadn't slept for days. She was pale and thin and hadn't eaten normally for weeks. She was literally being frightened to death.

I have forgotten some of the details of her story, but I do remember she had become involved with a local coven and had inadvertently offended their leader, a warlock. He asked her to do something illegal and she had refused. Whatever it was, after she refused to comply, he put a curse on her and told her she was going to die.

We knew about this coven. They were a powerful group of witches and warlocks, well known by the local young people who came to us, especially the college and high school students. Many years later, I reconnected with a friend who used to visit His House when she was a high school student. She remembers how afraid they made everyone feel, and yet how they attracted people with promises of power and drugs and a sense of belonging to something larger than themselves. But there was a price to pay. Members became possessed by an evil they were not able to control.

The curse placed on the girl's hands made them bleed. It began happening inexplicably at home, where she would run to the bathroom to hide it from her parents. Other times it happened in school. Her friend told us they were together in study hall when suddenly her hands began to bleed. She excused herself to the restroom, and her friend went along and witnessed what happened. As she held her hands under running water the sink filled with blood and yet there was no visible sign of wounds or cuts. When it finally stopped, they were both shocked she was still alive. What happened night after night was almost worse—evil beings would peer through her bedroom window and advance toward her bed. She was convinced they would devour her the moment she closed her eyes. She pulled the shades and hung sheets over the window, but didn't dare sleep for fear of what they would do to her.

The only thing she knew from the story of the Bible was that Jesus healed people and was supposed to be the Son of God. I told her about his love, his divinity, his coming to earth as a man, and his ability as Savior and Lord to rescue her from the power of the darkness that was devouring her. As she heard about what Christ had done, the forgiveness and salvation offered because of his death and resurrection, and the new life she could have, she began sobbing.

We took her into the prayer room where one of the other women and I prayed for her, encircling our arms around her as she reached out to Jesus in faith, opening herself to him. We bound evil from her, and asked God to fill her with the love and protection of the Holy Spirit. I could see the change in her whole body from terror to peace as it descended on her.

From death to life. I can't describe the joy of seeing this lost, dying little girl come to Jesus—of the privilege of being there with her. In the following days she reported being able to sleep and eat like normal again.

The warlock who had cursed this young girl had a large underground coven devoted to him. As some of his followers deserted and came to His House, it put us on a collision course with him. People feared and believed him because he could perform miracles, and it was even rumored he had caused the deaths of some who had crossed him. He used his occult power to punish anyone he considered an enemy. When people joined his orbit, they had to do exactly as he bid or suffer the consequences.

Late one night, when His House was filled with conversation and music, the door was thrown open and the warlock pushed in, wearing a black cape. His entourage, all dressed in black, flanked him as he threw back his hood to reveal flaming red hair that rose in a halo around his head, adding to the dreadful aura that surrounded him. The disturbing thing about his entrance was that everyone froze and silence fell on the entire room. Some visitors escaped through the door behind him. Around us, people huddled closer to one another.

He shouted a challenge to Richard and Denis. He taunted them, proposing a contest to see whose god was greater—Jesus or Satan. My heart felt like it had plunged into darkness. I had no idea what could be said or done to meet this challenge. It was scary. All of us who lived at His House silently pleaded for God to be with us, to help us. It was Richard who stepped forward and began to speak in a calm, earnest voice. "In the name of Jesus, we accept the challenge. Our God is greater than yours, and anything you think you can do or say, or anything Satan can do or say is like nothing since he has been defeated by Jesus Christ."

The words were so quietly delivered it is difficult to describe what happened next. Out of nowhere, something formidable and fierce fell on the room. We could feel the presence burning our faces. Instantly, the warlock shrank back. A look of terror flooded his face. He spun around and ran for the door with his minions following. The door slammed behind them and we never saw them again.

The hair on my neck and arms rose, my heart filled with awe, and everyone in the room pressed closer in a tight circle around us and began asking questions about what had just happened. They wanted to know more about this

Jesus Richard was talking about. What did it mean? What should they do? How could they become part of this story? It was a night straight out of the Acts of the Apostles—a remake of the jailor's question to the Apostle Paul after a terrifying earthquake: "What must I do to be saved?" (Acts 16:30). The love and joy that swirled through the living room was wild and holy. I never dreamed such things were possible or that we would be a part of them.

I'd read missionary stories of men and women who faced evil spirits who oppressed people with darkness, illness, and suffering. These were things that existed elsewhere but not in the West, and particularly not in our country, "one nation under God." But as recently as the day I edited this paragraph we received a letter from a young couple working in Nepal. They wrote: "Most of us raised in the modern West find in our gut a sense of implausibility when it comes to the reality of the supernatural, spiritual warfare, and the like. But those outside Europe, North America, and the world's megacities see us as the naïve ones."

One young man I'll call Trevor began visiting us. He and his girlfriend had been regularly tripping on LSD. Their trips had been beautiful, with intense colors, patterns, and sounds, and left them feeling euphoric, in love, and at one with the universe. Then, a trip went very bad. Trevor descended into a frightening nightmare of deep darkness where he found himself at the base of a cross on which Jesus hung in a tortured, bloody mess. Jesus looked down at Trevor and called him by name. "Trevor, why have you done this to me?" Jesus' question pierced his soul, and he began to weep inconsolably. Jesus told him he needed to find a place called His House and talk to the people there to find out what he should do.

He found us and began eagerly studying the Bible with Denis. He knew almost nothing of the story of Scripture. Of creation. Of sin and redemption. Of the coming restoration of all things. One day he showed up with a question. He'd been reading his Bible and had come across a word he didn't understand. "We write unto them, that they abstain from the pollutions of idols, and from fornication, and from what is strangled, and from blood" (Acts 15:20 ASV). "What is fornication?" he asked. Denis explained it was an old word for sex between people who are not married. Trevor was shocked. "*Why* haven't you told me about this? This is exactly what my girlfriend and I are doing." Denis responded, "It isn't our job to tell you how to live—that's the Holy Spirit's job." We trusted that in time God would convict and teach his people new things about how to live as we walked alongside them.

A few months later Trevor and Jane married.

I would never add, "and they lived happily ever after," because I don't know. I do know they became missionaries to South America and we lost touch with them. At His House, it was not an isolated incident where someone encountered

Jesus on an LSD trip that changed his or her life. In each case it was a call for them to leave behind what they were doing, to come home, to come to Jesus. It changed them. The experience was never seen as an invitation or excuse to take drugs in order to contact God. What it proved to us is there is no place on earth nor any human experience where God cannot enter. God was demolishing every limit we had placed on him. It was both shocking and thrilling.

One day Hells Angels roared up to the house on their choppers. They slammed through the front door in black leather jackets, with flames and demons tattooed on their arms, and chains rattling on their belts. The young hippies who were our housemates shrank into the shadows of the living room and the women escaped to a bedroom—for good reason. Numerous police and international intelligence agencies classify the Hells Angels Motorcycle Club as a dangerous motorcycle gang in which members carry out widespread violent crimes, including drug dealing, trafficking in stolen goods, gunrunning, extortion, and prostitution. It was well known that bikers loved to beat the crap out of hippies just for the sport of it.

The Angels looked around and saw a curtained doorway that led to our private quarters. Early on, I had hung a sign with bold letters *PRIVATE. HOUSE MEMBERS ONLY!*, but this was like waving rotten meat in front of hyenas. One of our housemates meekly pointed out they were not allowed past that curtain, but the intruders turned a steely eye on him and no one else dared utter another word. They disappeared through the curtain, clanking down the stairs toward the lower level. Later, Denis related that like frightened deer, they all gathered in the living room to pray for protection. They had no idea where I was.

I was downstairs doing something in the kitchen, unaware of what was going on. I had never seen a Hells Angel. I wasn't even sure they existed. I'd only read about them. I was making my way up the narrow stairs as they made their way down. I was pretty advanced in pregnancy and in no mood for shenanigans of any kind, and I was astonished at the audacity of this group of guys coming down our stairs in obvious violation of our rules, of *my* sign. I met them midway and began aggressively stabbing the leader in the stomach with my forefinger. "What?! Can you not *read?* This is PRIVATE! Turn around and get back upstairs *this instant!* They began stumbling backwards, apologizing, "Mamma, it's okay. Be cool. We're leaving. Sorry. Sorry. Mamma! Calm down!"

They clanked across the living room and out the front door with me in pursuit. They mounted their choppers, revved their engines, and roared down the hill as I firmly closed the door.

Feeling restored, I turned to a stunned silence and then applause as cheers broke around me. I was surrounded and declared a hero or something like. People wanted to hug me and touch my stomach. Again! Some even tried to rest their heads on it. They laughed and called me brave. I had no idea why until someone explained they were Hells Angels. These were men who cared for no one and no thing and were as happy to rape and kill you as they were to wreck your home and kidnap your women.

Once again God had protected us, this time in spite of my ignorance. It would have been nice to think of myself as a hero, but it was hardly that. I knew I was not brave. I was simply a crabby, pregnant woman who needed very little provocation to confront strangers foolhardy enough to break practically the only rule we had for visitors.

Each month, when rent came due, we all met together to pool our cash and hope we had enough. Most of the time it was just the right amount needed. The process made me anxious and I usually vacillated from trust to panic. No one had a steady income. Some had little odd jobs here and there or some birthday money they shared. Denis and I occasionally received a gift from his aunts on the East Coast. Then a month came when we couldn't scrape enough together no matter how many times we checked our pockets or the mailbox hoping for a miracle. It didn't seem like it was the right time to give up and move elsewhere. Our location was perfect. On the morning the rent was due, as Terry and I cleaned up from the previous night as usual, I found an envelope stashed between the sofa cushions. It contained the exact amount of money needed to make up our shortfall. We speculated it may have been accidentally left by a dealer or perhaps it was an anonymous donation from someone who cared about us. Whatever the case, we chose to believe God intended us to use it for rent.

There was another month when again the deadline rolled around and we didn't have enough money for rent. As we were cleaning the living room, we found three twenties tucked under a sofa cushion. Then someone found another stash, and another. We discovered more and more bits of cash hiding between books, under the rug, until it felt like a treasure hunt. It seemed like everywhere we looked there were bills—ones, fives, tens until at last, when we added them up, it was $500, the exact amount we owed for rent. It was a providential gift, generous and extravagant, arriving at the perfect time.

On evenings when visitors filled our living room we were all sensitive to the atmosphere in the house. Was there a sense of welcome? Were people antagonistic? Afraid? Curious? Calm? Most of all we wanted people to feel like they were in a safe and loving place. As our reputation spread, there were a few youth pastors who thought it was a good experience in evangelism to bring their youth groups on a little mission trip down to His House where they could engage hippies about the faith. Sometimes this worked out fine, especially if they listened and quietly observed. But one Saturday night, when the place was filled with visitors, a Baptist youth group showed up and decided they would sing a little concert. Think of the songs popular at Christian camps years ago. "Kumbaya, My Lord," "This Little Light of Mine," "Heaven is a wonderful pla-ace, full of glory and gra-ace." It was horrifying. They had not been invited to sing. They were in a room where people were trying to hold serious conversations. Most of them listened to musicians like Jimi Hendrix with his screaming guitar, Led Zepplin's acid rock, and The Beatles. Those of us familiar with Christian camp songs knew the kids' songs would be as incomprehensible as a foreign language to our guests and would have nothing to do with anything relatable. We had no idea how to handle these well-meaning youth without hurting their feelings. None of us had the guts to ask them to be quiet or leave. Apparently, had they been Hells Angels I would have had no problem.

One of our housemates suggested we lay our hands on the roof. She reasoned that we often placed our hands on people and prayed with requests or thanksgiving or blessing. Whatever the occasion, it was met with prayer and laying on of hands. So why not do the same thing on the roof of the house and pray for help?

We could get onto the roof through a window in the third-floor bathroom. Sometimes we sat up there in the darkness and watched the moon shine bright over the city, over us, over the world. I scrambled through the window with several others. Side by side we laid hands on the roof of His House and asked God to please intervene and cause these kids to either stop or go away. Perhaps both. We didn't know. When we arrived back downstairs to our astonishment they had moved outside to the veranda where they strained to quietly finish a song. Then they left.

A few days later, the youth pastor saw Denis and commented he had been down to His House with his group on Saturday night and they had a strange experience. They came, intending to help out by singing, but for some reason in the middle of a song they felt compelled to move outside and shortly after that they left. It was odd to him and he couldn't explain the weird feeling they had experienced. Denis smiled, but didn't tell him what we had done.

These stories may give a wrong impression. Our eight months in His House was not a series of days filled with sensational, spectacular events. The miraculous did not define most days. Most were filled with the mundane things of community living. We cleaned toilets and vacuumed floors. We rose to eat breakfast and make coffee. We welcomed visitors and sat to listen and talk. God was at work in the midst of our ordinary, everyday lives, teaching us that all days are holy, not only the days when we witnessed unusual evidence of God's presence.

Being pregnant was still interfering with my mind and body. I hardly recognized myself anymore. Nor did Denis. On several occasions he mournfully announced, "You're not the girl I married," which did not comfort me or improve our relationship. I channeled unpredictable emotions. There was still no wise woman to walk with me as I drew closer to my due date, larger and more breathless. I wished my mother was there to assure me *This is normal! You'll be okay.* After all, she had six miscarriages in addition to six births. We didn't communicate very often. Long distance phone calls cost money, and my mom didn't write very often—nor did I. There were times when I was overcome by great love and tenderness, not only for the life growing inside me, but for anyone who stepped into His House. Other times I was obviously possessed by a fierceness even the Hells Angels didn't dare confront. It was true in the midst of hormonal changes, I was more bossy, but I liked to think of it as simply being more assertive and not as evidence of moral failure. In those days, being kind to myself was not something I trusted or even knew how to do without becoming too self-centered. The kindness and acceptance I couldn't give myself was often given by those who lived with us—an unusually sweet gift.

Visitors often stayed until one or two in the morning, so by the time we fell into bed, we were exhausted. One night Denis and I settled down, hoping the house below was also slipping into quietness; we were nearly asleep when the guys pulled out their guitars. This was not unusual, except on that particular night they parked themselves on the landing outside our bedroom door, even though there were a million other spots in the house where we wouldn't have heard a single note. Not that I didn't love them or their rock music—I just didn't love it at three o'clock in the morning when I was hoping for a couple hours of precious sleep. I fumed and counted to one hundred while they continued jamming. I tried to get Denis to ask them to stop, but he said if I wanted them to quit, I should tell them myself. He claimed it didn't bother him. When I could no longer stand it I dragged myself from bed, opened the door, and told them to go somewhere else and play. I thought I hid my spleen, but they could tell I was irritated. "Sorry. Sorry," they whispered holding their hands out in apology, then sheepishly crept down the stairs to the living room. From that time on I was known as "Marge the Sarge."

No one knew it took courage to step outside my fear of being disliked to tell them to either stop or go away. Pleasing everyone, especially God, was still my primary motivation in life. No matter if their music made me lie in bed grinding my teeth and wishing they would move to Siberia, I needed to endure. I must never be angry. Telling them to go away left me feeling guilty. There were exceptions, of course, but pleasing everyone, especially God, was a potion I drank every day. Being pregnant reduced my ability to pretend nothing bothered me, including Denis' refusal to help me solve that particular problem. It hurt. It felt like he was indifferent to my needs. I tried to explain this, but he didn't understand.

This might have been a reasonable discussion between a more mature couple, but I interpreted it as rejection. He didn't love me.

I loathed myself for being so needy. It eroded my image of being strong and the helper of others, *not* the receiver of help. The larger I grew with child, the wider the crack inside opened. I was pregnant, fat, and ugly. I wanted my mother. I felt sad and lonely.

Overcoming pride and looking for reassurance, I crawled back into bed and asked Denis, "Do you still love me?" Even as I asked, I knew it was a mistake to verbalize the question. He was silent. If I needed to ask, what could reassure me? If he said, yes, I love you, I would dismiss it because I knew it wasn't a spontaneous declaration, but one I had forced from him because of my need. If he were to express anything short of I-love-you-forever-you-are-the-light-of-my-life, what would I do? If he was honest and said no, I don't love you, where would I go?

During that time of doubting, late one night I suddenly woke from a sound sleep. Someone had called me. I distinctly heard my name. *Margie. Margie.* I was instantly wide awake. It was a voice filled with deep tenderness and love. I was sure it had to be Denis who had called. Was there anyone else who could possibly say my name in the way I yearned? I looked over at him and whispered, "What? What is it?" But he was sound asleep, breathing regularly. Never in all our years of marriage has he talked in his sleep.

In the silence, it felt like somehow a universe of goodness and love had pressed into our little room and surrounded our bed. I thought, *Jesus, is it you?* I said nothing out loud. But there it was. There he was. Or so it seemed. The voice of God. It came during a time when I desperately needed the reassurance that someone loved me unconditionally. It took a long while to go back to sleep, as I waited to see if I would hear anything more. There was only a comforting silence. I settled down, believing if God loved me, that was all I needed. With whatever power we have as humans, and unable to respond perfectly, I loved him back.

Loving God was not a new path for me. I had loved him since I was a little girl and had decided to become a martyr for him, and wouldn't he love me forever for *that*? But here, as a woman far from her roots, living in an unfamiliar world in what was to shortly become a very unstable community, I was given a level of reassurance no human could give.

There was another night after Denis and I had gone to bed, tired and late as usual, when I sensed he was oddly wide awake. When we were with Team Outreach, nights had been our time for talking and sharing our thoughts. But now this wasn't normal. He usually fell into bed and drifted off immediately. I thought perhaps he wanted to chat. I could tell he was in a good mood and it felt nice to lie together holding hands.

The next day I learned he'd been stoned on acid. I've forgotten how I learned this—I think he told me. In any case, later, Denis did tell me all the details. Dave, one of our housemates had received some LSD in a letter from a friend in Germany. The drug was applied as drops on a piece of blotter paper. Each drop could be torn off and eaten. Dave knew his friend only purchased high quality product, and though Dave was no longer using, he offered to share one hit with Denis and be with him while he was high. Denis was interested because we were both familiar with the thinking of A.E. Wilder-Smith. He was a British organic chemist who had a theory about sensory perception and drugs which went something like this: We think of our sensory perceptions as opening us up to sense and taking in everything that's going on around us. Wilder-Smith argued, instead, that when humankind fell in the Garden of Eden, God placed a filter on our sensory perceptions. It was to spare us from being overwhelmed by the glory of creation and spiritual realities, both of which can overwhelm fallen creatures. Taking drugs such as LSD partially lifted that filter and allowed more of those sensations and experiences to pour into us. Denis and I both thought that in the experiences people related, there was a spiritual connection to the use of LSD and other psychedelic drugs. So he was interested in trying it.

I flipped out and cried. Mostly I was a little scared and definitely angry at myself for assuming his being awake was an expression of love for me. To learn he was high, couldn't sleep, and was enjoying being together, touching my skin, watching the colors and patterns that tracked across our ceiling, and the sound of music floating up to our floor, ran a stake through my heart. I went to Terry and demanded, "Get me some acid. If Denis is going to do this, so am I!" I was not interested in the effects of the drug so much as I wanted to punish Denis for this breach of trust. I would teach him a lesson! Alarmed, Terry, Diane, and Lauri put their arms around me to soothe and reason with me. Terry had the most convincing argument: "You're carrying a child so you must not do this to your baby." No one knew at the time what drugs could do to a baby in utero. Finally, I quieted down and backed off my plan, but it took a while to get over my pique.

Later Denis told me he was very sorry for upsetting me and his only regret was that I was pregnant and we couldn't take it together. Although he would never do it again, and never encourage anyone else to do it, the experience had been profound. Creation was far more beautiful than he had ever imagined. The veil between the visible and invisible realms felt permeable and immediate.

We continued to see so many conversions there weren't enough of us to care for all who needed love and teaching and mentoring. It was like leaving a new baby on the street and telling her to find her own milk. Most were unchurched, so the biblical narrative held a freshness for them. They were eager to learn all the stories and apply them to life. We poured and poured water into hearts that, like thirsty ground, welcomed it. But we were not enough. We needed help.

So Denis and Richard went to churches, asking pastors and ministers if they were willing to befriend and help these new Christians. When it became clear they were talking about hippies and druggies and street people, the pastors wanted nothing to do with us. Some claimed interest but hesitated because their members were frightened of hippies or simply didn't like them. Hippies were evil and drug-addicted and dressed weird. They were different from us. One couldn't risk having them walk into church on a Sunday morning dressed in sandals and patched blue jeans, smelling of patchouli oil.

Ah. We understood that only too well.

It was discouraging, until finally two churches came forward who were willing to help—Grace Bible Church and Heights Christian Church. The pastors leading these churches took a real risk in reaching out to us and promised to welcome any who wanted to attend their services or Bible studies. Staff members came down to His House to meet people and see what was happening. They began personal relationships with our guests and invited them not just to church services, but into their homes.

All these hippies whom others thought of as offensive and undesirable were people made in the image of God, and their very existence was connected to the deep joy and call God had given Denis and me: *this is your calling, these are your people, this is the place where you are to stay and love and serve.*

It was what Frederick Buechner speaks of when he says, "The place God calls you to is the place where your deep gladness and the world's deep hunger meet."[5]

UNTO US IS BORN

"I need a towel. I think this is it. Don't tell anyone. I *don't want* to be hugged and my belly patted before going to the hospital," I pleaded, as Denis bent his head over mine to hear my whisper. He immediately turned and ran up the stairs to our room on the third floor.

Supper was over and our housemates had left the table. Diane and Lauri were clearing dishes and cleaning the kitchen. I was about to rise from the bench, when it suddenly felt like a warm puddle gathered under me. I stood up and took a quick peek at the bench to see what in the world? The surface was shiny and wet. Shame gushed through my body. Had I lost all control? Did being eight-and-a-half months pregnant mean I was now going to regularly wet my pants? Then like a storm dumping rain, I remembered hearing that water breaking meant labor was beginning. The leak of amniotic fluid was not something you could control.

When Denis returned, we wiped the bench, and I fled to the bathroom on the landing. I had to be sure I wasn't simply incontinent. I wasn't. Denis ran back up to our bedroom and grabbed the overnight bag I had packed for the occasion. Quietly, we left the bathroom and as much as a heavily pregnant woman can sneak, I tiptoed up to the main floor and tried to nonchalantly pass through the living room. As I escaped through the front door cheers rose along the driveway. Everyone had lined up and all our housemates insisted on touching my swollen belly and giving me a hug. Like running the gauntlet. Not what I wanted. As we drove away, I could hear them shouting, "Praise God. We'll be praying for you."

In hindsight, I regret that this upset me, because it was evidence of their concern and affection for me. *"Who* did you tell?" I demanded. Denis sheepishly confessed he had told Terry, who was also pregnant and about a month behind me. "I didn't think she would tell everyone." A few weeks earlier, without my knowledge, he had promised to let her know when my time came. On hearing my labor had begun, she excitedly spread the news until everyone in the house knew, and they all gathered to wish me well.

There were some legitimate reasons for the emotions I displayed during my first pregnancy. Hormones were running amok, certainly. But I was also anxious about the entire process of giving birth. I wasn't sure what to expect. No birthing classes were offered at the time, although they were coming soon, I had not learned to breathe, and pant, and push, and do all the other things to help me bring a baby into the world. To prepare myself, I had read books about child-birth. The photos of smiling women with large bumps made the process look and sound like childbirth was magical. Nothing more than a tiny tummy ache. I wasn't entirely convinced. Growing up on a farm, I'd seen plenty of cows groan and moan while giving birth. I thought it might take all the courage and resolve I could muster. Surely my ability to be focused and stubborn would help me through the worst part. But how could I be certain? My mother had never talked about her birth experiences. I was determined that when the moment came, I would control my body and all distractions. At that moment, as we hurried out the door, friends were the first distraction of the night, and I was as fierce as a badger with a hole to dig.

During prenatal exams, I had told the doctor I wanted to have a natural childbirth. Surprisingly, my doctor agreed. "Fine," he said. "You can have your natural childbirth." This meant I was choosing not to take any pain medication during labor and most especially there would be no anesthesia that forced me unconscious in the delivery room. With all my heart, I wanted to be present when this child arrived and it made me happy that he agreed.

After settling into a labor room, I was given an initial pelvic exam to find out how far along I was. Periodically a nurse popped in to offer pain meds and I kept taking a pass, thinking how much better this would be for my baby. As each contraction subsided I told myself: *You've come this far. You can do it. Just keep on.*

We had arrived at the hospital around 8:00 pm. A first baby can take hours, sometimes even several days to naturally descend into the birth canal. My body, however, quickly amped up, and soon the contractions came hard and fast. They were lasting longer than a minute and were only a minute apart. I was struggling to control the pain when Denis became my second distraction. In an effort to comfort and help, he tried to hold my hand and reminded me to breathe. "DON'T TOUCH ME!" I yelled. Managing the pain was taking all my concentration, and I knew if I let up for one second I would start screaming and never stop. He forgave me this outburst, but never forgot it. He retells it with great relish.[6] From the stories told about women in books and movies, it was clear we women had a reputation for loud, piercing wails while giving birth. This was also something I was determined *not* to do. I would not conform to that stereotype *no matter what the cost*. As the pain mounted, cutting like a knife through my middle, I became a little more sympathetic toward the screamers.

There were others on the ward that night who were also laboring hard. We could clearly hear a Latino mother shrieking over and over, *Jesus, Mary, and Joseph, if you love me you will help me now!* We laughed at this until another contraction rolled through my body.

About 11:45p.m., I reached the stage of childbirth called transition. Unexpectedly, in less than four hours I was fully dilated and ready to push the baby out. My nurse meandered in asking, "How are we doing?" I didn't need to answer. From experience, nurses quickly recognize this phase and she jumped to warp speed. Instantly the room filled with staff who threw me on a gurney and ran me down the hall to the delivery room while poor Denis was left to anxiously pace the halls.

Shortly after midnight, I was unceremoniously spread, draped, and told to resist pushing until the doctor arrived. I knew the baby's birth was close and after making it that far drug-free, I was excited to think I could make it the rest of the way. I imagined the baby's first cry was only seconds away. Staff were still busy arranging things when the doctor pushed through the door. At his nod an anesthesiologist clapped a mask on my face and told me to breathe deeply. I struggled to push it off, but was held down. "Please, no, no. I want to be here. Please." It was useless. I lost consciousness.

My doctor had lied. He hadn't for a moment meant to allow a natural birth in his delivery room. He used forceps to pull the baby out, which left broken skin and bruises on my baby's cheeks and head and left me torn and in need of stitches.

I regained consciousness in a recovery room, feeling heartbroken. Somehow, while under anesthesia, my subconscious self had misinterpreted the events in the delivery room. I was certain I had delivered a baby boy and there was something wrong with him. At any moment, I had expected to hear a newborn cry, but when I entered that dark world, there was nothing but silence. Denis stood beside me and announced, "We have a little girl and she is perfect and beautiful."

"No," I insisted, sobbing, "we have a boy and he's not well. Something's wrong with him." Nothing comforted me. I did not believe Denis.

I didn't see our daughter until I was moved from recovery to a room several hours later. The nurse brought in a little red-faced bundle. I couldn't understand. I couldn't reach present reality. What had happened to the baby boy? I was confused. I held our daughter for a moment and, still weeping, handed her to Denis. She didn't seem to be mine. It took twenty-four hours to process this new truth. I had a baby girl. She was healthy. She was truly ours. Gradually, as my mind adjusted, so did my body. Powerful mothering instincts broke a dam and flooded my heart. As I held her to my breast, I was bonded forever to Marsena Joy, my first daughter.

Studies now show there is something physical and visceral that happens to a mother when she is conscious for the birth of her child and able to hold the baby next to her skin the moment that child is born. There is an actual hormonal response that occurs and it is still something of a mystery to scientists. It saddens me a little to remember those mixed-up, confused feelings following Marsena's birth.

Denis' first response to the birth of our daughter was altogether different from mine. As I tell you why it may seem like a tangent in the story, but stick with me.

Marsena was born during the Vietnam War. It was a time when her father could easily have been drafted. His draft number had come up during our first year of marriage and he was required to appear for a physical. He passed and was told to go home and wait until his number was called. That possibility hovered in the background for months. Young men everywhere waited. Some waited with dread, wondering how they would cope when the command to appear arrived. Some escaped to Canada to avoid induction. Others volunteered or waited with anticipation, never imagining what would happen if they survived long enough to return home to a country that would treat them with cruel heartlessness.

The reality of going to war crept into Denis' heart and all during the waiting time leading up to his draft call, he began thinking about Just War theory and the consequences of conducting an unjust war that turned out to be a disaster for our soldiers and our country.

Denis gradually came to believe he could not join the military and end up killing the people of Vietnam. Or kill anyone. Violence of any kind was out of the question for him. So he applied to be a conscientious objector as a pacifist. When he appeared before the draft board to defend his position, his application was denied, so as the war dragged on, we waited day after day for him to be called up.

But the first time Denis held his daughter, traced her soft cheek, held her tiny finger as it curled around his, and looked into her deep violet eyes, he was overcome with love for this helpless little bundle. A feeling of intense joy filled him, and in that moment he knew if anyone tried to harm this child, he would kill them. Shocked by this revelation, unexpected as it was, he realized he could no longer claim he was a pacifist. But thankfully, Denis was not called up because his classification changed when he reached the age of exemption.

Three days later I left the hospital against medical advice. At that time doctors were still keeping new mothers in the hospital for at least five days after the

Denis and Marsena

birth of a baby. But as medical costs mounted, costs we couldn't afford, we chose
to leave early to save the money.

I was wheeled to the entrance holding Marsena, and the nurse helped me
settle into the car. These were the days before car seats. I was gingerly seated on
the passenger side, my bottom burning from the stitches and holding a swathed
bundle that began screaming the moment the door closed. Who could imagine that a package that small could deafen the world? I had not heard her cry
much at all until then. It became immediately apparent that mothers are hard-
wired to instinctually respond to a baby's cries. Those cries hurt. They create
panic. Something *must* be done immediately to find the cause and stop it or this
baby will die! There was not one thing I could do or even knew to do on that
drive back to His House except to gently murmur and jiggle her up and down.
When the volume reached epic proportions, Denis couldn't take it any longer
and shouted, "DO SOMETHING!" I had no idea why she was crying or what I

could do to stop it. She was dry and had just been fed before we left. His bark made me begin to cry, too.

We arrived back at His House and tried to sneak in with a howling baby, up two flights of stairs to our room where we slammed the door and I began trying to nurse. Soon housemates came knocking, wanting to welcome us home and meet Marsena Joy. Denis held them all at bay except Terry. I wanted to see her and tell her all that had happened.

In my new role, I took on the protectiveness of a mother bear. I didn't say aloud, "No, you may not hold her. Do not even breathe on her." But I felt it. Who knew what sorts of germs she might pick up? With great reluctance, later that day, I allowed my housemates in to meet her. Then safeguarding her was beyond my control. Everyone held her, passing her from person to person, kissing and breathing on her face. After a short introduction, they quietly left so I could rest.

Denis settled me in with juice and a sandwich, wrapped the baby in a blanket, placed her in the bassinet. Then, to my horror, he prepared to leave for work.

Yes, work outside His House. This was another cataclysmic change in our lives. There came a point when we realized he would need to find a job to help meet our bills. We couldn't avoid those extra expenses any young family faces. He was hired as a front desk clerk at a Holiday Inn where he worked the evening shift from 3:00–11:00 p.m. It paid little, but was better than nothing.

I dreaded him leaving. I needed him to be with me. I wanted to be grown-up about it, but that was beyond my power. When he left, I cried and cried as I went about tending to Marsena. No one had told me about postpartum blues. Thus, on that first day home with a new baby, while Denis was off at work, I finally pulled myself together and settled on the bed, cradling my hungry, three-day-old daughter. She whipped her head back and forth in an effort to find the nipple as I directed it to her mouth. When at last I helped her latch on, her gums clamped down so hard I laughed, thinking she must have a metal vise in her jaw. After a few minutes, I switched sides and let her nurse as long as she wanted.

Satisfied and with a glazed look in her eyes, she fell asleep in my arms, and I pulled out *The Womanly Art of Breastfeeding*. I needed to refresh my memory now that my baby was depending on me as her sole source of life support. I wanted to be sure to do everything right. I reviewed my diet and made a grocery list of nutritious foods we should buy to make certain the quality of my milk would meet all her nutritional needs. Whole wheat bread. Milk. Juice. Eggs. Oranges. Spinach. Chicken. The book reminded me a mother should allow her baby to nurse for as long as she wanted.

This began a twenty-four-hour cycle for her: nursing, napping for only about sixty minutes, crying, nursing again. In between, I only had time for what was absolutely necessary. Use the bathroom. Eat. Drink. Change her diapers. Nap. As the first two days and nights passed with no change, I became more exhausted than I'd ever been in my life. When Denis was home, visiting with housemates and friends was much easier. He was a wonderful buffer, protecting me from too much social interaction and encouraging me to rest as much as possible. When he was gone, I hid in our room and ignored any knocks on the door.

The next two days were a blur of exhaustion and excruciating pain. I began crying, not just out of exhaustion or loneliness, but because my nipples were bleeding and lacerated. Even taking a shower hurt. Whenever Marsena began to cry from hunger, I began crying, too. Just the thought of her latching on made me shudder with dread. I didn't know what else to do other than keep on trying. Because of what I read, I seriously thought she would die if I couldn't succeed at this simple thing mothers had done since the beginning of creation.

In desperation, I reached a member of the local La Leche League by phone. I hoped she could help me. The woman listened to my problem and recommended I slather my nipples with lanolin and simply keep on trying until I was better. "Don't quit," she urged.

When Denis came home after work that night, he found Marsena screaming and me sobbing as I tried to feed her. That's when he . . . I don't know what to call it. Insisted? Commanded? Yes, commanded. "You have to stop nursing her right now. You have some sample formula they gave you at the hospital. Fix it and give it to her. You can use a bottle. She won't die. That book has made you crazy. You have to stop."

It's true. I had become convinced that formula was like feeding her poison, but I had no strength to disagree. Marsena was so happy to have that milk in a bottle, she drank all four ounces and for the first time, slept for three hours. So did I. When I woke, rather than feeling better, the pain had grown so much worse. My breasts were hot and swollen nearly to my chin. I was dripping milk like a broken faucet. Everything, including the bedding was sopped. I had a fever and could barely move.

I arrived at the doctor's office with a bath towel wrapped around my middle to soak up the milk beneath a loose maternity smock and was ushered into an exam room to see the same physician who delivered my baby. When he walked in and pulled back the sheet he actually exclaimed, "My God, I've never seen anything like this. Nurse! Come take a look." I couldn't believe my ears. He was treating me like a circus freak. Okay. True, I had never been a size 32A, but that remark was as rude as any I'd ever heard. If I had been in less pain I would have cursed him, and taken my engorged mammaries elsewhere for treatment. Instead, I began crying.[7]

Of course. That's all I seemed able to do.

The doctor told me I needed to stop nursing and recommended I bottle-feed exclusively. After giving me a hormone injection and some pain medication, he told me that milk production would slow down and stop in seven to ten days. Three days later I was feeling better physically, but emotionally I knew I had flunked the first major test of good motherhood. I had to give up nursing my baby. I had failed.

BOOK IV

[1971–1972]

The Sandia Mountains

In 1540, the Spanish discovered the southern ranges of the Rocky Mountains in New Mexico. They named them the Sandias, which roughly translates as "watermelon" in Spanish. Reaching 10,478 feet, the Sandias form the eastern border of the old City of Albuquerque. They can be seen from nearly every point in the city, and as the sun goes down, its rays are reflected by the granite in rich hues of pink and red. Every day we watched the setting sun as it flamed against the Sandias' peaks, cliffs, and canyons.

They brought to mind Gregory of Nyssa, a fourth-century desert monk, who contemplated a mountainous cliff. He discovered it was a place of beauty where you see the majesty, greatness, and glory of God. He also discovered it was a place of uneasiness where we are confronted by our own frailty. As you meditate on its existence over thousands, maybe millions of years, you ask yourself a question: How did that mountain change on the day my personal world fell apart? You find, Belden Lane writes,

it didn't change at all . . . It was waiting, staying there as if for you, in the same way that God does not change. That stone cliff, a metaphor of God, invites you to pour out all the grief and anguish you can muster, then accepts it all without rebuke, receives it all right there in the desert.

Something amazing happens at that point. When you become silent enough and empty enough, pouring out your needs to God in that desert place, you are able for the first time to hear what you had never heard before, and that's a single word whispered by Jesus: love. It's one of those words you can't hear until you are utterly silent and utterly empty.[1]

DON'T YOU, DENIS?

"You agree, don't you, Denis?" When my husband was thirteen years old, his father spoke these words to him. They were talking to a group of young soldiers from a military base in the Philippines near where his parents were missionaries, and his father had just stated that Denis loved archery. This was so far from the truth it could have been a joke. But as his father continued speaking, gripping Denis' shoulder tightly as he smiled at the soldiers, it was clear he wasn't joking.

"Yes, he loves it so much he begged me every day to take him to the target field to shoot arrows. You agree, don't you, Denis?"

Denis knew from past experience he must instantly agree or face punishment that could last for days. "Yes, I love archery," he lied.

Denis often insisted he remembered nothing about growing-up, and yet now and then a story surfaced, a dark memory emerging from the hidden recesses of his mind. In time we pieced together a patchwork quilt of his growing up years.

In a way, his experience was similar to mine. He had a father, and I had a stepfather, and both were men we never understood, even as adults. We never learned what shaped them or what caused them to behave as they did.

The man who became my stepfather, after my own father was killed in a plane crash before I was born, helped shape my understanding of God. God was someone for whom you must work hard in order to gain his approval. It wasn't until my mid-thirties that I began to grasp the deep affect my stepfather's rejection held over me.

From an early age, I had sensed this man didn't care for me, not the way he cared for my siblings when they came along, though I couldn't have articulated this as a child. Also difficult to verbalize was why I was so passionate about winning his love. Growing up on a farm, I thought the chores I did without being told—restacking the woodpile, cleaning the cow barn, and peeling cedar fence posts would cause him to love me. Throughout my childhood, those efforts never made a lasting difference. Even at the end of his life, when a stroke stole his speech, when my own children were grown and I had become a grandmother, he was still able to communicate his dislike from the moment I walked into the room. It was some comfort to know my mother and some siblings witnessed this pattern, so it wasn't just my interpretation. And yet no one was able to convince him to change his attitude, least of all me.

Family dynamics such as this spread and stain our hearts like watercolor paint slowly seeping across the years. I believed God loved me. I was convinced of it, but for many years felt compelled to earn his love by being the best girl ever. There was a futility in these efforts because perfection is impossible for anyone. As a child, I spent many nights staring at the ceiling, confessing my failures: the mean tricks I played on my brother, my envy and hostility toward classmates who were rich and owned many pairs of shoes, the times I missed prayers and was dead bored in church. And worst of all, the times I didn't tell someone God loved her because I was embarrassed to admit I was a Christian. I thought for sure I was a big disappointment to God.

It was shocking to discover God loved people in a way I didn't understand. In a way my stepfather couldn't. I often heard people say the God of the Old Testament is an angry God. He is vengeful and judgmental. He does not forgive. He dislikes us. But the entire reason Jonah ran away was because God was a loving God who cared about the Ninevites. God didn't dislike them. Jonah was angry because God *forgave* the people of Nineveh, a people Jonah hated.

> Isn't this what I said, LORD, when I was still at home? That is what I tried to forestall by fleeing to Tarshish. I knew that you are a gracious and compassionate God, slow to anger and abounding in love, a God who relents from sending calamity (Jonah 4:2).

This was an important revelation because it confirmed that God loved people in the way I wished a father would love his daughter. God was everything I ever hoped a father could be. If he accepted me, I could relax a little. When life went off the tracks, as it is bound to do, there might be love for me even when I failed in some way.

When I first met Denis, I had no idea he, too, had father problems that shaped him and his relationship with God. The abuse he endured sickens and destroys children. It has taken Denis a lifetime to unpack the consequences of having had Milton Haack as a father. There has been a measure of healing, but it isn't totally complete. None of us are entirely healed in this life. So we wait in anticipation for that day when the Healer returns.

As a seventh grader, Denis attended a missionary school in Manila where for the first time he discovered a world of wonder in stories and began bringing books home from the library. Soon after this discovery his father found him reading in his bedroom. Milton demanded to know what Denis was reading and snatched the book from his hands. When told it was a library book and not an assignment, he looked at it with disgust, threw it on the desk, and sneered, "Why are you reading a good book when you could be reading the *best* book?" From then on Denis never brought a library book home. He did all his reading at school and left his homework to complete at night. Appearing diligent about his homework was an acceptable activity and good for one's Testimony.

One Christmas, Denis received a woodburning kit from an aunt in the States. He was excited as he opened the box, gathered the materials and, following a pattern, began to burn a little Scottie dog onto a piece of balsa wood. As he was finishing up this first attempt, his father walked in, picked up the piece, laughed, tossed it down, and said, "Let me show you how this is done." When his father left the room Denis carefully replaced everything in the box, put it away, and never brought it out again. In the following months when they needed to move from Manila, everything they owned was brought before Milton who decided whether it was to be kept or given away. When the woodburning kit appeared his father asked him why he wasn't using it and then berated him for being so ungrateful and selfish. "I don't know why your aunts bother to buy you anything."

Somehow that sweet little Scottie survived, and now sits on my desk as a reminder of Denis' survival. His father missed a perfect opportunity to give confidence and encouragement to a boy who sorely needed it. No matter what he did, Denis was always aware of what a disappointment and failure he was. It filled him with shame.

The tropical weather of the Philippines is brutal for people not used to heat and humidity, so each year Milton took the family to spend a week in Baguio which is higher in elevation and cooler in temperature. There was an American military base nearby and citizens with an American passport were allowed to use its recreational facilities, shops, and restaurants. There were simple cabin accommodations nearby which allowed visitors to escape the heat of Manila. Milton warned the family to never mention this to anyone back in the States because it might be perceived as a vacation. People who donated to his work might not understand and it could ruin his Testimony.

The recreational facilities on base included an archery range. Each day at a certain time, Milton emerged from the room where he slept and studied and insisted Denis accompany him to the range to practice some target shooting. Denis dreaded this excursion since he was terrible at archery and his father was quick to emphasize what a poor excuse he was for an athlete. Denis rarely hit the target, but succeeded in burning his arm with the bow string when letting arrows fly. Each time he tried, his father scolded, grabbed the bow and shot to prove how easy it was to hit the target. This was repeated many times. Each day, the humiliation continued back at the cabin when Milton insisted Denis report to his mother and sister how he had done. His father kept score and wrote down the number of times he hit the target versus how many times Denis missed.

Denis confided in his mother how much he hated it and didn't want to go. She tried to intervene, asking his father to allow him to stay home. Denis could see where this was leading and at that point he began to cry. Milton predictably became angry with both of them and asserted he was training Denis to be a man. "Men don't cry." From this point on, he was more determined than ever to make Denis go. He humiliated him for days afterwards, laughing scornfully and announcing, "Here's the little boy who can't hit the target."

When they returned to Manila after the week away, as often happened, they hosted a meal in their home for American soldiers. This is when Milton called Denis from his room to tell the soldiers what he had done in Baugio. He clamped his hand on Denis' shoulder, squeezing the muscle, and before Denis could answer, announced, "I've never really liked archery, but Denis loves it. Every day in Baugio he begged me to take him out to target practice with bow and arrows. I was happy to do it because Denis loves it so much. You love it, don't you, Denis?"

"Yes," he replied.

The young men left impressed with how much this man loved his son and what a great model he was.

It was a moment of terrible enlightenment for Denis. It was shocking to see his father brazenly lie. It was the first time he consciously wrestled with the re-alization that his father was not a truth-teller and could not be trusted. Truth to Milton was whatever his opinion happened to be. It was also shocking that his father forced him to lie in order to make himself look good.

These are only some of the many incidents that forced him to begin ques-tioning his father's opinions. Until then Denis assumed his failure to please was his own fault. From his earliest memories he cannot remember a time when he was able to please his father. He did not receive praise or acceptance for any-thing he did or tried to do, whatever the outcome. Milton always knew what was right and what was wrong. There was never anything in between or outside his control. His legalism offered no grace or mercy.

When Denis first told me he was never able to please his father, I thought this had to be an exaggeration. "If we search hard enough, surely we will find there is *something* for which you received praise and support." As much as we explored their history and observed their relationship, right up until the year Milton died, we never found evidence that Milton had approved of or praised Denis.

I hated to think Denis had the same experience I had—a father who never approved of him. For many years I kept hoping I misread my stepfather's dislike of me. Or that he would change and approve of me. Not just me, but my husband and children. The times when he approved were so rare I can only think of one. When I was a junior in high school, I shot a deer with a .410 shotgun using slugs. Mom told me he bragged about it to his hunting buddies. I was a girl and they were getting skunked. But he never told me. His prevailing response was either silence or sarcasm, like when I brought home straight A's on my report card. He would say, "I suppose you think you're pretty smart now." Never, "You done good."

Clothing was another part of Denis' life that his father controlled. I was shocked to learn that even when Denis was a junior in high school, Milton made his mother lay out all his clothes in the morning. Denis had no choice. So when the 1960s began an era of sweeping fashion changes, Milton sharply condemned the new styles. Bell-bottoms, miniskirts, and sandals were worn by young people everywhere. It's easy to forget that before that time, men and boys never wore sandals in our country. They were considered unmanly and effeminate. No longer. People wore their blue jeans patched and torn. Boys wore their hair looser and longer. Peasant blouses made long-haired girls look like gypsies. Like most young women, I did not hesitate to dress as I pleased, even though many people considered miniskirts scandalous. Wearing make-up was another questionable custom. Milton forbade his wife to ever wear any at all.

One time, when Denis' parents were in their sixties, the four of us were driving somewhere and I was in the backseat with Denis' mother. She leaned over and whispered some version of the following: "If I outlive him," she pointed at Denis' father, "the first thing I'm going to do is learn to drive, buy a tube of lipstick, and wear pants." At first I thought it was funny, but that quickly gave way to grief. Wearing lipstick? Really? But she never dared oppose him or act on her secret desires. Milton had ways of punishing her for any resistance, whether real or imagined. Using Scripture as support, he made certain she remained subjected and obedient to his rule in every little thing. She made little comments like this throughout her later years.

According to Scripture, it isn't only the wife who is to submit, we were to "submit to one another out of reverence for Christ" (Ephesians 5:21). The idea of *mutuality* means making decisions together. We can think, pray, struggle, and decide together. This was a teaching Milton firmly rejected. It seems especially poignant that life could have been very different for Denis' mother if he had not ignored the verses that firmly establish that a husband and wife are also to be subject to one another.

Denis and Margie, 1969

"Husbands, love your wives, as Christ loved the church" (Eph. 5:25) deeply impacted me. What Jesus did was radical in so many ways. Christ gave up his status and his position of power; he suffered pain and death for the sake of his bride the Church. As an analogy for marriage, this is not difficult to understand. But I don't recall this ever being emphasized or taught in the circles where I grew up. The years of bondage Denis' mother experienced nearly erased her sense of self. It was an appalling example of how the abuse of authority in the name of God leads to destructive acts of unkindness and injustice.

Both Denis and I had yet to fully accept the reality that neither of us had or ever would please our fathers. We both continued to believe that our desire to follow Jesus would be understood and applauded by his parents. I especially thought because they were missionaries they would not only appreciate our desire to give up everything and follow Jesus whatever it cost, they would be thrilled when we joined Team Outreach. Then I thought they would understand when we left the Team to begin living at His House. I assumed they would see our desire to help young people—runaways, drug-users, those searching for spiritual answers or who wanted to become Christians—as a kind of missionary work.

It didn't occur to me that they, his father in particular, would vehemently disapprove of everything.

While we were living in His House, someone snapped a photo of Denis and me (page 122). We were leaning back against a built-in bookshelf in the living room, standing side by side. Denis was wearing a nice tab front shirt and I had on the skirt and top I made in Arizona. I was seven months pregnant. We sent them a copy, thinking how happy they would be since Denis' mom repeatedly asked for pictures.

The bitter response we received from his parents felt like a viper strike. It came in a letter written from his father. Denis' hair told them everything they needed to know about our decadence. It was long. It was unkempt. It was following The Beatles, who had been condemned by all Christians. This especially puzzled me because compared to all our housemates and friends, his hair looked positively conservative—more like that of a member of The Bill Gaither Trio. This criticism seemed so short-sighted and unfair. I knew I had seen old sepia portraits of Denis' great-grandfathers and grand-uncles hanging in the upstairs hall of his grandparents' home. They all sported some version of long hair with sideburns, huge mutton chops, and mustaches or beards. Here was Milton's son, with his dark hair no longer short and slicked back with hair cream, but casually falling forward with sideburns that had grown out a bit.

Milton wrote that Denis' mother was in the next room sobbing because of the picture we had sent. Much later we learned the reason she cried was because Milton took out his rage on her whenever he received news about us that met with his disapproval. But we didn't know that then. "You don't need to become a prostitute in order to win prostitutes to Christ. But this is what you, Denis, have done—you have compromised with the world, and have become someone we are ashamed of. You have ruined your Testimony."

I was chagrined for encouraging Denis to stay in touch with his parents. Denis did not want to write to his parents, but I thought it was what a child must do to honor their parents. I also hoped we could persuade them that we were following Jesus. So far, efforts to communicate with them half a world away gained nothing, nothing but more disapproval. This was not new to Denis since it had been the way of things since his earliest memories. To me, it was entirely grievous. I just couldn't comprehend why we would be so thoroughly rebuffed. After all, we shared the basics of the faith. We agreed that Jesus was the Son of God, that the Scriptures were the inspired word of God, that salvation came only through Christ, that the universe was created by God. This was common ground. But Milton's disdain only increased and grew worse.

Even after this, I continued to push Denis to write to them, which increased his perplexity. He was at a point in his spiritual growth where he did want to do the right thing, that is, to honor his parents, but how? If he wrote, nothing good came of it. If he didn't, nothing good came of that. Sadly, I only added to the pressure of a no-win situation. So I wrote to them instead—until I began to understand they wanted to hear from him, not me. They wrote back asking, "Why doesn't Denis write to us? It's nice to hear from you, but why doesn't Denis write?"

I wish we had explanations for Milton's behavior. Did he have a terrible childhood? Was there some traumatizing experience in his past? If so, I might have been more understanding. But if there was an explanation, we were never granted that insight. Among the Assemblies, Milton was respected as a preacher and Bible teacher. He was admired as a missionary who established Assemblies in the province of Pampanga where there had been none. After three decades of work, he left behind numerous local churches and an indigenous leadership.

And yet, he was disliked by his wife's sisters who knew him well. His own brothers were not close to him. He was stubborn. In private he was abusive and unkind, not only to Denis, but to his wife. All her life she feared him and was afraid to express even the smallest opinion. She panicked when answering our most trivial questions. If we asked, "Did you have a dentist appointment this week?" she would glance nervously at Milton and wait for him to answer for her. She had to request money for the smallest necessities. There were times when she secretly slipped us a twenty-dollar bill she saved from buying groceries with a whisper not to tell. She was not allowed to buy nice clothes because her position wasn't public like his. Milton's public comments directed at her were often subtly barbed and cynical. He laughed as he spoke, expecting others to laugh, too, and she would force a smile.

After his father's death, Denis' mother moved into a memory care center. She was often confused and sometimes forgot that Milton was no longer alive. When we visited her, she cried and worried that Milton would come to see her. "I'm so afraid of him and what he will do to me."

At other times, she sobbed, telling us how good he had been to her. Then she would pause, as if a new thought had occurred. "If he's so good, then why isn't he visiting me?" she asked. We gently reminded her of his funeral and of the Navy Ceremonial Guard who attended and how they folded the flag covering the casket and handed it to her before the coffin was put in the ground. We kept the flag in plain sight in her room, hoping it would help anchor her memory.

But even as her memory continued to fail, she had days of clarity that were delightful. Several times she told us she wanted to go to church with us. We asked her if this meant she wanted to attend the Plymouth Brethren Assembly— we would have been glad to take her there. We reminded her that our Anglican Church was very different from what she was used to.

"I *know* that!" she retorted. "I want to go to your church!"

She squinted her eyes and stabbed her finger at Denis saying, "Don't you get smart with me, young man!" Then she threw back her head and laughed. He had often heard her say this when he was a boy.

We wanted to bring her to church with us, but her mobility declined to the point where she could no longer be safely taken out. Even when she was in hospice toward the end, she still complained to the chaplain about us not taking her to church. She asked him to speak to her son about it. "He refuses to take me!" she declared.

There were times when her clarity brought up moments of deep sadness. "Why," she asked, "did Milton always make me feel this high?" She held her finger and thumb about a half an inch apart. "Why did he never make me feel important or a part of his life?" It was heartbreaking to hear her express this as she wept inconsolably. We would pray with her and read a psalm together, asking God to comfort her troubled heart. And no matter what her condition, Denis was somehow able to make her laugh. She never stopped thinking he was hilarious.

Throughout her life she continued to play the role that was required of her. Her sister, Aunt Ruth, once told us that on the night before Marge's marriage to Milton, she confided it was a mistake to marry him, but by then she felt powerless to do anything about it.

It is difficult for us, in an age where women are more free to go public with the injustice and abuse they have suffered, to understand why a woman would remain in such circumstances. Psychologists tell us that some who suffer in extremely difficult relationships find it is easier to remain in the troubled life they know rather than court the troubles and problems of a life they don't know. Denis' mother grew up in an era when women, especially women in the church, were taught to go home, pray, and submit. There was no way out. Who would believe her? Where would she go? It was painful to witness her sorrow.

She did outlive Milton by two years, but sadly, at ninety-three, with the exception of a few changes, it was mostly too late for new possibilities.[2] At the care center where she lived, she got her nails polished. She told us to buy her things like a warm winter coat to replace her worn dirty one. She wore pants anytime she pleased. We arranged for her to get her hair cut and styled regularly. All these were things Milton considered either sinful or unnecessary luxuries for a woman. "I have the money and I can do it!" she declared. It gave us joy to spend time with her and to see to these small matters until her death in March of 2019.

Both Denis' and his mother's experience left me with a troubling problem. I have hated my father-in-law. Each Sunday, as we recite the Lord's Prayer, *Forgive us our trespasses as we forgive those who trespass against us*, I am reminded of my obligation. I don't want to miss being forgiven because I can't forgive him.

It has been difficult coming to terms with Milton's life. I've read books on forgiveness, met with a counselor, and had endless conversations with my husband. It's true that righteous anger can and should exist against evil. But my anger can easily spill over into bitterness, with a desire to punish Milton. There were times when he angrily told Denis he couldn't wait for the "Judgment Seat of Christ" where Christ himself would condemn Denis for his theology, his decisions, his interest in reading fiction, his disgusting enjoyment of movies, and his compromise in leaving the Plymouth Brethren. "We'll see *then*," he would gloat.

I didn't mind so much when he told Denis he never liked me and that I was the cause of his poor decisions and backslidden condition. But I resented his continuous scoffing at Denis and his rejection of our daughters. His exclusive and preferential treatment of our son because he eventually chose to worship in the Plymouth Brethren Assembly with my family in northern Minnesota made me more angry.

I often reverted to justifying my hatred. Yes, I argued, but . . . he did that . . . he said this. Then, one night I had a dream that felt so real, it helped me lay some of this to rest. In the dream, I was wrapped in the softest quilts, protected not only from bad weather and danger, but from strife and criticism. It was a place of comfort and peace. I knew it was a holy place belonging to God. I was invited to stay there and rest. It existed because God was powerful and strong and had all people and events under control. In that place I was expected to let go of all responsibility for righting the world's wrongs because God was going to take care of all injustice and suffering. He would heal problems with both justice and mercy. So in whatever way he dealt with Milton, it would be exactly the right thing for him and for everyone else involved. I didn't need to fuss about it. I'm not sure this means I've completely forgiven him for what he did to Denis and my family, but it feels like progress and the right place to be right now.

This family dysfunction has not been only my problem—it has been the arch enemy of my husband. Denis' journey as the son of an abusive father whose standing in the church was respected and powerful was bound to affect him both as husband and father. The most difficult question he has faced regarding his father is, what does it mean to honor him? Denis has struggled to right the wrongs in his own life, and together we have experienced much growth and tender grace. That Denis did not reject the faith altogether, but became a devoted follower of Jesus, is a story of redemption and love. I can only tell it in part.

I wish there were clear answers. We tried to establish healthier boundaries with his father while he was living. Our visits to Denis' parents were limited because after about two hours things deteriorated. We insisted that when they visited us, they didn't just come in unannounced and expect us to drop everything for the day. We needed to plan ahead. Denis also received help from a therapist who provided some direction on what it means to honor a parent. It did not mean tolerating hateful or sinful behavior. It was good to protect our children from him, especially our daughters. Because he did not like them, we never pressured them to visit their grandparents. When Milton began to scoff and yell at Denis, he did not try to defend himself or argue. He left. I so dreaded visits with them, Denis never demanded I go with him. For the record, most of the time I did.

We gained some wisdom. We found a measure of peace believing God is in control of our stories even when things are difficult. Sometimes God surprises us with a gift that feels like he is saying, "I know that was hard." That's what I thought when we unexpectedly became owners of a new bike.

Years ago, when Denis was living in the Philippines, his grandparents sent him money for a bike. He loved riding down the hill beside their house. He rode the way young boys have always done, racing the wind, hair whipping, shirt flapping, with a powerful sense that a boy might even be able to fly.

There were many household rules he had to rigorously obey to stay out of trouble. One of them was the warning to be careful when riding his bike: *Be very careful so you don't have a fall and ruin your pants or damage the bike. These things cost money, and repairs to clothes and bikes can easily be avoided if you're careful.*

One day it had rained torrentially, as it often does in the tropics, but when the rain stopped and things began to dry out, Denis went out to ride. At the bottom of the hill, the rain had washed piles of sand into the intersection. When Denis flew down the hill, he could not stop in time to avoid skidding, and he wiped out. Picking himself up, he saw he had dirtied his clothes, torn the knees of his pants, and skinned his elbow. But worse, he had dented the headlight and scratched the frame of the bicycle. With a heart full of grief and fear, he pushed the bike up the hill and into the garage, hoping to sneak into the house to see what could be done about his pants. For several days his accident went unnoticed until his father saw the dented light. Denis will only say there was hell to pay. He never rode the bike again, even though Milton said he was an ungrateful boy for not using the gift his grandparents had given him.

Fast forward to one year before Milton died. By then, Denis was in his sixties. Our next-door neighbors were cleaning out their garage. They had a dusty old bicycle that had sat in the shadows for a long time and offered to give it away just to be rid of it. Denis researched the brand and model and learned it was an English manufactured Raleigh 3-Speed AMF—the exact model of the one Denis had been given so many years ago as a boy. We were stunned. It was in beautiful shape and only needed to be cleaned and tuned up. I promised him he could ride breakneck and ruin as many pairs of blue jeans as he owned as long as he didn't leave me a widow. It was as if God was telling Denis, "You see? I can restore life any old time, anywhere I choose, and do it in a way that will blow your mind. You agree, don't you, Denis?"

It was critical to my growth, and to Denis' that we both moved beyond the failures of our fathers. God is not like them. His love never wavers. He accepts us as we are, even with all our idealism, our accidents, and sticky messes.

DEATH

Only the very young believe that community means harmony.
We are born to pride, every one of us. Is it likely that we should
be at peace with each other?
—Bruce Ray, *Winter Light*

The door to His House creaked open and two handsome young men in their early thirties walked in. They were from Dallas, Texas, and had somehow heard about us. They said they were called by God to join us and teach us about a deeper walk with Jesus. No one knew them or had seen them before. In their soft Texas accents, they explained there was so much more to be had when you allowed the Holy Spirit to take complete control of your life. They had come to share those truths with us.

We listened and invited them to move in with us, and at first they seemed a wonderful addition. They were gentle and charismatic and spoke with authority about every aspect of the Christian life. Our housemates were ecstatic about them, but it didn't take long for their teachings to begin making Richard, Terry, Denis, and me feel uncomfortable.

The beliefs they taught so enticingly reduced the complexities of life to simple formulas. They began by encouraging us to fast regularly in order to cleanse ourselves spiritually. Fasting is certainly a time-honored practice in the Bible and the historic church, even though I admit I've never been very consistent or good at it. Their own fasting went on for nearly four weeks. They declared it led them closer to God, not only to know his heart and mind, but to enable them to speak his words to us. They taught new doctrines, undiscovered and unknown in the history of the church until they revealed them. By placing their hands on ours and somehow reading our spirit, they could determine whether or not we were ready to become more empowered by the Holy Spirit.

As our young housemates began following these two men like puppies and devouring every word as if God himself was tossing them bones, we became increasingly alarmed. Before long these men declared no Christian should ever be sick. This did not make sense to me. I asked, "Do you mean, then, that if you are pleasing to God you should never have to die? Theoretically, you would live forever unless an accident took you? So, if I get sick it will be because I don't trust God or have done something that deserves punishment?"

"Yes," they said, "You don't *need* to get sick if you have faith."

I pushed them. "Who have you seen do this? Everyone who lives to get old eventually gets sick and dies no matter how godly they are." They began speaking in tongues and moved toward me to pray for my unbelief. It gave me the creeps.

Each day, they held sessions for healings, learning to speak in tongues, seeing visions, and being slain in the Spirit. These things became a litmus test to determine whether you were genuinely filled with the Holy Spirit or not. Richard said, "Something about this is not right." Denis agreed: "It's becoming a new kind of legalism."

Then they began to teach that the ultimate gift of power and Christian maturity would be confirmed when you leaned the secret name of your personal angel. This was even more alarming because there is nothing in the Bible to suggest such a thing. It was a warning to us that this was about to become a cult. And it sickened us. As leaders, we wanted to kick them out, but they were already firmly embedded and adored by the rest of our housemates. What we didn't know at the time was that one of the men was already having a sexual relationship with one of our women, who was only nineteen years old and a new Christian. He told her that God's love was so great it can come to us sexually through another person who has dedicated his life to the power of the Holy Spirit. She was she was sworn to secrecy because, he told her, others in the house might not be mature enough to understand this relationship.

The sessions to receive your angel were kept from us because we were doubters. We were given the details later by those who left shortly after we did. The idea was appealing to someone like Manny, who was a kind, tender-hearted, paranoid, ex-druggie who had experienced many encounters with the spirit world. He had terrifying flashbacks and his nightmares often featured demons preparing to eat his soul. When he heard these teachings, it seemed too good to be true. He felt an angel could give him much needed peace and protection. When the two men thought he was ready, they took him to the prayer room and quizzed him about his spiritual life. The two then laid their hands on his head and prayed that God would reveal the name of the personal angel who would be assigned to Manny. They told him if he prayed and believed, the name of the

The Two from Texas

angel would suddenly come into his spirit and he would say it aloud. This angel would not only protect him, it would do whatever he bid. Manny could send him on missions to fulfill his will. The angel could do many things, from thwarting evil to finding a good parking space. Manny said when the name came to him he had a rush and felt something enter his body.

It was only a short time before the presence of these spiritual beings became strangely dangerous and uncontrollable. We were aghast, but had no experience dealing with demonic powers operating that openly around the lives of Christians.

Denis and Richard continued to question and refute these teachings, while warning our housemates there were Scriptures that addressed these very issues. The book of Colossians was especially relevant. We were astonished by this letter from Paul written two thousand years ago to early Christians. It was if he knew exactly what was happening in our commune.

Paul warns against false teachers, imposters who come in disguise declaring special fast days, subjecting the body, and hijacking the faith of young Christians, sending them down a path of destruction. We were witnessing

heresy, new revelations blatantly adding to Scripture, a sin that was condemned
by the Bible and church leaders from its beginning.

> Let no one disqualify you, insisting on asceticism and worship
> of angels, going on in detail about visions, puffed up without
> reason by his sensuous mind, and not holding fast to the Head,
> from whom the whole body, nourished and knit together through
> its joints and ligaments, grows with a growth that is from God …
> These have indeed an appearance of wisdom in promoting self-
> made religion and asceticism and severity to the body, but they
> are of no value in stopping the indulgence of the flesh. (Col. 2:16–
> 19, 23 ESV)

We were outmaneuvered as the Texas Two rallied our housemates to their
side. They began having Bible studies and meetings without us. Compared to
the sensational possibilities they offered, our objections just didn't seem attractive. They explained that Denis and I were not really filled with the Holy Spirit,
poor things. Richard and Terry didn't fare much better. We were devastated. In
retrospect, our housemates' response shouldn't have been surprising. We were
living in the midst of a generation that prized transcendence, but they were so
open to spirituality, they would accept anything if they didn't have a solid base
of truth to help discern what was of God and and what was not.

Back in Minnesota I had felt that the Bible or Christianity didn't have much
connection to reality. Here, seeing the real power of spirituality, I didn't know
whether to be terrified or joyful. I found comfort in the thought that whatever
happened, it was not a surprise to God. I reached for that comfort often, as the
two cult leaders began to cast more suspicion on the four of us "quasi" leaders.

All this was happening just before and right after I gave birth to Marsena.
Then another sudden devastation: Richard and Terry moved out. Her military
father was being posted overseas and needed someone to house-sit. For them,
it seemed perfect timing. Terry's baby was due soon and this would give them
a place of rest as a couple and time to prepare themselves for a new baby. We
understood, but, oh, it was hard to see them leave. They invited us to live with
them, but given the size of her parents' house, that didn't seem workable.

Other circumstances made Denis and I think we needed to move out. Denis
was still working 3:00–11:00 p.m. each day at the Holiday Inn, which meant he
was gone during our busiest time when visitors dropped in by the dozens for
coffee and conversation. The Texas Two were completely in charge now. With
Richard and Terry suddenly gone, I felt utterly alone in the evenings. I missed
Terry's bright laughter and her salty talk. During the day, Denis felt ostracized

from the rest of the household. He missed Richard's steady presence and dry humor.

Although there was no one to rescue us or our friends from the false doctrine that was growing by the hour, even so, God continued to work in our lives. I poured over the Scriptures. The New Testament lit up in a blaze of fresh light. Denis and I discussed how amazing it was to find whole portions that spoke directly to our lives and the troubles we were experiencing.

Our final days in His House dragged on with mounting stress and disappointment. While I was struggling to care for Marsena, Denis began looking for another place to live. We needed to get out. About a month after the birth of our daughter, we moved into a little apartment behind His House. As soon as we left, the Texas Two declared Denis and I were emissaries of Satan and anyone who continued to have contact with us would be in spiritual danger. We were now the enemy.

Despite those dire warnings, some of the house members began sneaking down to our apartment under the cover of darkness. Sitting on our couch, fidgeting nervously, tearful, and peeking out the window as if some*one* or some*thing* was going to fly down the hill from the House, they told us what was happening amidst their growing confusion and fear. The angels they had received began to pressure them to do things they didn't want to do. Some experienced terrifying nightmares and heard voices urging them to commit suicide. Others experienced urges to kill. They lived in fear of being punished by their angel if they didn't obey. Several said they could physically feel the presence of their angels come and go. It filled them with dread and a sense of evil. It was heartbreaking to listen to their stories and witness their pain and fear. All we knew to do was to pray for them in the name of Jesus to be freed from the power of Satan.

Whether their experience was a kind of demonic oppression, I don't know. I do know that after we prayed together, our apartment was filled with a warm presence of holy sweetness and peace. No one wanted to go back to His House and we advised them to move out as soon as possible.

The days that followed marked the closing of His House. Our housemates and regular visitors dispersed in different directions. The Texas Two disappeared and were never heard from again. It was the end of a fleeting era that changed our lives in a thousand ways that would last us a lifetime. We had witnessed miracles and dangers. We were filled with a love for God we had never known. We had met real heresy and escaped, becoming wiser for the encounter.

RESURRECTION

From the front door of our little apartment, we could look up and see the windows of the third-floor bedroom where we had spent eight of the most significant months of our life. I wondered who was sleeping there now. Our little two-bedroom apartment was shabby, but charming.

I was ecstatic to have our own place again for the first time in nearly two years. Life seemed far more manageable, and surprisingly vacation-like. Even our baby's projectile vomiting that hosed everything within a radius of three feet was not so bad when there was a washing machine available and no eyes on me as I shed clothing and cleaned the mess. One of the small joys of those first days of being just us was opening the refrigerator to find the pitcher of orange juice still there and still half full. I had become accustomed to food and drink mysteriously disappearing, even when labeled, "Do Not Touch or Margie Will Kill You." That threat was invoked only after "For Pregnant Mothers Only" proved ineffective.

It took us time to decompress and begin navigating a whole new stage of life: parenting. Life seemed workable now that I was feeling so much better mentally and physically. As the oldest of six children, I had plenty of experience taking care of babies as I grew up.

As a couple, we shared similar interests, goals, and experiences that helped us bond as partners. Our gifts and personalities, brain types, and families were not alike, but some of those differences added an attractive chemistry to our relationship. They made us interesting to one another and, like a team whose individual skills make them stronger together, we could fill out what the other lacked. However, we found other differences that were not so compatible. Ones that chafed. Nothing heated my temper like Denis' naïve approach to parenting. He didn't seem to understand I was far beyond him in expertise.[3]

Throughout my childhood, my siblings and I ran barefoot on a 160-acre farm, with no helmets, no insect repellant, and no sunscreen—we only knew suntan lotion as the enticing whiff of coconut you noticed on pretty girls at the beach. My mother was easy-going about what shenanigans we kids were up to when we played outside. We roped and rode anything with four legs. We climbed to the top of swaying trees. We swam in the lake without supervision. We were stung by nettles and bees. We threw rocks and rotten tomatoes at each other. We had lots of freedom and time for play, but we also had work. We had tasks and chores to do every day and they weren't busywork as can be the case today; we made necessary contributions to our farm's livelihood. When it was twenty below zero outside and the barns needed to be cleaned, we didn't get a pass on work assignments.

Accidents were a part of life and they weren't your fault unless you did something really stupid. I rode horseback all the years of my growing up and was thrown from a runaway or bucking horse more times than I can remember. Once, when galloping through an alfalfa field in the early morning when it was sopping wet with dew, I wasn't paying much attention to the mare I was on. She was a horse who habitually found excuses to shy away from the smallest piece of trash fluttering in the wind. That morning she jumped about six feet sideways over a white gum wrapper and took off like a rocket, heading for the barn. Caught by surprise, I gradually lost my seat and fell to the ground. Dad had drilled into our heads that you never, ever let go of the reins even if you get bucked off, so I clung like a tick to a dog's ear as she dragged me across the field. When she finally stopped, I got up drenched, covered from head to toe with green stains on my pants and white blouse. Mom praised me for hanging on to her. My ruined clothes were of no importance.

Denis' home was such an extreme opposite, I could hardly fathom it. He was taught that accidents could *always* be prevented because they only happened when he was not doing what he was supposed to be doing or was somewhere he shouldn't be. If his clothes got a little stained from rolling down a hill, or he fell in the gravel and came up with cuts and scrapes while playing, he was treated like a felon. Clothes cost money and his carelessness was the result of disobedience. When Denis was a child, anything that interrupted his father's study of the Bible was inexcusable and deplorable. Running, rolling, playing, and loud laughter were strictly forbidden in the house and were a punishable offense. This dumbfounded me. It didn't seem like any way a child should be raised.

The first time these differences in our upbringing became really apparent, our daughter was three months old. I had placed her on the couch with her feet against the back and her head toward the edge. She couldn't roll over yet and I had no idea she could kick hard enough to push herself headfirst off the couch, but that's what happened. I was beside myself, reproaching myself for being so careless. We were both crying, although she was frightened, but obviously not hurt. Denis was very upset with me when he learned of this and repeated the family-of-origin philosophy that "accidents can be prevented." In spite of how horrible I felt, and the fact that the fall *was* my fault, I knew in my bones there was something wrong with that idea. Of course, we must not be foolish, we must take precautions, but isn't the definition of "accident" the occurrence of something unexpected, unpredicted, a mishap or an injury out of your control?

But what if he was right, even though I had my doubts? It was confusing. There was so much to lose now that it was about someone I was responsible for. At the time I said nothing. I filed it away in my head and anxiously told myself: *You know, Margie, someday something terrible might happen and it is going to be your fault.*

Marsena's fall off the couch prompted us to begin working on what every relationship needs—learning to listen, being willing to grow and compromise, and loving your partner despite the differences that make you crazy. Parenting was just one area where we disagreed. There were others, and I admit we haven't always worked them out well. For as long as we have been married, the effort to understand and get along with one another never seems quite finished. On the other hand, it has grown easier, and that has been encouragement enough to keep on trying even when differences threaten to undo us.

At first as we settled into our apartment, I couldn't imagine wanting to live with people again. You'd think we'd be *so done* with communal living. Not true. We'd been bit. It didn't take long for us to miss the intimacy and daily interaction of living with others. Besides, we loved those who survived the collapse of His House. And there were still hundreds of young people wandering the streets—lost, stoned, and searching for home.

There were some members of the House who missed us as much as we missed them. We began carefully inviting some of them to think and talk and pray about whether God would lead us to live together again. And if it seemed right, where? We were not open for just anyone to join. We wanted them to be serious about growing in their faith and willing to set aside some money each month to help us with expenses. They had to be on the same page, agreeing that Denis and I would make final decisions about who could live with us and who would lead. We didn't want a repeat of what had just happened.

Ten months after we moved into that little apartment, Denis and I found an old, five-bedroom house for rent in a rundown neighborhood in the valley near the Rio Grande River. Rent was cheap enough for us to afford, and it was month-to-month, so we didn't need to sign a lease. The apartment behind His House had served a purpose. It provided some privacy and gave us time to recover from our daughter's birth and from what had happened at His House. We began attending one of the churches that was friendly to us and made new friends who were straight, conventional, and conservative—conservative in that they had professional day jobs, owned homes, drove decent cars, and didn't go to rock concerts. But they were people we enjoyed. Our horizon was expanding beyond hippies.

We packed up our belongings and moved to the house in the valley, a place obviously unloved and unkempt for many years. The yard was a desert of sand and dust. The dirt basement had walls of woven spider webs and multitudes of cockroaches that scurried into the darkness. But with a fairly big living room, it was perfect for large group gatherings. We were prepared to once again to open our home to others.

Soon there were nine of us including Marsena. We were all in our early twenties or barely out of our teens, but Denis and I were accepted as leaders because the old age of twenty-three made us slightly older and hopefully a bit wiser. We named it His House again, because it was a name known among the crowds who had frequented the first house. We wanted it to once again be a safe place to explore ideas, study the Bible, and find out if Christianity was relevant to everyday life. Denis had quit his job at the Holiday Inn and was now working a day job at a service station, which meant he was around in the evenings.

Soon people made their way to us again, and in the evening, our house was filled with the voices of seekers and skeptics, the sound of music, and the joy of young converts.

Of the housemates and friends who followed Denis and me to the new place, many had been deeply wounded by the Texas Two. It made us so happy to be with them again. We, too, had been hurt by what had happened, but not in the same way. Their faith was more shaken for having trusted two men who took advantage of their youth and lack of scriptural knowledge. Denis and I had a different kind of mending to do. To us, it was storybook stuff about wolves sneaking in among the sheep, wrecking lives, and getting away scot-free. At the time, we thought this tragedy was probably a one-off and wouldn't happen again in our lifetime. We were naïve about that, too. We didn't know that in ministries and churches—wherever Christians gather—there is always the possibility of things going terribly awry.

In the wider culture, changes were taking place across the country. As the riots protesting the Vietnam War spread across American college campuses and across the nation, the police and National Guard became very aggressive towards protesters, hippies, and anyone suspected of using drugs. In Albuquerque, hippies were pushed out of the parks, beaten, and arrested at demonstrations and other public places. Sometimes they were harassed and arrested because they merely looked suspicious. Drug use was also changing. At first many of the users who made it to our door were searching for answers to the big questions of life or spiritual enlightenment through the use of psychedelics. We began seeing more high school students and even junior high students using drugs for recreational purposes, not because they were looking for answers, but simply to be cool and get high.

The push by law enforcement caused many young people to flee from the cities. Over the next few months, visitors to His House began dropping off as fewer and fewer traveled across the country. Many hippies, including the Jesus People, headed to California or to communes being established in remote areas. From Vermont to the West Coast, young people who had dropped out of society were still trying to find their way to a better place. Northern New Mexico became the destination for many who wanted to live communally, but most of the communes didn't last long. Initially, the countercultural vision was so appealing: live off the land; reject bourgeois, suburban American life; hold all things in common; and replace conventional relationships with free love. But the experiment soon failed. Lack of work skills, money, food and health services, unfair and unequal work responsibilities between members, internal politics and even romantic squabbles—the lack of rules and safeguards did not bring about a utopia.

It was the early 70s. At the second His House, we began doing what was before us, small things that didn't look like much. Not like the World Evangelism Project that was sweeping the nation, hosting seminars that taught thousands of American churchgoers how to evangelize, and predicting that in a few years, every tribe and nation was going to hear the Gospel. We were in a small corner, simply loving those who showed up and allowing our friends to process and move on with their lives. We fed them, hugged them, listened to their stories and prayed together. Marsena played in the mud with the hose in the front yard and we had a garden in the back with tomatoes, beans, and onions. Evenings were spent in study and Denis often lectured on a passage from Scripture. Nothing sensational at all—just living our ordinary, everyday lives.

LORD OF ALL

I was twenty-two when we rented the little apartment behind His House. At that time, I hadn't banked a lot of hospitality experience, and didn't have the words to express its full meaning or significance. But my mother taught me back on the farm that what happened around a table was important, so it was part of my DNA. Sharing a meal could be a way of saying, "I love you. I care." In spite of Denis' and my relative poverty, I saw hospitality as a way of walking with others and treating them as whole persons.

Then something happened that caused it to become a keystone for the rest of my life.

One Sunday we impulsively invited a couple, Scott and Marilyn, for lunch after church. What we shared in common was an interest in spirituality, how God might be connected to ordinary everyday life, and what difference it could make in how we lived.

For our meal, I made the simple potato salad I learned from my mother. I fried hamburgers—fried because we didn't own a grill. I spread a homemade barbeque sauce on them. I opened a can of baked beans and upgraded them by adding chopped onion, green chile, and a little brown sugar. I served whole wheat bread I had baked the day before. Dessert was brownies from a box mix. I served water to drink. That was all we had.

We sat at our rickety table in the kitchen and later moved to our living room to sit on an old, worn couch and chair. They were hand-me-downs and roadside pick-ups. The furniture would probably now be called "shabby chic," which makes me laugh. That was probably the only time I was ahead of the fashion curve. At the time, I didn't have many options for home decorating. My main accessories were paisley fabric tacked to the walls, black fishnet, and glass balls hanging from the ceiling. As we sat talking for the rest of the afternoon, it became clear something magical happened and our hearts opened to one another.

Later, the couple told us how much they enjoyed that Sunday afternoon and hoped we could do it again. They said it was rare to be invited to someone's home and were touched by our interest and kindness. Somehow our conversation stimulated them to reflect more deeply on what it meant to be a Christian across all of life and culture. And so, our friendship grew, and it all began with a simple meal shared in humble surroundings.

Not long after, they invited us to their home. They were hosting a dinner party for friends and wanted to include us. As we drove into their neighborhood, I felt a sinking sensation. The homes were all southwestern adobe style, designed by architects. We approached their front door on a path leading through a wooden gate, to an inner patio, past a perfectly landscaped desert garden with a fountain to arrive at a large oak door with a knocker. Very Zen. As we waited for an answer, I experienced a wash of uneasiness. These people were way out of our economic class. He was an engineer working as a researcher at Sandia National Laboratories, and she was an administrator for the school district.

What had we been thinking when we invited them to our tiny apartment? If I had known their decor was Persian rugs and teak furniture, would I have presumed to invite them for a meal of canned baked beans with The Beatles' *Sgt. Pepper's Lonely Hearts Club Band* playing in the background?

We sat around a large oak table, eating from bone china and drinking from crystal. Marsena was with us, but she was such an amazing little baby, I could tuck her into a blanket on the floor in a quiet corner and she would fall asleep for an entire evening. When we were through with dinner, the women moved to the living room to play mahjong while the men talked in the den. I had to admit, "I don't know how to play mahjong." I'd never even heard of it.

As I took inventory of the differences in our life and status, I began to see this was a problem entirely of my own making, not theirs. Whether we are poor or wealthy, whether we drink from Mason jars or Waterford crystal, that should not be the concern when inviting people into our homes, into our lives.

In *by demonstration: God*, Wade Bradshaw reflects on the meaning of what should happen when we invite others into our home:

> The trick of real hospitality is not always to make a special time of the meal but to include people in it naturally. We should include others in what we do and drop entirely the effort to impress them. There is a place for the big feast (and we do have fun celebrating sometimes), but a bowlful of hearty soup and a thick piece of freshly baked bead on a drizzly day can be better than haute cuisine if they come with hospitality as warm as the food: a sense of comfort and welcome, and the wonder of simple pleasure.[3]

I was beginning to learn that participating in serving and caring for others meant, above all things, that I could not, should not practice hospitality for the sake of entertaining or impressing others. I didn't need a Viking range to cook. Nor did I need to know the meaning of "frisée" to reach out to people of any race or class. When we take the risk of inviting people into our lives and homes, we find God at work in everyone. Not only in the lives of the poor and broken—we find him at work in the rich and successful, whose lives are just as messy as ours.

I couldn't have defined it back then, but we were slowly learning to practice a rhythm of hospitality that has remained with us through all stages of life. Too often, women have been expected to carry the weight of this directive alone, but hospitality is clearly something we should all be practicing—men as well as women. As we invite strangers into our lives, we answer a call from Jesus: "I was hungry and you gave me something to eat, I was thirsty and you gave me something to drink, I was a stranger and you invited me in" (Matt. 25:35). For me, this was another way of affirming the sacredness of the ordinary and routine. Following Christ wasn't going to be the sensational let-me-be-a-martyr life I had imagined. It was more about being faithful now, in this moment, in this small way right in front of me.

Sometimes we've been tempted to ask whether the interruption to our life is worth the sacrifice. Is this person deserving of my efforts? Shouldn't I be fixing the leak in my roof rather than listening to this guy whine endlessly about his vasectomy? And what if when I invite someone in to stay awhile, my shower drain gets matted and clogged with creepy hair and slime, and pages are turned down in my favorite book, and the drill is never returned to the tool box because "I forgot"?

When we engage a stranger, we can't know the risk involved, and we shouldn't demand to see long-term results of our hospitality. The early church fathers viewed acts of hospitality in the same light as welcoming the Incarnate Lord. Long before modern humanitarian relief efforts, Augustine argued *against* the tendency to gauge whether any particular person was worthy of relief efforts by saying: "Let in the unworthy, in case the worthy might be excluded. You cannot be a judge and sifter of hearts."[4] He goes on to teach that our giving to others should not be based upon their moral worth since we ourselves were taken in by Christ when we were dark and broken. We show strangers hospitality because in doing so we are loving Christ as he loved us.

It has been a great inspiration and comfort that walking spiritually with others does not require me to be wealthy or particularly gifted in chit-chat or even to keep a perfectly presentable home. I don't need to be a "professional" in some Christian ministry way. I love the way James Houston describes the Christian life as a realm that belongs more truly to amateurs and dilettantes, lovers who take delight in God.[5] That means that as flawed and as unqualified as I am in so many ways, I'm in!

It has often been the case that the person we met at our door and invited in became a friend who gave back many times over. The difficulties and joys of hospitality lie close together and we experienced both—the unexpected blessing and the struggle of our limitations.

We had been living in the house in the valley for several months when there came a barely discernable knock on our front door. Denis answered to find a slight young woman with blue eyes and straight blond hair down to her waist standing on the steps, clutching a worn backpack. Denis called me over because she was asking to stay with us and we had a "No Crashers Allowed" policy. I picked up our one-year-old daughter and carried her with me to the front door. Denis introduced me. "This is Nancy. She's asking to stay with us."

"But we're not a crash pad," I said, with a note of frustration. I looked at her and thought, sure, another traveler passing through, looking for a place to drop acid and find a "Stairway To Heaven."[6] I was annoyed that Denis hadn't just sent her away. The two women and four young men already living with us were funny and charming, but their all-night jamming sessions and the amount of food they devoured were taxing my patience. In that moment I was all about boundaries, not hospitality.

"My dad dropped me off over there"—she pointed to the Piggly Wiggly parking lot across the street—"and I told him I'd be staying here. He's gone back to Las Cruces." She looked forlorn. "Please? I heard you were Christians, sort of like L'Abri, and you took people in." She was barely twenty and spoke with an appealing lisp.

There was a vulnerability about her and it seemed uncaring and dangerous that her father dumped her off in the middle of one of Albuquerque's run-down neighborhoods. Denis and I looked at each other and a slight nod passed between us. "You can come in and stay the night, but I'm not sure after that. We don't have a bed for you, but we have extra blankets and there is the floor." Her face brightened, and she entered our home, and claimed a corner of the living room.

We had read about L'Abri, which was run by Francis and Edith Schaeffer. We knew that they lived in a chalet in Switzerland and that young people from around the world were flocking to their home in the Swiss Alps in order to study and be mentored by them. Visitors and students included people of other religions, agnostics and atheists searching for Truth or merely a place to argue with someone about Christianity. What was appealing about their ministry is that all were welcome and any honest question was taken seriously and discussed.

We learned more about L'Abri as we got to know Nancy, who had been there. When Nancy visited L'Abri, she had arrived as an agnostic and a skeptic. She used her formidable intellect to argue with every staff person who lived and worked there. By the time she left, she was not intellectually convinced that Christianity was for her. But back home in New Mexico, she began realizing what she missed most was the reality of love and respect that permeated every part of life in their community. None of the leaders or workers, including the Schaeffers, were dismissive or annoyed by her questions and arguments. She was surprised by how much Francis and Edith valued art and creation and beauty. They believed that people were created by God to enjoy God's gifts. Those gifts were found in every part of life, including gardening, music, fresh bread, and candles on the supper table.

The Schaeffers never denied the brokenness of the world, but insisted that its condition was never something God intended. Rather, it had been the choice of humankind to turn away from the truth. For Nancy, in the end, it wasn't theological arguments or philosophical answers that changed her heart, but the kindness of hospitality and love that caused her to give her life to Jesus. So there she was, sitting on our living room floor, a new Christian trying to find her way, looking for the love and community she had found at L'Abri.

That night Denis led a Bible study and discussion that was crowded as usual, and Nancy made some precocious, insightful comments. They were enough to capture our full attention. Late that night after everyone left, she told Denis he needed to read more of the works of Francis Schaeffer.

Though we found many reasons to love her, we owe Nancy gratitude for that one small suggestion. Our lives were shaped and changed through the books, the lectures and lives of Francis and Edith Schaeffer.

Nancy stayed that night and the next day and the next, and that summer was the first of several summers she spent in our home as a loving part of our family.

Reading more of Schaeffer's books and listening to tapes of his lectures opened entirely new perspectives on the questions we had been asking. The Schaeffers' L'Abri work began almost by accident when their college-age daughter began bringing friends home on holidays. These students were asking questions about the meaning of life and the relevance of Christianity. Did it have anything to say to a world that declared God was dead? The Schaeffers were moved by the students' efforts to make sense of life, to find reasons for hope when there seemed to be none.

Their work grew naturally as more and more young people from all over the world began showing up at their chalet. The Schaeffers taught that Christ is Lord over all of reality, including all the arts, all our callings and vocations, from gardening to medicine. This was new to us. It was shocking to think God was as pleased with me when I went about my daily work changing diapers, doing the laundry, writing a letter, as when I prayed and read the Bible. I had been taught and believed I was most pleasing to God when I was practicing spiritual disciplines. It would take time for us to reckon with these intriguing ideas.

During our college days at the University of Minnesota, someone at school gave us a copy of *The God Who is There*, suggesting it might answer some of the questions we were asking about Christianity. At the time, we understood very little of what Francis Schaeffer was saying, but Nancy helped us make sense of it. Schaeffer was more of an oral communicator and writing wasn't something he felt gifted to do. He had initially refused to allow anything to be put on paper, but a student hid a tape recorder in the flowers on their dining room table to capture discussions and then transcribe them. Many have benefitted from that act and it paved the way for some of his later books.

Many of the taped lectures we heard began with a question from a student. As Dr. Schaeffer taught, he modeled that questions were not only acceptable, they were a necessary and important way to grow. Christians didn't need to fear them. As Schaeffer often said, "Honest questions deserve honest answers."

This was completely new to us. It was in direct contrast to what Denis had experienced when he brought questions to the elders of our Assembly. There, the elders saw questions as a problem. A lack of faith. Doubting meant you were harboring sin. "Is your heart right with God?" they asked. They quoted the book of James as a warning to have faith and not doubt: "But when you ask, you must believe and not doubt, because the one who doubts is like a wave of the sea, blown and tossed by the wind" (Jas. 1:6). Philosophical questions raised doubts; we ought to avoid asking them. "See to it that no one takes you captive through hollow and deceptive philosophy, which depends on human tradition and the elemental spiritual forces of this world rather than on Christ" (Col. 2:8).[7]

We became more familiar with the Schaeffers and the work of others associated with L'Abri. Jerram Barrs, for example, was converted there as a young man. He went on to write many books and to teach at Covenant Seminary. Eventually we came to know him as a friend. We were surprised when the Schaeffers taught and wrote freely about anything and everything as it related to everyday life, including philosophy. We learned there was a Dutch theologian, Abraham Kuyper, who famously said, "There is not a square inch in the whole domain of our human existence over which Christ, who is Sovereign over all, does not cry: 'Mine!'"[8]

We began to see that life was not limited to activities that were a justification for sharing the Gospel. It was permitted to raise a garden because you loved gardening, not just because the produce would be an excuse for witnessing to your neighbor as you shared the harvest. We felt released from the narrow confines of a sandbox to explore the ocean beach as far as the eye could see.

When Dr. Schaeffer taught about how deism, for example, gave rise to existentialism, even the history of ideas became exciting. Christianity wasn't just a small club people joined because they needed a private moral framework to live by. Rather, Christianity was pivotal to all of human history and human thriving. This didn't mean everyone would be persuaded to accept it as true. Christianity held sufficient answers to all the great worldview questions that have been asked by each generation since the beginning of time.[9]

Denis eventually distilled the questions down to their essential elements, making them easy to understand and think about:

Who am I?
What went wrong?
What's the solution?
How will the story end?

These questions capture the concerns, the hopes, and the fears every human being faces, even if not verbalized. These questions may not be experienced or asked all at once, but at some point in life, they are bound to surface for every person, no matter what philosophy or religion they live by. The answers to these questions will determine not only how we think but how we live out our lives in real time.

It was immediately clear based on my own experience that I wanted, no, needed to find answers to these questions—especially when facing a crisis of some kind. Death. A debilitating illness or depression. A lost job. Too many hard choices. Even while lost in the mire of changing diapers and feeding small children. When enduring any of the uncertainties life brings, we want to know how our story will end.

These worldview questions perfectly fit the biblical narrative of Creation, Fall, Redemption, and Restoration where, according to Christianity, we find the beauty and comfort of answers and the hope that one day, as Julian of Norwich declared, "All shall be well, and all shall be well, and all manner of thing shall be well."[10]

Denis posed them this way:

Creation:
Who are we?
What is the nature of things?
Is there a God?
Is there meaning, morality, knowledge?

Fall:
What went wrong?
What is the result?
Can we solve it?

Redemption:
What is the solution?
How can it be accessed?
How do we know?
Is there meaning to life, to suffering?

Restoration:
How will the story end?
What happens at death?
Is there hope? Why?
How realistic is it?
What evidence do we have?
What does it promise?

We had not known Christians—to say nothing of a church or ministry—who welcomed and accepted skeptics, atheists, agnostics, and Buddhists the way the Schaeffers did at L'Abri. Those who came to L'Abri included Christians who had the same doubts we did. When Jesus was on earth, it was not the religious leaders and the morally upright who were drawn to him. It was those who were needy, outcast, marginalized, and asking questions. This was the kind of Christianity we had been searching for. The more we learned about the Schaeffers and L'Abri the more excited we were that their message spoke to our hearts' deepest desires.

Their emphasis on hospitality was also a gift. In some instinctive way it was already part of me because my mother modeled this gift, but the Schaeffers connected it to the practice of Christian faith where it wasn't done to impress or entertain, but rather as a welcome to join just as you are. Although Denis and I never made it to Swiss L'Abri as students,[11] their influence moved us deeply and helped us see that our home could be shared with others as a place of love and beauty and safety. We trusted that what Jesus said would come true—when the kingdom of God arrives in all its fullness, it will be our final homecoming and our complete restoration for the way all things were meant to be.

In the same month we met Nancy, a fifteen-year-old girl came to live with us. Mandy Garcia[12] had nowhere else to go when she found us—or maybe we found her. I don't remember how we met the first time.

Mandy had been addicted to heroin and was living on the streets for a year before Teen Challenge accepted her into their program, where she gave up drugs and made a profession of faith. Having experienced the power of the Gospel, she really wanted a new life in Jesus. When her time at Teen Challenge was over, she was expected to move out and live on her own because her parents didn't want her back.

Mandy's parents were both professionals who had grown tired of her troubled life and kicked her out of their home. She often spoke of their detachment and wondered why they didn't love her. She remembered her father, how when he was home from his office, he always sat in a chair, hiding behind the newspaper. He rarely spoke to her and met her comments or questions with silence. In an effort to gain her mother's attention, Mandy dropped syringes and needles in the hallway or on the front steps, hoping her mom would find them and be alarmed. Her mother never noticed or at least never mentioned them. Mandy was deeply troubled and wounded. With nothing to offer except a desire to care for her, we invited her to live with us.

We loved Mandy, but not perfectly. She was a huge trial, combining little girl needs with sexy streetwise attitude. Sometimes she annoyed me. Other times she made me uncomfortable, asking personal questions about my sexual relationship with my husband. One night as I sat on her bed saying goodnight, we talked about little things, nothing profound. She suddenly began sobbing and couldn't stop. It was my sitting there so casually, tenderly, absently-mindedly stroking her arm that undid her. It was something her mother had never done.

After living with us for a few months, Mandy left because she couldn't stay away from drugs or from the men who used her body. We felt like we had failed her.

During the next four years we occasionally heard from her. Often she called in the middle of the night, crying, wanting us to pray for her or needing us to come pick her up from some dump and rescue her from a man who was beating her. She wanted life to be different, she wanted to quit heroin but was never able to overcome her terrifying addiction.

One day as I prepared dinner, I was listening to the local news with half an ear when I heard that a young woman had been shot by an ex-boyfriend in a lover's quarrel. I turned to the television and learned it was Mandy's body lying on the sidewalk, covered with a sheet. A pool of blood seeped out from under it. I was so shocked I dropped the dish I was holding.

Had she been ushered into heaven that day? I prayed so. All her wounds would have been healed by the time of the newscast. I imagined her fresh and virgin in a way that wasn't possible here on earth. Jesus would have held her in his arms and healed her body and soul forever. Someday, I hope to see her again, hug her, and laugh about the way she sometimes shocked me.

So many we meet do not carry their hunger on the surface of their lives. They remain secret, buried beneath layers of enculturated behavior. To be present to such need requires unhurried time to listen, and gentleness in peeling back layers of protection long in place. It can only be done with the help of the Holy Spirit and the patience God alone can give.

In the midst of both joy and pain, we were learning that hospitality could be practiced in a thousand little ways. We might never know the result of a small act of kindness, or even one that is sacrificial. God is under no obligation to show us the effects of our living for him. When he does give us a glimpse, we're amazed because we know how inadequate we are in so many ways.

Recently, we received this message from a woman we knew as a teenage girl way back in those Albuquerque days. She wrote:

> You both need to know the fruit of that time and season of harvest yielded within me a biblical foundation of stamina that kept me walking in the ways of Christ for over three decades. I for one, am eternally grateful for God's university while being in fellowship with you all! The seeds planted then still produce the gifts of the Spirit in my life now and until eternity.

It's painful to admit that during this time, Denis and I were struggling. Even though we were learning so many good things, there were problems causing stress in our relationship. It would be nice to report how wonderful everything was, how easy to love one another, how victorious we were in all our troubles.

Our schedules were split. Each night I went to bed before visitors left because I had to get up early with our baby. Denis stayed up late until everyone left and the house settled down. I was beginning to resent him because I didn't think he understood why I needed his help with some of the household responsibilities and the people who lived with us. At the same time, he was working a full-time job, coming home after work and interacting with all our housemates and evening visitors while also trying to prepare for talks and discussions.

We rarely had time alone together. I assumed he didn't seem to notice or need it. Often I couldn't sleep as I waited for him to come to bed, hoping we could have a conversation. When he finally fell into bed exhausted at one or two in the morning, I was wide awake, wanting him to ask how my day was, or ask me anything. When he instantly fell asleep, I lay there, growing more discouraged by the second. No self-talk was making it easier.

One night I snapped. I sat straight up, gave him a hard push, and told him what a rotten husband he was for not caring about me. "Oh yes," I said, "you have time for everyone else, but none for me." He claimed to have *no* idea what I was talking about. When I tried to explain that I felt lonely for him, he pointed out that he was around most of the time, what more did I want? He didn't know what more he could do than what he was already doing. Neither of us was able to cross the barrier rising between us. I wasn't expecting to have my hand held every second of the day, but I didn't know how to explain that our marriage needed tending without sounding petty and demanding. It filled me with a weary hopelessness. I resorted to prayer, asking over and over again, "Please help, please help."

Evenings at His House were changing. By the fall of 1971 fewer visitors were showing up for coffee and discussions. The culture was shifting again as many of the young people who had been on the road quit traveling across the country, found jobs, new partners, and new places to live. We weren't certain where God was leading us or what we should be doing differently.

The house itself was also beginning to reveal serious physical problems. The foundation was cracked. The toilet leaked. The place was infested with insects. The problems were serious enough to make us wonder if we needed to move again. The house was feeling less like a home and more like a place we needed to escape. That thought left us feeling close to despair.

We were stretching our money trying to make ends meet. Denis had left a part-time job in a greenhouse to work for a man who owned a gas station. The pay was so low that showing up was hardly worthwhile.

In the midst of these uncertain times, a little person lit our days. Beautiful, bright, and a clever trickster, she was making her presence and opinions known. When Marsena was around thirteen months old, her high chair sat in the kitchen beside a door with an old-fashioned keyhole. One noon as I prepared her lunch, she began crying loudly with real tears streaming down her cheeks. When I turned, I saw her tiny finger was stuck in the hole. Alarmed, I ran to her and gently tried to maneuver it out without further hurt. At last it slipped out and her finger looked okay. I turned back to the counter to finish making her sandwich. Again, she began to scream. I turned to see her finger was back in the same hole. As I hurried to her, she pulled it out and laughed at me. She had made a joke and it was on me. Anytime I forgot to pull her chair out of reach of the keyhole she performed her trick again. It made us laugh like fools and think we were raising a genius.

BOOK V

[1972–1973]

Piñon Pines

There are certain living things that can survive the adversity that would wound or kill others. One tree that is able to withstand drought and years of dormancy is found in many parts of New Mexico: the Pinus Edulus, commonly known as the piñon pine. There is a particular spot in Owl Creek Canyon near Fort Collins, Colorado, where a grove of piñons exists miles from any others. They owe their existence to a cache of nuts left by Native Americans some 400 years ago. The piñon's growth is slow. It's not majestic like the ponderosa, as it only reaches 15–60 feet at maturity, but what the piñon lacks in height, it makes up for in beauty. The trees are lovely in shape as their branches spread in a dark, green canopy beneath their rounded crowns, and on a good year, their cones produce pounds of delicious, buttery pine nuts. These nuts are prized for their nutritious qualities and are harvested and enjoyed by mule deer, black bear, birds, and humans. Native Americans steeped the needles for tea, and the inner bark was used to ward off starvation. The piñon can live for up to a thousand years. We sometimes burned piñon in our fireplace to enjoy the loud snap and citrusy, clean scent of its resin as it burned. One year I collected dozens of its unique shaped cones and made a wreath that has moved across the country and endured years in its box, and still, every winter it comes out to help celebrate Christmas.

COCKROACHES, POTATOES, AND PINTO BEANS

It was past midnight. The new His House in the valley was asleep. I turned the corner into the darkened kitchen, flipped on the light to get a drink and the entire room moved. I muffled a scream as cockroaches by the hundreds fled into cabinets and drawers. An entire phalanx headed under the refrigerator.

Suddenly I understood why each morning when I opened the cupboard where the plates were stacked, the top one seemed sprinkled with pepper. A closer look revealed that the sliver of black was a lost antennae. That dark line was a leg. That dot of pepper was cockroach feces.

I had been aware of a few roaches that wandered about the house; we often chased a running roach and crunched it under our shoe. But this revelation was so disturbing, I had to keep my hand clamped over my mouth to stop screaming. My visceral reaction to spiders, centipedes, and cockroaches has always been thus. It seems a little cowardly, because couldn't I butcher a chicken, clean a stinking calf pen, and tend a baby with diarrhea? On the Minnesota farm where I grew up, sure, there were insects. Flies, mosquitos, and the occasional beetle, but this, this was an Egyptian plague.

I fought them with Raid, spraying here and there, hoping to at least suppress them without spreading too much poison around the kitchen where a crawling baby was part of our family. Raid only seemed to inspire more flagrant breeding as all sizes began appearing: babies, teenagers, and old grandfathers the size of jumbo eggs running amok.

War was the answer. With toxic poison, we would attack all the cracks and crannies in the kitchen where, I was certain, they emerged from the dirt basement below the house. We prepared for battle one afternoon while Marsena napped. Denis and I moved every dish, pan, and utensil from the kitchen cabinets and drawers into the living room. We began streaming, spraying geysers of insecticide inside each cupboard, shelf, corner, under the refrigerator, and along the baseboards. We included the kitchen range because they always crawled out of the burners and oven when I turned on the gas. At first nothing happened and I thought we had just contaminated our kitchen for no reason. Then all hell broke out. Roaches began to emerge from every crevice, slowly, drunkenly staggering up the walls and across the ceiling by the hundreds and falling to the floor. They fell onto my head and scrabbled though my hair and I bolted to the living room where I stayed until Denis finished cleaning up. With the dustpan and broom, he swept piles of them into the trashcan. It was such a heroic act, I didn't know how I would ever pay him back. Then we washed down every surface in the kitchen.

We hoped this might get rid of them or at least diminish them a little. Not many days later they began reappearing, first one here, two there, and then multiplying by the hundreds.

I couldn't shake the dread of living there any longer, even though moving would probably mean the end of His House. It turned out, the end was near anyway. Financially, we were having trouble keeping up with our bills. The number of visitors dropped off, and only those in close relationship to us kept coming for studies, discussions, and the sake of friendship.

At work, Denis was facing our first experience with a Christian business owner who claimed the faith but had no reservations about exploiting others. This man owned a gas station and car repair shop and had assured Denis he could make a lot more money working for him. This was good news because Denis' minimum wage job at a greenhouse was not enough to support us. Working for a brother in Christ, we thought, was going to be much better.

Denis' job was to man the gas pumps and take care of the front of the shop. Before the modern era of self-serve gas, an attendant always came out to pump gas, wash the windows, and check the oil. Another daily chore was cleaning the mechanics' tools, which were dropped in a caustic bath. No gloves were provided, so after two days the unprotected skin on his hands began to blister and peel. In between all this, Denis washed semitrucks in one of the garage bays.

We eagerly awaited his first paycheck, thinking, yes, even though this job was uninspiring and soul-sucking, it would at least provide a way to pay off our medical bills. When he opened his first paycheck, we gasped. For more than forty hours of work he received less pay than at his former job. We thought it was a mistake, but the owner insisted, "Well, of course you can make more money, you just need to work more hours. I'll give you all the hours you want."

The next crushing disappointment was the vehicle we purchased from a friend of his. We were desperate for a reliable car and grateful when his boss introduced Denis to a friend who sold used cars. He had one he claimed would be perfect for us. Not only was the Buick a great deal, it was going to last us for years. When Denis hesitated because the price seemed high, the man insisted as a favor to us he wasn't going to make any profit from the sale. In addition, he'd be glad to let us make payments until we paid it off. We could trust him because he, too, was a Christian. We bought it.

Several weeks later the universal joint unexpectedly went out. It was expensive to repair, but such things happen, don't they? A short time later it went out again. That time we took it to a new mechanic who told us we'd been sold a car with a bent frame. It had been in an accident. The mechanic said, "Whoever sold this car to you knew it was a lemon. I can put in a new universal joint, but it'll go out again in a few weeks." We said to go ahead. We still owed money on the car and there was nothing we could do except keep making the payments and hoping somehow the second repair would last longer than the first.

Disappointed and disillusioned, it became clear we couldn't trust the owner of the gas station. We had assumed he was a friend. It was bewildering. We didn't think a Christian would take such advantage of others. We felt stupid, like somehow we should have known better. We had no power to change him, but we learned an important lesson the hard way: just because a business owner claims to be a Christian doesn't necessarily mean he will treat employees or clients with justice or compassion. We are still cautious and even skeptical of businesses or services advertising themselves as "Christian."

All these circumstances taken together made us wonder if we were entering a new phase of life and needed to face some changes. We didn't know what God was doing or where he was taking us. One thing gave me courage: Denis received some advice and he took it seriously. A friend, a man who was older than us and who visited from time to time, observed how our schedule was stressing our relationship. He took Denis aside and counseled him that in marriage, setting aside time for one another is not only crucial, it's pleasing to God. No matter how demanding your life and ministry, making family a priority is essential. Denis told me about this conversation and agreed it had been a problem and he was going to try to be different.

We now felt it was time to close His House and Denis and I began looking for another place to rent. We read every want ad and noted every "For Rent" sign as we drove around the city. Nothing affordable turned up until we found a one-bedroom house the size of a postage stamp near the university. It had been on the market for months, so the owner was willing to rent it with the understanding that if it sold, we would need to move out quickly.

We were ready to be just us, a family of three for a while again. When I walked through the living room with its outrageous African wallpaper with zebras, giraffes, and lions in warm colors and black accents, rattan furniture, and

floor pillows, I felt a longing in me for a home where beauty, creativity, and surprise infused you with pleasure. I wasn't only tired of roaches, I was weary from
having so many people in our home day after day. The rooms of this rental were
all midget-sized, but I thought one bedroom would do us just fine. We could all
snuggle in together for a while. And who knew, perhaps it would be months
before it sold?

Once again we packed our belongings and moved—just the three of us.
Denis quit the gas station and spent every day and all our gas money looking
for another full-time job. But day after day, he only had sad news. There was
nothing; no one out there who wanted to hire him. Our cash dwindled to almost
nothing.

Each evening, he would ask hopefully, "What's for supper?"

Each evening, the answer was, "Potatoes and beans."

I had ten pounds of pinto beans and a sack of potatoes. For three weeks I
cooked beans and potatoes every way I knew. Baked, mashed, fried, and soup.
We had run out of eggs, cheese, and fruit. We had enough milk for the baby to
last a few more days and little else. There was nothing to do except pray and
keep on trying. Denis had to find a job and I had to make meals from nothing.

We began doubting everything. Had we misread God's direction and timing?
Should we have stayed among the roaches in the Valley? Should we bail from
New Mexico altogether and move back to Minnesota? Where was God in all of
this?

We had been in the rental for only one week when the owner contacted us.
The house had sold and we had two weeks to get out. Those weeks with no job,
no money, and now no place to call home, torpedoed our last hopes. It was as if
we were calling God on the phone and the phone just rang and rang.

And then. Denis came home beaming early one afternoon. One of the two
churches in all of Albuquerque who welcomed new converts from His House
had contacted him. Ron Miller, the pastor of Grace Church, was a great big guy
with a heart as generous as his girth. Somehow he learned that Denis was looking for work and he had this crazy idea that Denis would make a great youth
pastor. By the time he approached Denis, he had already met with his elders and
gotten approval for bringing him on staff. They were enthused about it, thinking
we were exactly positioned to help their young people navigate the immense
changes in our culture that were affecting all families.

Denis was to begin immediately and to our astonishment, we were even giv-
en a small advance to tide us over until his salary began in two weeks.

You know how when you reach a point where you're terrified nothing will
ever work out and you'll end up homeless, sick, and begging for bread? Your
child will starve? Your car will *never* stop breaking down and protein will never

be on your table again? You doubt God loves you and you know he's tired of your complaining and is going to stop listening? You've done all sorts of wrong, and actually, you deserve this poverty because you're a big loser? In fact, you deserve nothing?

Then, God hands you a plate full and overflowing with things you couldn't imagine even existed, or if they did, they'd only be going to the saints, or the perfect, or the rich. Suddenly you. You are among the favored. You are rich. I went to the store and came home with ground beef, frozen corn, fresh strawberries, and bananas. We were going to feast.

I've tried to find words and have put down many, but can't find ones big enough or powerful enough to express how our hearts cried with joy and how we confessed we had grown exhausted and full of doubt. Never again would we question God's goodness and faithfulness. From then on, through all the years to this day, when we face discouragement or crisis, I am reminded of this time and repeat the following: "Now to him who is able to do immeasurably more than all we ask or imagine, according to his power that is at work within us, to him be glory in the church and in Christ Jesus throughout all generations, for ever and ever! Amen" (Eph. 3:20–21).

CHRIST'S LITTLE WAY[1]

We left the house with the zebra wallpaper and quickly found another rental. Thanks to Denis' salary, we could afford it. This was the fifth time we had moved in two-and-a-half years since arriving in Albuquerque. It wouldn't be the last. The new house had four bedrooms and a large den. Oddly, you could tell the den had been converted from the garage but it was going to be perfect for youth group meetings and other gatherings.

People from Grace Church helped us move. I was not used to such kindness and generosity from church people. It made me feel wary. Did their expressions of love have a dark side? Did I need to wait for the other shoe to drop? Denis and I soon agreed this church was going to be very different from Garfield Gospel Chapel. No one would be rejected or escorted out the door because of the way they dressed.

When we moved into the house on Pampas Street, the few pieces of shabby furniture we were glad to own made the rooms looked bare and dingy. A crib here, a mattress on the floor there, a rickety table, a stained easy chair covered by an old afghan to hide the stuffing that was popping out. It was all functional, but none of it was attractive.

The day after we moved in, a church elder stopped by and looking around at the spartan décor gruffly commanded, "Get in my pickup, I have something for you to look at." He wasn't asking.

Having no idea what was up, we arrived in the parking lot behind the church where there was a locked storage building. He unlocked the door, threw it open and issued another command, "Take what you need." From floor to ceiling, it was stuffed with furniture and lamps and a few rugs that had belonged to a lady who had long since left for the mission field and no longer had use for it.

This ex-Marine with his stocky body, burr haircut, and brusque attitude proved to be altogether different from what I imagined when I first met him. He represented one of the first in a long line of precious lessons about not judging a person by his or her demeanor, dress, or hair-cut. His tender heart was exposed as we learned more about him. He had lost a daughter in an accident when she was just a young girl and that grief was never far from him. Later I would witness him quietly slip out of the kitchen where he had been cooking for a youth retreat. His eyes would tear up as he listened to Denis' talk (what it was about, I don't remember). Later, he would thank Denis for caring for this group of rowdy, sweet, and sometimes impossible teens. This master sergeant was one of the kindest, most generous Christians we ever met.

With mounting excitement, we pulled out a bed, a of couple lamps, some area rugs, and bedroom furniture hidden in the stacks. Several days later, this man returned to our house with a green naugahyde couch his wife was getting rid of. As we set up housekeeping, I kept a sharp eye on the corners and crevices in the kitchen. With traumatic memories of cockroaches crawling out of the cabinets and across the ceiling still fresh in my mind, I began each day with a rush of thankfulness after not spotting a single one. Our house was furnished and it looked far more pleasant. We were set.

This began a new stage of life where we were suddenly involved in the life of a church that seemed to want us as much as we wanted them. Our home became a gathering place for high school students who hung out as often as their parents allowed. They constantly dropped in to listen to rock music, talk about life, and consume our food. Three of our housemates from His House moved back in with us and, as former druggies, they were subjected to a lot of scrutiny by the youth group.

The hardest part of our former ascetic lifestyle was doing without the small things that warm a living space and make it feel like home. Rugs to soften the floors. Mirrors that extend space. Art on the walls. Soft blankets, clean and unstained. Attractive dishes, even if unmatched and chipped. We were still processing what we were learning from the ministry of L'Abri and the lives of Francis and Edith Schaeffer. They had challenged us to see that God is Lord of all life. We understood this intellectually. We now believed there was no division between the spiritual and the material, and their ideas encouraged us to see and practice creativity and beauty in everyday matters. God had made a world that was both pleasing and inviting. We could do the same. I was loving the chance to make our home pleasing and inviting. Being made in God's image meant we, too, were legitimate creators. It felt glorious.

When I thought about everything we had gotten rid of back in St. Paul, I realized something phenomenal. God had gradually replaced every single thing we sold and provided more besides. We did not pay a single penny for any of it. It was all gifted to us. We still own a beautiful solid oak buffet, an antique highboy dresser with Queen Anne legs, and bookcases that came from the church's storage shed. A woman who was updating her kitchen appliances from avocado green to black gave them to us. I didn't care that black was the fashionable new color, I was thankful to have a range and refrigerator that worked perfectly. Friends who grew tired of eating at our card table and sitting on folding chairs surprised us one Christmas with wooden benches and a harvest-style table made especially for us. They were functional *and* beautiful. From others here and there over the years we received more beds, dressers, couches, and easy chairs than I can count.

Many years later, after we had moved back to Minnesota, I finally gave myself permission to purchase our first piece of furniture that was brand new—a leather easy chair. The act felt monumental. Nearly everyone my age had done this many times; for them it was as natural as turning on the water tap. You went to the store, pointed out the piece, chose the color, and it was delivered a few days later. For me, it was a big deal. I learned it didn't need to be a slippery slope after all: it was God's overflowing and generous permission to enjoy something well-crafted and handsome that wouldn't break apart the first time our teenagers threw themselves down in it.

In time, I met a friend whose lovely companionship helped creativity explode into other areas of my life. She was an artist and a mother of three just as I was. She taught me calligraphy. She inspired me to learn tole painting. Together we gathered piñon cones, weeds, and dried flowers and made beautiful natural wreaths. We shopped flea markets for picture frames. We refinished furniture. We sewed. We cooked. How we cooked, baked, and canned! Each year we bought a gunny sack full of Anaheim green chile. In the back yard we heated a charcoal grill to blister their skins, then we peeled and chopped them to make tons of tasty salsa. During our first salsa-making marathon, I grew tired of wearing plastic gloves and chopped chile with bare hands. On my way home that evening, they began to burn. I spent the entire night lying flat on the floor with each hand in an ice-filled pie plate, trying to relieve the pain. And yet, it was so satisfying, such joy to be set free to create. It was as if God was blessing us, saying *I am calling you to a life that is rich in relationships and beauty—not in the way you imagined. In love, I am providing what you need to make a home and a life that isn't just functional, but also beautiful.* That God permitted more than four whacked-together walls and a cement floor is something I will never take for granted. God gently moved us past our asceticism and redeemed it.

While Denis and I were growing and changing in some ways, we still had a long way to go. It's not unusual for someone who is passionate about a cause to become self-righteous. Both Denis and I were quietly judging others, especially those who seemed wealthy.

It's embarrassing to admit our arrogant attitudes were directed toward a particular couple who had been good to us. As old as I am, I've never quite reached the point where I can say for certain: *Got it. I'm done with that problem, praise God. I am now the person God has meant me to be.* I continue to be confronted with the ways I deceive myself and harbor bad attitudes and prejudices against others.

The man who kindly challenged Denis to spend more time with his family happened to also attend Grace Church with his wife Cheryl and their three children. Ken was a highly educated nuclear physicist who worked for Sandia National Laboratories. He and Cheryl owned a modern ranch style house and drove a Volvo. *A Volvo?* I asked myself. They were really expensive. From all this, Denis and I assumed they enjoyed a very large salary. We wondered how they could really be dedicated to living as disciples of Jesus if they were so wealthy.

Gradually, we learned more about them. Together they often traveled to the Soviet Union where Ken was hosted by scientific societies and where the KGB kept a cold eye on them. Wherever he gave lectures, Ken always mentioned having faith in a Creator. This invariably caused a ripple of curiosity and skepticism through the lecture hall. A few reached out secretly to speak with him. How was it possible for such an intelligent, internationally-recognized scientist to hold impossible beliefs such as man being made in the image of God?

After he delivered one of his lectures, a couple overcame their fear of surveillance and met him in a safe place where they could speak freely. They asked many questions. "What god?" they asked, for they were all atheistic materialists. "What is faith? What do you believe?" When Ken explained the Creator God, who in love sent his Son to earth, their hearts blew up in that uniquely Russian way accompanied by tears and many shots of vodka. Astonished, they told him the more they studied and observed how scientific principles worked, the more they began to think there must be a designer behind the order of the universe. The most incredible thing to them was the human hand. Who could have imagined a hand with four fingers and an opposable thumb that allowed humans to easily touch their fingers, firmly grasp, and delicately manipulate objects of many different shapes? They began to think of this unknown designer as a being they called "The God of the Thumb." Suddenly, they learned who that God was. The astonishing answers they found in the Gospel of Christ made them weep with joy.

So okay. Ken and Cheryl told others about God, Creator of the Universe and about Jesus, his Son. Still, I judged them for being rich even though I liked them and they were generous and kind to us in many ways. They invited us for meals where hearty chunks of protein were served up in amounts I hadn't seen since I'd left my childhood home on the farm. They babysat for us occasionally. They gave us gifts of money and it was no tax deduction for them. They ministered to us spiritually by praying for us.

Then one day we learned a shocking fact—I've forgotten how. This couple regularly gave a significant portion their income away. I was stunned. If God himself had stood before me and said, "You see? I told you not to judge others or underestimate my power to work in ways you can't imagine," I couldn't have been more mortified or repentant. As Denis and I stumbled along with remnants of legalism still clinging to us, God, rather than sending us packing as harsh zealots, continued to teach us with patience and grace.

At Grace Church, the way Denis and I ministered as a couple shifted. He learned the administrative skills which would serve him well when he became an area director for InterVarsity, a college campus ministry. It would also help us when we moved back to Minnesota and began Ransom Fellowship, our own non-profit ministry. He was good at it. Denis also became an accomplished speaker under Pastor Ron's mentorship. This large, beautiful man was never threatened by others' success. He was a true lover of God and a great teacher. Occasionally he scheduled Denis to give the Sunday evening sermon where he sat in the front row, nodding, laughing when appropriate, and taking notes. Denis knew that on Monday morning he would be given the notes Ron had taken while he preached. They would compare them with Denis' notes. "This is what I heard you say. Is that what you meant for me to hear?" Ron would ask. Going over the text, the illustrations, and the points Denis made, Ron taught him as no one had before.

The kids in the youth group listened to Denis because he won their hearts by listening to them. He challenged them about what they believed, knowing from his own experience that when you grow up in a Christian environment and are sheltered from real life, getting launched into the world can be exhilarating, but it can also be a dangerous walk in the Serengeti at night. Denis and I wanted them to learn there were good reasons to believe that Christianity offered what every heart needs. A first step was allowing doubts and questions to surface where they could be acknowledged and examined. We also knew from experience that questions could be seen as rebellion, but we welcomed them. We wanted honesty. We knew that repressing doubts didn't make them go away. We longed to prepare young people for the temptations and harsh realities they were bound to face in life, but to also taste the deep love and joy God gives to his people.

Denis loved this new challenge of leading the youth group, teaching them, studying the Bible with them, pushing their beliefs, and asking questions. It was a challenge for me, too, but not in the same way and not quite as welcome. At His House we had worked together; now that he was youth pastor, I almost felt we were no longer teammates. Even though he tried to reassure me that what I was doing was important, I often rolled my eyes and mocked Denis for all the compliments he received.

Being home alone with a toddler was different from being in a household where many people came and went throughout most of the day. Some had come to see me specifically, and I had loved them for their stories, their dreams, and their difficulties. Even in the kitchen I hadn't been alone because both young men and women helped out. But now I struggled with my significance and worth. Managing a home, having babies, caring for physical needs, while important, ranked lower in my mind than what Denis was doing. Although life was definitely richer and more creative than it had been, I had not quite shed the belief that praying, reading the Bible, witnessing, and making disciples were more significant callings in life than raising children. I made this problem more complicated by wanting to be and do something exciting and sensational which would surely bring the approval I craved. I recognized there was something rotten about this self-centered attitude. I sincerely wanted to be different. More kind. Patient. Content. More like Christ. The trouble was I wanted change to be immediate and permanent. We are conditioned to expect this because we live in an age of instant everything. Whether we're talking about construction, art, education, or any of the character flaws or bad habits we host, we value getting things done quickly. No surprise.

John White, a Canadian author, once likened our efforts to eradicate what is wrong with our lives to a ball of tangled, knotted string.

> God has his own program for reshaping our lives. No exact hierarchy of sins is laid down in Scripture.... In dealing with you and me, God is doing what we do ourselves when we try to untangle a knotted string.[2]

It never works to tug and pull furiously at an end. You must patiently, gradually untangle all the knots bit by bit, one at a time. That, White says, is how God works in us. We would prefer him to clean up the whole mess at once, but he works slowly, giving us time to process and grow.

That's the story of my life. In fact the same knot can often reappear again, but God's patience is infinite as he untangles me one more time.

Years later, I heard Zack Eswine, the author of *Sensing Jesus*,[3] say in a lecture, "God says to us, 'Shhh-shhh. I see you. I see you. Follow me and you will learn to do small things slowly, over a long period of time.'" It seems inevitable that the process of growth is slow and painful. Maturity is never quick, never easy. Slowly, over time I began to recognize the holy and the sacred in my ordinary, everyday life. In the end I grew to love it and even found enough embedded humor to make me laugh nearly every day.

ACCIDENTS CAN
BE PREVENTED

Dust rose in a trail behind our car. We were first in the line of vehicles pulling into Camp Del Chapparal on a forest road near Cuba, New Mexico. The school bus rocked in last, carrying a load of teenagers eager to begin running amok. It was the summer of Denis' first year on staff at Grace and the first camp he would direct.

Denis had prepared hard for this week, recruiting counselors, the ex-Marine who was also a cook, his kitchen helpers, and a song leader. Denis created a schedule that included serious Bible study and times of physical activity, rounded out with creative art projects. Anticipation ran high in the church because this was the first camping experience for the youth group that anyone could remember, and Denis was already appreciated for the work he was doing.

The land surrounding the camp was typical high-desert basin with low hills leading to higher elevations up to 7,000 feet. Rocky cliffs bordered the camp with dry stream beds and boulders strewn about as if giants had a rock-throwing fight. Piñon trees, sagebrush, yucca, and prickly pear cactus covered the ground, adding rich texture to the land. The sharp scent of pine and sage made you breathe deep and wish your skin and clothing always smelled of pure air, sunshine, and wild mountains.

I had few obligations. I would help in the kitchen when I could and keep an eye on our two-year-old daughter as she played. There was little to concern us—only the occasional rattlesnake sunning itself on a path. The weight of the city melted away to a countryside where the iconic sky of the American West glowed brilliant turquoise blue. Nights were cool and from horizon to horizon, the Milky Way shone in a way I hadn't seen since leaving home in Northern Minnesota. Our room was on the second floor of an old adobe home with a door leading to an outdoor balcony. Denis carefully tested the railing around the edges to make sure it was secure. He knew there would be times when I sat in the freshness of that place, enjoying the shifting desert light, allowing Marsena to play with her dolls and books. The distant view of the blue Jemez mountains was so vast, the experience so pleasurable, it lifted my heart to the heavens.

Four days into our week-long stay, Marsena and I were on the balcony watching the campers and counselors play capture the flag. It was perfect terrain for the game with granite boulders, hiding places, and little thickets. There were shouts of victory when the flag was stolen and screams of dismay when prisoners were taken. Marsena plunked her potty chair beside me, which at the moment was not for elimination, but served as repose for a little body to sit and read. Perhaps this was the beginning of a lifelong bathroom habit many of us secretly enjoy. Not being quite satisfied with its position, she stood up to horse it past my feet to the other side. As I reached forward to help her, she tripped, rolled under the rail and fell approximately twenty feet to the ground below.

Denis heard my scream and knew instantly what happened. I flew down the stairs and through the house. In those few seconds, my heart ruptured and fell into a dark place. Words left my body, replaced with one long, piercing howl.

Denis ran up the slope, arriving breathless and panicked. By then our dear friends Pete and Mary Swearengen, who were helping run the camp, arrived. I was bending over our daughter, whose head was resting on a half-buried boulder. Blood was seeping through her hair. She was conscious and crying as she reached for me with her little arms. Somewhere in my brain I knew I shouldn't move her in case her neck was broken. Mary tried to stop me from picking her up, but I couldn't resist. The only thing that made sense in that terrible moment was that I must hold her. Carefully I cradled her in my arms and brokenly tried to comfort her.

The fact that she was conscious gave us hope. We quickly decided Pete would drive me to the small clinic in Cuba run by a young moonlighting resident from the University Medical School in Albuquerque. He was kind as he gently examined her and checked the pupils of her eyes. He would have taken X-rays, but their machine was ancient and broken. Since she seemed stable, he suggested we take her to Albuquerque to be seen by our pediatrician.

We left the clinic and headed to Albuquerque, leaving Denis behind. As camp director for forty teenagers, he needed to make arrangements before he could leave. On the one-and-a-half-hour drive back to the city, I held her in my lap and several times with the few words she knew, she told me the story of what had happened. She made motions lifting her arms up and letting them fall down. She kept repeating, "Fall, fall, fall. Up high. Up high." Later Mary told us she witnessed Marsena's tumble to the ground as she did a summersault on the way. I knew I had to remain calm for our daughter's sake. I couldn't allow myself to sob because I wouldn't be able to stop, but my tears would not listen as they silently fell.

Our pediatrician examined her, stitched the scalp wounds, and decided on an X-ray just to be thorough. That meant going next door to the University Hospital. "She looks okay. This is just precautionary," he assured me. At the time X-rays were not instantly readable, so they sent me home to wait for results. I was feeding Marsena yogurt and applesauce when the doctor called. "You need to return immediately. Your daughter has a large T-fracture of the skull."

Pete was still with me, waiting to hear she was going to be alright. With the doctor's news, Denis needed to know the result of the X-rays immediately. I knew I wouldn't be able to speak to him without crying. I didn't want to see him either. The accident was my fault and our daughter might die. Pete kindly took the phone and called the camp to tell Denis what was happening. Denis left to join us as quickly as he could and Pete headed back to oversee to the rest of the week.

Marsena was admitted to the hospital where in her bed she looked like a fragile little doll. Exhausted from the trauma, she was allowed to fall asleep. A surgeon came in with our pediatrician and explained some of the bones in the skull were over-lapped and she might require surgery, but they didn't dare proceed until they learned how much swelling and pressure would form on her brain. They would monitor her condition for at least the next twenty-four hours.

Word of the accident spread through the church and to our friends. I sat for hours watching her lashes rest against her cheek and her thin blue-veined lids twitch as she dreamed.

The dreaded moment came when Denis walked into the hospital room. All I remember is that he hugged me and assured me over and over—this wasn't your fault. *This wasn't your fault.* I didn't believe it—it was my fault.

That evening a couple walked in. I don't remember who they were. I can't think of their names no matter how I try. They asked if they could pray for our daughter. We said yes, of course. They stood beside her, their hands on her silky hair; Marsena watched me, her eyes filled with questions. They prayed that God would heal her, then they left.

Marsena remained stable through the night. The next morning we waited for the results of more X-rays. When the team came into the room, we prepared ourselves for the worst. But who can do that? In spite of our efforts, our breathing sped up and our hearts hammered. They smiled and the doctor holding the X-rays said, "We didn't expect this at all, but the broken bones in her skull that had overlapped have somehow slipped back into place. There's no bleeding or pressure on the brain that we can see. She won't be needing surgery after all.

We'll observe her for a while longer and if she shows no further symptoms she can go home."

I'd like to say the medical staff used the word *miracle*, but I can't remember if that was the case. But we did. A miracle. An amazing miracle, we called it. Our daughter fell twenty feet, landed on a boulder, and all she needed was some stitches for a gash. And who was the couple who prayed for her? I'll never know.

You would think after this, all would be well and we would go home rejoicing. Marsena was healed! Denis didn't blame me. That was a relief. But I wasn't well. I fell farther into a dark place, blaming myself over and over. My mind was filled with what-ifs. I remembered the times when Denis had insisted accidents could be prevented. He was right! If only, if only, if only. How could I forgive myself? The malaise spread. I was a failure. I was not a good mother and I could not be a good wife either.

BOOK VI

[1973–1981]

Turquoise

All Native Americans believe the earth is living and all things in it are precious. Turquoise is no exception. It represents life itself and is highly revered because of its color-changing properties, so they named it The Sky Stone or The Stone of Life. Turquoise colors are surprisingly varied, from rich shades of blue-green to deep blue and even shades of copper. Most turquoise contains remnants of its host stone, which often leaves a matrix of veins embedded throughout the stone reminiscent of spider webs. What would be called flaws or imperfections in other gemstones can make the turquoise all the more valuable. Among many turquoise mines in New Mexico, there is one called Cerrillos about ten miles south of Santa Fe where research has proved that Native Americans worked the earth to dig the rocks that hid veins of turquoise as far back as prehistoric times.

When we first came to New Mexico, I couldn't see anything lovely or inviting about it. It was no place I wanted to be. That feeling was gradually replaced with deepening love and gratitude for this high desert country. Among the many things we grew to love were The Stones of Life.

I KNOW THE WORST ABOUT YOU

Paralysis gripped my body. I was trapped on a narrow bridge that forded a raging river. On the opposite shore, the path to safety led through a darkened wild land. I sprinted, trying to make it. Beneath the bridge, wraith-like demons rose from black water. They floated up, their cold skeletal hands reaching for me. I screamed and pointed a cross at them. *In the name of Jesus, in the name of Jesus. In the name of Jesus.*

Denis shook me. I was groaning, my arms were lifted and my fingers were still making the sign of a cross. *Shhh. Shhh. You're okay. I'm here. I'm here.* I didn't feel okay or safe. Satan had entered my dream and was determined to catch me on that bridge.

The same nightmare repeated itself night after night until finally Denis suggested it must be a spiritual attack. We invited several friends to pray for me. They were understanding and supportive as they held my hands and filled our house with prayers of comfort and protection and bound evil from us. That night the dreams left and never returned. Peace flooded my body and I knew that somehow, mysteriously, Jesus had rescued me.

In the following weeks, physical problems began appearing. My hands wouldn't stop shaking. The slightest effort turned my heart into a pounding hammer that spiked my pulse. Overwhelming fatigue drained me, and yet I couldn't sleep at night as my mind spun round and round. I couldn't stop thinking. The simplest household chore brought on staggering weakness. I was convinced all this was caused by sin that needed to be confessed. Was I angry when my two-year-old spilled her milk? Yes. Did I really lust after that handsome man who stopped by? Yes. Was I a lazy slob? Maybe. I combed through the pages of my life, examining attitudes, looking for the tiniest transgression. In misery, I pleaded with God to forgive me.

I didn't ask for it, but friends showed up to help with some daily chores I couldn't manage. At church Denis mentioned I was having trouble keeping up at home because I didn't feel well. When a woman came by to pick up our dirty laundry, I was so humiliated I tried to pull the basket from her arms. Her response was gentle but firm. After she left, I sat on the couch and bawled. I was becoming everything I despised—unable to shoulder responsibility, a slacker, a shirker, a complainer, and worst of all, a weak emotional person who cried about everything. I was mentally ill. Denis thought so too, but quietly said nothing about that possibility. He plugged along, trying to hold us together while keeping up with his job.

As if I didn't have enough to complain about, back pain added a little more to the pot of torment. We thought it might be due to sleeping in our old, worn out valley bed. But when someone generously gave us a new mattress, the pain didn't improve. Finally, I made an appointment with a chiropractor who examined me and thoughtfully reported, "You need to see a medical doctor." That seemed strange and a little worrisome. I erroneously assumed chiropractors and medical doctors were adversaries.

A week later, I sat on the exam table, weeping, as my physician checked me over. She didn't say much about what she was thinking, but when she ordered blood tests, I began to wonder if perhaps there *was* a physical explanation for the mess I was in. When the tests came back, she referred me to an endocrinologist who diagnosed thyroiditis. He was kind as he took my hand and assured me I would get better soon. He explained that historically many patients with thyroid disease were committed to mental institutions because no one understood it could be treated with medication. Mine had given me a crazy back-and-forth whipping as it cycled from hyperactive to hypoactive.

The gland needed to be ablated. I like that word. Ablate. It means remove. Take away. When the thyroid gland is unable to regulate hormones, radioactive iodine is injected into the bloodstream until the high concentration burns it out. From then on a patient relies on synthetic hormones to do the work of controlling metabolism and calming the brain. I stopped obsessively confessing sin.

The effect was miraculous. It's interesting how brain chemistry can affect us. I was so certain this had been all my fault. It not only affected my belief of how God viewed me, but it also stirred up childhood insecurities about being unlovable. But now I began sleeping better. I stopped crying over every little thing. I was even restored to grocery shopping—a domestic task I never enjoyed. Now I thought pushing a cart up and down the aisles was so pleasant I could do it forever.

It soon became clear we needed a reliable car—one that didn't blow its universal joint every time we turned a corner. We had no savings and no money for this. All our income went to daily living and paying our bills. There was a lot of evidence that God was taking care of us: we were not homeless. We had been able to furnish a house with generous gifts and free cast-offs we picked up along the curb. Our daughter had been healed from a bad fall. Denis had a job that actually paid him.

I thought about what Jesus said regarding everyday needs: "For the pagan world runs after all such things, and your Father knows that you need them. But seek his kingdom and these things will be given to you as well" (Luke 12:30–31). We needed to get rid of that old Buick. We believed God knew about this and could provide, but exactly *how* was that going to happen? We had no extended family to function as a safety net and no one we wanted to ask for advice about used car purchases. It was embarrassing to admit we'd been duped. The Buick was a big mistake. How stupid was that?

The Buick from hell.

Denis and I agreed to wait and move ahead carefully. We didn't want to make the same mistake twice. As the days passed with no text messages from God about what to do, Denis grew frustrated with waiting, and one morning he was done. He declared he was going to go to a car dealership, get a loan, and buy a used car off the lot. He didn't care how much it cost.

Being a responsible provider weighed heavily on Denis. He was trying hard to do the right thing, but it was complicated because in the background he heard the voice of his father playing on a loop telling him what a failure he was. I was concerned about making a decision that would put us heavily in debt. I urged him to wait longer and pray God would somehow provide a car. Not what he wanted to hear. He insisted I was being pious and unrealistic. Maybe true. I was never good at debate, but I extracted a promise from him to wait until Monday. "After that," he said, "I'm going down to the lot. I'm sick of this."

Four days. God had four days. Nothing was happening. By Sunday morning, I felt pretty discouraged. We dressed for church and drove automobiles as far out of our minds as possible.

Then.

When Sunday school was over, a young couple casually asked Denis if we could use a car because they had a little blue Subaru they no longer used. It was fairly new and in good shape. We made plans to meet with them the next day to make it official.

When the church service was over and we were leaving, another couple stopped us. They had a station wagon no longer in use because their kids had left for college; it was just sitting in their driveway. They wondered if we could use it.

We laughed all the way home. In less than an hour we had become owners of *two* cars and had paid *nothing* for either one. We were going to be rid of that clunky, junky Buick. Those cars became worry stones in our pocket, reminders we have rubbed smooth until this day. We learned that in any situation, especially one that seems impossible from our perspective, God has an infinite number of ways to care for us. He is author of possibilities we can't imagine. I remind myself of this especially during times of distress when I have no idea what God is up to. To be honest, there have been times when it seems nothing good is ever going to come from a situation. Then I must concede we may never understand or know God's purposes until years from now, or maybe not even until the next life, when we have the promise that everything that has ever gone wrong will be made perfect and whole again. In the meantime, he brings events, people, and even cars into our lives to teach us that hope in him is not foolish or misplaced.

The next summer, Denis and I moved again and for the time being no one else was living with us. Marsena turned three and Denis' parents returned from the Philippines on furlough to tour the US and report on their work. They sounded excited to meet their first grandchild, but their arrival in Albuquerque resurrected old problems and stress. Both of us anticipated more disapproval because to his father, being at Grace Church was not much better than living in a hippie commune and entertaining prostitutes. Denis still hoped that at least we could convince them we loved God by the way we lived our lives. I suggested, "Perhaps their opinion of us will change if they see us reaching out to others and leading Bible studies."

In order to convince them that befriending young people who were considered hippies was a way of loving our neighbor, I proposed, "Let's invite Michael, Manny, and Bill over for supper to meet your parents. What better way to convince them than by introducing them to some of these delightful young men whose lives have been changed by the Gospel?" Denis thought it was a great idea. The night arrived. The young men made their way to our house and got caught behind an older man driving very slowly. When he approached a corner, he made an illegal left turn from the center lane, nearly causing a collision. When they finally passed him, they rolled down their windows, gave him the finger, and yelled: "GET OFF THE STREET, OLD MAN." Of course, due to their speed they arrived at our house first. They were looking out the window as Denis' parents parked out front. There was a stunned silence, then actual cries of anguish as the "Old Man" got out of the car.

And so, one of the most uncomfortable evenings I've experienced commenced. The guys apologized profusely, but what could erase such an obscene gesture of disrespect and demonstration of bad manners? Milton pursed his lips and frowned. Denis' mother looked down at her plate the entire meal. Denis tried to make up for it by talking brightly about the weather. Conversation lagged. Marsena was unaffected as she chattered and laughed with Michael, who was always sweet to her. Even my fresh strawberry pie, which is pretty phenomenal, couldn't save the day. Everyone left early. As Denis and I cleaned up, we looked at each other and started laughing at the irony of it.

After this, we could no longer defend ourselves to Denis' parents. The evening couldn't have provided more damning evidence against us, proving to his father that the work we claimed to be doing was a failure. In the boys' defense, their reaction underscored that maturity is not instantaneous. It requires patience and grace to walk alongside young Christians.

At the church office, Denis mentioned his difficult relationship with his father to a staff member who had a counseling degree from Dallas Theological Seminary. The staff member's advice was *You need to stop looking for daddy because you're never going to find him. God is your father.* We weren't sure what to do with that counsel. Was this the way to take heart and be comforted?

During that same furlough, another incident occurred; I was recently reminded of it when we visited Marsena. She had a small framed photo of herself being held in the arms of her grandfather. Denis' mother stood beside him smiling. They posed on the front steps for a picture. Marsena was obviously unhappy as she glared at the camera. I remember that day and she did too, which surprised me. Milton wanted to hold her for the picture. Marsena was adamant. She did not want him to hold her. She declared in front of them, "I don't *like* him!" Looking back, I'm quite sure it was a photo op that made him look good—here I am, the loving grandfather holding my beautiful granddaughter.

I still marvel at my cowardice and the fear I had of offending Denis' father. I totally caved and told her she had no choice, so stop acting spoiled. I apologized to him and insisted she didn't mean it at all. Well, she did mean it, and you can tell by the look on her face in the photo. She intuitively sensed something unpleasant about him, but not because we talked about him in front of her. When

Marsena held by her grandfather.

I asked why she now kept a copy of that photo on display, she said she kept it as a reminder to listen to your instincts and not allow others to bully you into a bad situation. I'm a thousand times sorry that my unresolved issues meant I couldn't stand up for my girl.

Four years later, his parents were once again in our area on furlough. By then our family had grown to five, and holidays were always something we looked forward to. Thanksgiving was coming up and we knew his mother mourned she was never with family to celebrate holidays. We asked them to join us for a Thanksgiving dinner. We invited two other couples: reliable, professional, up-standing Christians who would be good company, and able to diffuse uncomfortable silences with stories and laughter.

It's almost comical how we prepared for their visit. We hid things that might offend them, like Denis' pipe collection. We pushed a bottle of wine under our bed. We turned certain books to the wall. The day came and his parents arrived first (one must always be early). The crisp, brown scent of roasting turkey was in the air. Apple and pumpkin pie lined the counter. Fresh rolls were warming in the oven. The children were dressed in their best and the table was set with as much finery as we owned. So far it was going well. Then came the knock on the door. Without waiting, Tim, our pharmacist friend, kicked open the door and shouted, "HAPPY THANKSGIVING!" He entered, holding high a magnum of wine in each fist. Not just a bottle—a magnum.

It took a moment for our hearts to resume beating. That was when Denis and I concluded there would never be a way to raise our status in their eyes. There would always be something or someone to expose our shortcomings. From then on, we gave up hiding evidence that we were hopeless sinners keeping company with other degenerates, and probably on our way to hell besides. There was no way to convince them otherwise.

It was easier living with this painful reality when they were half a world away. Having them back in the States and knowing they would want to see us always brought tension to the surface. On one occasion, when Milton came through town, he expected to stay with us during the days of his visit. The thought of having him in our home was so stressful I panicked. Any time he arrived at our house, he expected to be greeted with a hug and a kiss. Suddenly that felt so hypocritical—a betrayal of all that affection was meant to represent: love, friendship, and trust. I just couldn't do it. How could I honor my husband's father with a kiss, knowing he neither liked nor respected me? Wasn't it dishonest, a lie, to pretend something so intimate as a kiss represented affection for another? I couldn't think how to deal with this and I had no one to advise me.

When his car pulled into our driveway, Denis was not home. Dismayed, I snatched our eighteen-month-old son—Marsena was still at school—and walked out to meet him, my stomach in knots. I dodged his grab for a hug and a kiss and held out my hand for a shake. That was the most I could manage. I lied when I said, "Welcome, I was on my way to the store, go on inside and I'll be back later." At the supermarket I seized a cart and stumbled up and down the aisles, praying for help because I didn't know how to survive him sitting in our living room reading his Bible and staring at me all day from the easy chair.

This might sound ridiculous. Why couldn't I have been strong enough pay no attention to this man; just swat him away like an annoying mosquito? Perhaps because I am a two on the Enneagram,[1] at least that's what I tell myself now. According to the Enneagram way of way of defining personality by nine types, I am among those who consider relationships more important than almost anything. Twos can be extremely critical of themselves for not being as loving as they think they should be, so I felt tremendous guilt. At the same time, I reasoned, this was *not* the way relationships were meant to be between parents and adult children. My feelings toward Denis' father were creeping toward hatred, which made me feel worse, but I couldn't seem to stop the shift.

In a mysterious way, the problems I faced were beginning to coalesce as I stumbled through the debris of daily living. My sense of being unworthy, my nightmares, thyroid disease, pregnancy, the problems with Denis' parents, and troubles with my stepfather were gradually pushing me toward a deep and meaningful change in life.

With my thyroid now functioning properly, my body decided it was time to add another member to our family. I had just been to the doctor and she declared it had been five years since Marsena's birth and because I hadn't been using contraceptives, it wasn't likely we would have another child. She was wrong on two counts. First, when your hormones are messed up with thyroid disease, pregnancy is rare and if it does occur, most babies are miscarried. When hormones return to normal, chances of conceiving go up. Second, unbeknownst to us, on the day of this appointment, I was already several weeks pregnant.

By this time, Denis had completed an undergraduate degree at the University of New Mexico. He had left his position at Grace Church and we managed to pay tuition and keep ourselves out of debt with a cleaning contract for a large building that housed dentist and insurance offices. It paid well and together we cleaned the entire building every night in about three hours. On weekends we put in eight. After graduation, he was hired by another church to become their youth pastor and we gladly said good-bye to janitorial work.

On a morning shortly after Denis accepted the position at this new church, when I was about seven months pregnant with Jerem, I had managed to rise, make breakfast, see Denis out the door, and get five-year-old Marsena coloring and cutting at the table—the same table loaded with egg-encrusted plates and dirty glasses I planned to wash later. The previous night we had hosted a small group, and I hadn't cleaned up from that either. Folding chairs, coffee mugs, and plates with cake crumbs were scattered about the living room. Marsena was still in her pajamas and her long braids were matted and frayed in a halo around her head. I had gone back to bed in my comfy pink quilted bathrobe with snags and stains down the front when the doorbell rang.

I screamed, *"DON'T ANSWER THE DOOR!"* But it was too late. Ever the friendly host, my daughter had already opened the door and invited in whoever was there. I contemplated just not coming out of the bedroom. Nervously, I zipped the robe up over my belly, steeled myself, and walked down the hall. Three older women from the church were standing by the front door, surveying the living room and kitchen.

They looked shocked. Or did I imagine that? Finally, one announced, "We make a practice of visiting people who are new, so we thought we'd drop in to welcome you to the church."

Without calling beforehand? Without notice? Everything about me, my home, my child was so unfit for guests I didn't even bother making excuses. I offered to make coffee but after glancing around, they declined. Whether they were afraid of some disease from my messy house and disheveled self or were just being polite, I didn't know. After a short, strained conversation they left.

This was a massive moment of revelation. I'm quite sure these women did not mean to humiliate or expose me, but that's how I felt—I would now be seen as a negligent mother, a poor housekeeper, unkempt, and lazy. My public image was shattered. I was not only a fraud, I was a pathetic failure. Now everyone would know.

One result of this encounter has always remained with me. I never judge a person for the way their home looks. Its condition is irrelevant. There may be reasons for the way it looks beyond what I can know. Dirt and disarray are not moral issues. But until this happened I wasn't aware of how much pride was embedded in how I looked and in how I kept my home.

After the women left, I sank into an easy chair and admitted defeat. I needed help. I had worked hard to maintain an image of myself as a good Christian. I read the Bible and prayed almost every day. We hosted a small group in our home—a group dedicated to Bible study and discussion. I served homemade refreshments. I tried to be a good wife. I wanted to be the best mother. I had worked side by side with Denis while we vacuumed, dusted, and swabbed toilets so he could finish a degree. I excelled at making our home hospitable to everyone. I loved the teenage girls who came every week to hang out with me and take cooking lessons. I went to church to support him. I was friendly and helpful to everyone who crossed my path. We often had a needy or lonely person living with us. All this was for God. I wanted desperately to please him. I wanted him to see everything I did and approve of me. I wanted him to love me. I was killing myself for him, so why was I so miserable?

Suddenly, everything was too hard. Everything. Life. Being a mother. A wife. A good neighbor. Keeping up appearances. My failures scrolled across the screen of my mind. I was jealous of Denis' success and opportunities. In my pride I even thought I was beyond the temptations of ordinary people, and how I despised those who succumbed to them, only to be totally devastated the day a male friend walked in. Denis was gone, and I suddenly knew if he came any closer I would fall all over him. I was a hypocrite. When we were with Team Outreach, I dreaded going door-to-door doing literature evangelism. I hated it. It seemed so pointless. Wasn't I supposed to love telling others about Jesus? This was only a fraction of my failures.

I tried hard to be responsible and right about everything. It was important to be right even about the smallest things, like what is the shortest, fastest way to your destination? To this day, I argue with Google Maps about the best route. Being right meant I was doing life well. But it is *exhausting* to need to be right all the time, especially when you live with a partner who knows you intimately and confronts you when you're wrong.

Confrontation only revealed how angry and hostile I could be, even while outwardly serving others. The tendency to react this way was always present, but if you didn't tap into it, you might never know I was not the kind, gentle-hearted person you thought I was. Obviously, even keeping my own standards was impossible, to say nothing of God's.

Denis had majored in psychology and one of his class assignments was learning to administer personality tests to family or friends. I love that sort of thing. Tell me who I am so I can seem more gifted than average. I loved tests that ranked me as exceptionally intelligent. The tests I had taken in high school were, after all, standardized tests. They were administered nationally and I really had scored in the ninety-ninthth percentile. So even though I had trouble in college, I concluded I wasn't that stupid after all. The Taylor Johnson Temperament Analysis (T-JTA) is a test that measures nine personality traits and their opposites, traits such as "Nervous versus Composed." The scores were calculated and placed on a scale between the two extremes. The well-integrated personality would fall somewhere in the middle of the chart and be considered healthy. If a score landed in the red zone at the top or bottom of the chart, there was a warning to the administrator that this person should be encouraged to find professional help. I settled down with a pencil and score sheet, ready to enjoy the good things I'd learn about myself.

When Denis showed me the results, my score in the "Tolerance versus Hostility" category was so high, it was off the chart. I was enraged. I insisted he had not scored it correctly and I should take it again. I did, but somehow I couldn't even pad the answers to get a better score. I was still off the chart. I didn't believe it, but Denis was nodding calmly, "Yes, you are a hostile person."

This problem had taken root in my life for so long I was hardly aware of its origin, but just as a window struck with a stone first shows spider web cracks spreading, until piece by piece the whole window falls down, the pieces of my life were falling.

My strategies for getting through life had made me hypervigilant, anxious, uncertain, and often disappointed in myself. Over time, without recognizing it, my disappointment turned to anger and impatience against myself and others. It was the church ladies' visit and the personality test that finally collapsed my defenses.

At the time, we owned two books I had not read. *Being Human* was authored by two L'Abri workers—Ranald Macaulay and Jerram Barrs.[2] Macaulay and Barrs had both been influenced and mentored by Francis and Edith Schaeffer and had been part of L'Abri for many years. The other book was *Knowing God*[3] by J.I. Packer, which has become a classic in Christian literature.

The day after the church ladies visited, I picked them up and began laboring through them. Gradually those books began a reorientation of my life and how it ought to look. They opposed my endless struggle for perfection and merit based on effort. Layer by layer, they stripped my misguided attempts to win a secure place with God. Through their teaching, I began a slow process of healing from the inside out.

As I began reading *Being Human*, I was astonished to find the authors knew and understood the questions Denis and I had been asking for years. We weren't alone in asking them after all. How is it possible to live in the world and not be a part of it? Why is it so difficult to put into practice? If the most important things in life are spiritual, then how can we please God if we enjoy the physical? Does "setting my mind on things above" mean I should be unconcerned about the present realities of such things as the economy or politics or pollution? What about sexual pleasure or the simple beauty of a garden, the comfort of a bed, a painting, a loaf of well-made bread? Can such things be enjoyed by the serious Christian?

"Set your minds on things above, not on earthly things" (Col. 3:2) was a Scripture I often heard quoted in sermons, at Bible camp, and conferences. This, along with "do not taste, do not touch" (Col. 2:21 NASB), proved we were to be set apart from the world. Didn't it?

These verses confused me because where does the "world" begin and our lives end? It seemed impossible to know. As early as fourteen, I seriously questioned whether I should enjoy swimming as much as I did when it had no spiritual value according to the teaching I was exposed to. God's highest and best for us was always spiritual. I was confused because so many parts of the world were beautiful and they kept tempting me. Art, love, sexuality, food, even creation itself—how could we keep from touching or enjoying those parts of life which God himself had made and called "good"?

I grew up immersed in a Christian environment described by the authors. It was characterized by "a denunciation of the mind and a rejection of all cultural activities. The mind has been seen as a boogieman, and creativity as wasteful luxury ... this spirit of negativism has been presented as a virtuous and religious attitude."[4]

Being Human maintained that the answers to our questions were found in just those words: being human. God had created us in his image and declared it was good. Although we are fallen and all our faculties, like eyesight, are impaired, broken, defective, that doesn't mean we are of no value. Rather, being made in the image of God implies "an affirmation, rather than a negation of life ... the Christian life should be viewed as life and liberty, recovery and restoration. Too often it has been viewed as a life of dullness and dryness, of repression and rigidity."[5] We are free to be creative in every aspect of life and culture. Only what is sinful is off limits.

This was amazing news. The authors went on to recount how the history of evangelical thought that developed in America had been influenced by revivalism. As if they were in my living room listening to my confusion, they went on to explain:

> People think that being a Christian—being spiritual—means giving up everything that is enjoyable and crushing whatever inner impulses they have simply because they are part of human experience… Those who are "too weak" for this asceticism imagine, therefore, that religion is against the experiences which make up their ordinary life—the enjoyment of food and drink, of husband or wife, of leisure and creativity. Religion appears to them to be a monster that eats up the self.[6]

References in the Bible to the *world* still needed to be explained, because what could it mean when, for example, John wrote: "Do not love the world or anything in the world. If anyone loves the world, love for the Father is not in them" (I John 2:15). This verse was often used as a proof text by those who confined spiritual experience within very narrow bounds of dos and don'ts.

Barrs wrote:

> … such a reading of the passage is quite wrong for John goes on in the immediate context to clarify what he means by "loving the world." He says, "For all that is in the world [that is,] the lust of the flesh and the lust of the eyes and the pride of life, is not of the Father but is of the world" (2:16). These are the things we are not to love. John is not excluding the enjoyment of God's creation and all its beauty, nor even the enjoyment of man's creation—music or painting—nor even the enjoyment of physical experiences in general, such as eating and drinking. He is simply excluding a wrong attitude which does not honor God and which fails to see that God is the ultimate origin of everything, the one who gives significance to all of life.[7]

An important chapter of our marriage was when we decided to give away everything we owned, and follow Jesus' call to be his disciple. For many years Denis was ashamed of that decision. He was concerned that any who heard of it would either be influenced to do the same or would think we were insane. We came to see it was an important part of learning what it truly means to be a disciple of Christ. In spite of our ignorance and misplaced zeal, over the course of a number of years, God was gracious to lead us through that ground to a more solid foundation. We had plunged into a life of asceticism in an effort to learn whether Christianity could fill our lives with meaning and give answers to our longing for authenticity and hope. It was our way of renouncing the world. Our austere disciplined life with Team Outreach proved it was not sustainable in the way we had hoped. Gradually God chipped away at our misunderstandings of what he required of humans who sought him.

When a rich man came to Jesus, he was prepared to affirm some, but not all the commandments of the Law (Mark 10:17–22). He loved the world in a way that Jesus exposed when he told him to give away all he owned. The man went away sorrowful because he was very rich and was faced with a choice to have a different center for his life, "a different integration point . . . to turn from whatever has been the center (another God, a religious system, a person, or things, to the living God of the Bible . . . it is never an easy choice. God must be at the center of our lives. In whatever way we may be rich, whether in possessions or in talent, we face the struggle to set aside these things and to be 'rich toward God'" (Luke 12:21).[8]

As I read the book, I realized I had never thought about the term "being human." Or the idea that being created in God's image meant as humans we were invited to live a fuller, more creative life because God had made us and desired to bless us in that way. This was the best news. There could be beauty and pleasure and joy after all for any who came to Jesus.

Learning we were free to live and love as God had designed was wonderful, but I still had doubts that God could love *me* in particular without my doing something to earn that love. This, in a tangled way, was connected to my sustained hostility. My failures made me angry. The failures of others made me angry.

For nearly as long as I could remember, I thought I knew what grace meant. From childhood I had memorized verses that declared Christ's love was *free,* and there wasn't anything I could do to earn it. Love, mercy, forgiveness—he had done it all. My part was to believe and accept this. I was always quite sure I understood this. Reality proved I could not apply this grace to myself. I did not understand or appreciate the depth of what it meant. My dilemma grew worse when I realized I did not truly understand God's grace or love. I did not know God.

The second book, *Knowing God,* began to address my weaknesses and ill-placed affections, the failure of my efforts, and the anguish of trying to be a perfect person. The dreadful personality test had exposed yet another layer of deficiency—the accumulation of hostility fueled by years of anger and disappointment.

As I read, I was overwhelmed by the combined impact of the Scripture verses Packer listed one after the other, in various sections of the book. Even though familiar, somehow, seeing them piled high and deep all together on page after page gathered them in an avalanche that poured over my heart.

I read these passages with fresh eyes:

> It does not, therefore, depend on man's desire or effort, but on God's mercy (Rom. 9:16).

> But because of his great love for us, God, who is rich in mercy, made us alive with Christ even when we were dead in transgressions—it is by grace you have been saved. And God raised us up with Christ and seated us with him in the heavenly realms in Christ Jesus, in order that in the coming ages he might show the incomparable riches of his grace, expressed in his kindness to us in Christ Jesus (Eph. 2:4–7).

> If God is for us, who can be against us? (Rom. 8:31).

> Who shall separate us from the love of Christ? Shall trouble or hardship or persecution or famine or nakedness or danger or sword? ... For I am convinced that neither death nor life, neither angels nor demons, neither the present nor the future, nor any powers, neither height nor depth, nor anything else in all creation, will be able to separate us from the love of God that is in Christ Jesus our Lord (Rom. 8:35, 38–39).

> And I ask [God] that with both feet planted firmly on love, you'll be able to take in with all followers of Jesus the extravagant dimensions of Christ's love. Reach out and experience the breadth! Test its length! Plumb the depths! Rise to the heights! Live full lives, full in the fullness of God. (Eph. 3:17–19 *The Message*)

Packer summarizes this with:

> There is unspeakable comfort—the sort of comfort that
> energizes ... in knowing that God is constantly taking knowledge
> of me in love, and watching over me for my good. There is
> tremendous relief in knowing that his love to me is utterly
> realistic, based at every point on prior knowledge of the worst
> about me, so that no discovery now can disillusion him about me,
> in the way I am so often disillusioned about myself, and quench
> his determination to bless me.[9]

In a way, Packer's words were devastating—God knows the worst about me?
Yes. And he is still determined to bless me. I let the words fall into me. They
infused all of my being with the peace that comes from *knowing God*, being
known by him, and most of all, being loved.

When I finished these two books, having been so steeped in my own efforts
to remain acceptable to God, I stepped away from all spiritual disciplines and
practices. For a year I did not pick up my Bible. I did not pray. I would have
stopped going to church if Denis hadn't been on staff. In the past, I would have
thought such a decision would damn me to some circle of Dante's hell. But having finally accepted there was nothing I could add to God's plan to bless me, it
became a time of rest and recovery. God didn't need help redeeming me. God
had done the heavy lifting. I was loved.

I slowly picked up spiritual disciplines again with a better understanding of
the seamlessness of ordinary life with the transcendent: my everyday life and
calling was filled with simple things. Coloring with my daughter. Picking wild
apricots. Walking the dog. Nursing my newborn son. These were as important
as praying before sleep. The year was over; God still loved me.

WOULDN'T TAKE NOTHIN'

Two years later, when our son was a toddler and our second daughter was a baby, Denis made another career change. He became the New Mexico campus staff member for an organization called InterVarsity Christian Fellowship. Our pilgrimage through doubts and questions about the relevance of Christianity, our time spent in a Christian commune, and our experience working with youth groups had uniquely prepared us for working with college students and faculty. Leading Bible studies, meeting with students, and training leaders was a perfect fit for Denis' gifts and interests. We still loved helping young people face our culture without fear—to learn, to listen, to think, to ask questions, and apply a thoughtful Christian faith to all parts of life. We also still desired to bring them into our home for food, music, and unhurried conversation. This was a form of hospitable love not many had experienced.

There was so much I appreciated about this new ministry. Working with IVCF was challenging and rewarding. We were privileged to work with college students during that stage of life when world views and attitudes will shape a young person for the rest of their lives. We prayed we could help them discover how rich and varied God's calling was for each of them. Part of Denis' responsibility was spending part of each summer in the breathtaking mountains of Colorado at Bear Trap Ranch. There he helped staff summer camps for student training. Our family was always included and it was a lavish gift that fed our souls.

Students who came to Bear Trap often had life-changing experiences, but so did we. Denis worked hard every day, but it was doing something he loved. It was there we made friends for life. For me, there was time for personal reading and study, conversations with adults, and evening sessions that allowed me to listen to challenging lectures after I tucked the children in bed. The place itself healed. The warm days and cool nights, wildflowers and butterflies, the garlands of clouds wrapping snow-capped peaks, the comforting food in the dining hall, the kindness of students toward our children—all were reminders of a greater beauty that existed beyond the troubles and stress of daily life. I was in the grip of creation's beauty and kept thinking, if we had to pay for such an experience in such a place, it would have cost more than we owned.

I needed a place like that where I could unclench because by this time we were not only a family of five, but the owners of our first home in Albuquerque. Thrilled to be proprietors and with no one to stop us, we transformed our backyard into a kind of urban farm. But in my everyday world, I regularly felt alone as I dealt with family emergencies while Denis' responsibilities kept him on the road for about half of every month.

One afternoon, a cloud of insects flew past the dining room window. *What the…?* It looked like a biblical plague. I drew closer and saw they were bees. Thousands. So many I could hear them through the window. I ran outside and realized what was happening, but had no idea what to do about it. Our bees were swarming. Denis was in Phoenix attending a student conference and wouldn't be home for another three days. *Were we losing the entire colony?*

Panicked, I called him. He tried to calm me down and make a plan, when our conversation was interrupted by a frightening alarm. The phone company had received an emergency call and an official voice commanded, "You must accept this emergency call." Denis was automatically cut off and my brain exploded. *What is going on? Has someone died? The bees are swarming. Denis is gone. How on earth am I going to handle another crisis?* Somehow, our neighbor had convinced a telephone authority that her circumstances were so critical, she needed to reach me immediately, even though my number was busy. I had no idea such a thing was even possible.

Our next-door neighbor was a retired widow and from the time we moved in, she made it clear how much she detested us and our friends.

Some of it was the compost pile behind our house which was contained, covered, and carefully monitored (and couldn't be easily seen from her side of the six-foot tall cinder-block wall between our yards). It was odorless and free of vermin and flies, yet she insisted we get rid of it because "rats will soon move in." Our yard *was* a bit unusual. We were a bit unusual, but the yard was groomed and neat. It wasn't as if we were *The Beverly Hillbillies.* Her attitude was bewildering. When our friends parked on the public street in front of her house, she emerged in a rage and chased them away with a broom, banging it against their doors and fenders. Nothing we did to befriend her worked against her bitterness toward the world.

Raising bees wasn't the only evidence of our move toward more ecological awareness and the use of natural products. We improved the soil in our small backyard and raised a vegetable garden. Our children still remember I gave them

Catching grasshoppers for a penny each.

a penny for each grasshopper they picked off the broccoli and fed to the hens. Those sticky legs and brown spit rather put them off that vegetable. We also raised rabbits and butchered them ourselves. Not very romantic—those bloody actions of backyard farmers. Our four hens laid brown eggs with the brightest sunny yolks we'd ever seen. Whole wheat bread emerged from my oven every week. And, yes, homemade granola was a breakfast staple. We didn't change the world, but it gave us joy to eat healthy foods and to try to care responsibly for the tiny bit of earth we owned. We were thankful for this first home and yard of our very own after wandering the city for so long.

It was during the "emergency" phone call I learned that thousands of our bees were circling the air space above our neighbor's front yard and had begun to gather in a basketball-sized cluster in one of her trees. You could hear the ominous humming from anywhere in the yard. On the phone, she screamed at me to *get over here and get every one of these bees off my property this instant*. I almost laughed. Swarming bees are not dangerous or interested in stinging anyone; they're only intent on following their queen and finding a new place to establish a hive. But there was no convincing her. Each time I tried to explain and assure her I would take care of the problem, she shouted me down. By the time I got off the phone, the police had arrived, much to my children's delight, who were outside observing this most interesting event.

They were not afraid of bees. In fact, my two youngest were so fascinated they nearly got themselves into a spot of danger over them. We had two hives

that Denis had placed on the flat roof of our garage. It seemed a brilliant location for the production of the golden, sweet honey we all craved. The hives
were out of the way and yet accessible via a ladder propped against the garage's
back wall. True, had we been more conscientious, we might have anticipated
the temptation a ladder would pose to our children. I was in the kitchen on the
day I heard high-pitched wailing and loud cries for Mommy, Mommy. I rushed
out to find them nowhere in sight. Following their calls of woe, I looked up to see
them precariously standing on the edge of the garage roof with bees buzzing
round their heads in a perfect Winnie-the-Pooh illustration. They had climbed
the ladder to visit the hives and were now too afraid to climb back down. Step by
step, I carefully helped them down the ladder. The bees were too busy to bother
them with stings.

The police quickly assessed the situation, witnessed the neighbor's unreasonable anger, and were kind. They even laughed. Apparently, swarms of bees
were not so rare in the city because they knew all about them. The precinct station kept a list of beekeepers who were happy to come and capture a swarm for
their own apiary. Eventually a bearded, scruffy-looking man in an old pickup
arrived with a ladder and a box. Undaunted and looking quite capable of anything bee-related, he climbed up to where the writhing mass of bees were hanging from a branch in our neighbor's tree and, without any protection other than
gloves, gently gathered them into the box, along with their queen. Our neighbor
watched all this through her window.

There were other disasters when Denis was gone. One morning I was getting the kids ready to leave the house and had placed my son, Jerem, in the front
seat of the car. These were the days before car seats were mandatory. I hurried
back inside to fetch Sember, who was waiting in her carrier. As I was button-
ing her sweater, I looked out the window to see our car slowly rolling down
the incline in our driveway toward the busy street. Jerem had moved the gear
from park to neutral. I slammed out the door and raced down the driveway. I
managed to jump in and apply the brakes a second before it reached the street.
I pulled it back up the drive and sat shaking with relief knowing he could have
been killed. Then I began to cry. I hadn't had time to close the driver's door after
I jumped in and it hit the Arizona cyprus tree at the end of the driveway, bent
the door around, and smashed it into the front fender. It was thoroughly broken
and impossible to close.

My arm was full of pine needles, which told me I had reached the tree a
millisecond before it would have blocked my jump into the car. A friend came
over, pried the unusable door loose, placed it against the opening, and tied it to
the frame with ropes. We could drive the car but because the ropes encircled the
body we couldn't get in via either front door. We had to get in the back and climb

Urban farmers. Jerem "helping" Margie pull carrots.

over the front seat to get behind the steering wheel.

The bees and the car door underscored a growing feeling of dissatisfaction I had with my life, which was exacerbated whenever Denis left town for work. While I was stuck at home mopping up emergencies, he was off seeing the world, dining out, having significant conversations with adults, and basically enjoying a vacation, or so it seemed to me. As my resentment built over his traveling, it became clear some things needed to change.

On another day, while I was on the phone with a friend, our weekly order of milk in two gallon glass jugs arrived from a local dairy. Jerem noted I was busy, so he opened the door and let the driver place the jugs on the carpet just inside. To be helpful, he called out "I hep you" and, with all his three-year-old strength, picked them up by their handles and begin staggering toward me. I moved quickly to stop him, but too late. He clanked the jugs together and they broke, sending a tidal wave of milk down the hall carpet toward me. I screamed, left the phone dangling by its cord, and ran for bath towels.

Again, where was Denis? Traveling. Having a good time. I was mad.

Before we could name what was happening and work on some solutions, I had a pressing need to work on another personal issue. The 70s was a time when nearly every woman was impacted by the feminist movement. I was no exception. Concerning men, I had plenty to complain about. An old problem resurfaced and I began to resent Denis more. I blamed him for thwarting my dream of going into medicine. From the beginning of our relationship, he had made it clear he did not want me to become a doctor, a nurse, or any other kind of health care worker. (There were reasons for this that were understandable.) I fell so in love with him, I easily gave up the dream. Now, seven years into marriage and three children later, I was angry he had not supported my dream. But I must be honest; it took time for me to see it in a more realistic light. As we became friends with students working their way through medical school, residency, and fellowship positions, I realized I didn't have the focus and incredible stamina it takes to become a medical doctor. Acknowledging this to myself, but not to Denis, made me a little more thankful for the freedoms I had in life. But it did not cure my resentment about other things, like his travel. Or his way of checking out when he got home from campus. His depending on me to take care of all the children's needs. There are more details, but this is enough.

My objections to serving men, and especially Denis, climaxed on a particular evening. It happened during a time we mothers sometimes call the witching hour—the time of day when the home universe is most vulnerable to breakdowns, anywhere from 4:30 to 6:00p.m. The children are hungry. Mom is in the kitchen hurrying to make dinner. Dad comes home from work and heads to the living room to read the newspaper. The toddler is in the high chair which unfortunately has a metal tray that he is pounding on with a spoon. The elementary school daughter is asking, no, begging to spend the night with a friend and arguing you must let her. The baby is crying. The phone rings as you are about to put food on the table. Just then your husband walks in with the baby, holding her out by the armpits. He hands her to you saying, "She stinks."

We could pause there. But pausing won't change the direction this was going to take. It was about everything, but especially the dirty diaper. I was angry. "What do you think, I have no olfactory nerves? Mine are the same as yours. Are you helpless? You can't walk into the other room and change a diaper? This is not rocket science." Then came the drumbeat, ka-ta-ta-boom, and I announced, "I'm leaving."

On my way out the door, Denis shouted after me, "If you leave, don't ever come back." Which struck me as so absurd, such a ridiculous threat, I couldn't help it, I started laughing. I walked around the block and came back. Leaving could have meant anything, including what I'd just done. Inside, I found the baby had a clean diaper and the kids were eating. The memories stop there. I don't remember how the evening went. I do know there were some changes around that time.

Edith Schaeffer had done so much to teach me about the importance of loving people through hospitality, of making room for beauty and comfort in the home. "Her passion for art extended to everyday aesthetics. She was a lifelong champion of all forms of human creativity, including 'everyday' forms of art such as cooking and sewing, because she saw all art as stemming from the creativity of God."[10] With all my heart I believed it was good until I had to honestly face some of the old hostility that festered inside.

Mrs. Schaeffer was famous for serving the tea and teacakes while Dr. Schaeffer led discussions, something every visitor to L'Abri looked forward to and relished. It was the very thing that annoyed me. We often hosted student groups and young people in our home. While I was in the kitchen preparing refreshments, Denis was in the den having adult conversations I wished to take part in. In one ill-considered moment I turned on him, announcing (not in public, so there was that), "I am so sick of serving 'the tea and the teacakes' while you sit in the living room with pearls of wisdom dripping from your lips. From now on, I'm not going to do it. And another thing. When you want something like a cup of tea or whatever, don't ask me. Get it *yourself!*"

There are legitimate reasons for women to call out men who expect women to provide them with maid service. But I was quickly convicted about my attitude after this contemptuous pronouncement, which had felt so empowering at the time. I heard the voice of God speaking to me when in my private study of the Bible, I "accidentally" came across the passages about Jesus serving his disciples.

In John 13, at the Last Supper, Jesus washes his disciples' feet. As an old Sunday school veteran, I can completely lose sight of context and its impact because the story is so familiar. To really be there in that room, to recognize how shocking this move was, broke my heart. It would be like (totally inadequate comparison) allowing Edith Schaeffer to clean out the bottom of my refrigerator. I simply could not allow her to do it. In the disciples' case, they had no choice. Jesus told them, "Unless I wash you, you have no part with me" (v. 8). Jesus emphasized it again: "Now that I, your Lord and Teacher, have washed your feet, you also should wash one another's feet" (v. 14). Think of it. On that night, sitting around the table, Jesus knew there was one man, supposedly a disciple and friend, who was going to arrange his murder in the next few hours. That didn't stop Jesus. This act of serving was not based on their worth or their perfection, it was based on love and fulfilling his mission and calling.

Jesus asserts again in Mark: "For even the Son of Man did not come to be served, but to serve, and to give his life as a ransom for many" (Mark 10:45).

I was so stirred by what Jesus said about coming to serve, not to *be* served, I saw no way around it. If Jesus loved me that much, then what did my loving Denis and all the others who came to our home mean? Don't assume I then had to pretend he didn't have any faults that needed to be addressed. Not at all. I concluded that even if Denis needed to get off his butt and help, it wasn't a viable excuse for me to be such a bitch about it. The problem was embroiled in gender role issues we needed to learn to navigate, but still, I needed to adjust my attitude.

Change came slowly, and not in an elegant way. It took time and multiple conversations, if you can call it conversation when you are yelling much of the time. We laid things on the table, picked them up and examined them.

Traveling half the month as Denis did was not the vacation I assumed it was. He helped me understand traveling was a challenge he actually didn't enjoy that much. Long hours, crowded airports, staff tensions, strange beds, and food that was sometimes difficult to eat. Once while staying with a campus worker who had planted a garden to save on food expenses, Denis arrived during a season of zucchini glut. It was the only vegetable available from the garden. In an enterprising fashion this young staff member made it a policy to eat every one of them, so each meal was some version of zucchini. After zucchini bread, zucchini pasta, zucchini smoothies (did I mention Denis does not like zucchini?), Denis pulled rank and took everyone out for steak. These challenges were all part of his job and he wanted to do it well, with good humor and love for both his staff and their students.

The ache in my bones was deeper than wanting him to be home when things went awry. I thought he loved being away from the family. Or, rather, he preferred it. It hurt to think work was his number one love and we were second place. I thought I could tolerate his travel more easily if I knew I was first in his heart—if our family ranked number one. It would also help if he understood and sympathized with the challenge of caring for the children and home when he was gone. He assured me he didn't want to be a slave to his work as so many Americans were. He wanted us to know he loved us more than anyone or anything and wanted to find ways to prove it.

Denis thought of a way to help me through the week. I could place our two youngest children in our church's Mother's Day Out program one day a week. It cost money and I felt guilty about spending it on something so luxurious, but Denis insisted. Part of my reluctance came when I compared my life to my mother's. I was a whiner. She had six kids, a tiny house with no indoor plumbing, and no Mother's Day Out. When she heard I hesitated, she rebuked me, insisting I *often* babysat for her while she and Dad took a break. Then Denis scolded, "I don't want to hear about your mother's hard life again. Each life is different." He made me promise not to use the time to catch up on household matters, but to do something nourishing. To read. To be quiet. To walk in a park. To think and pray.

We talked about our phone calls to one another when he was gone. He confessed he dreaded calling home because I always had a litany of complaints.

Backyard babes Jerem and Sember, 1979

Emergencies were an exception, of course, but I got it. My grievance was when he arrived at the airport exhausted, all he wanted to do was take a deep breath and ride home in silence, whereas I was eager to hear about his week and share mine. He learned to tell himself the trip was not over until we had debriefed and he greeted the kids. Then he could let down. We agreed to work on these things.

Then there was how to deal with the witching hour. We needed to do something about that. Normally when Denis arrived home from campus around supper time, he walked through the door, headed to the living room, picked up the newspaper and sat in a comfy chair while I dealt with hungry children and supper. We agreed to find ways to share that time equitably. We agreed to see our work day as continuing until the kids went to bed. So we split responsibilities. I continued making supper while he played with the kids, who were ecstatic to see him. Afterwards we cleaned up dishes together. He picked up toys and straightened the living room while I got children ready for bed. After we put them to bed, then we could sit down with the evening ahead of us. We didn't allow the children to stay up late. There were many reasons why this was a healthy approach for all of us, and that time became a sacred space for the two of us to be together or to pursue our own interests.

There was another change that soothed my irritated feminist soul. Remember, we had a janitorial business while Denis finished college? He had no choice but to learn how to vacuum and clean. The work couldn't be any old *give it a lick and a promise*. It had to be done well. This was a bonus for me.

Since Denis' schedule often included evenings, he set aside daytime hours each week to help me clean the house. Every Friday when he was in town, we cleaned together. Wonderful. Families have different priorities, I understand that. Yours may not be the same as ours. But for us to survive as young parents, these were some of the things we needed to do.

> How old must we be in order to recognize that preoccupation with ourselves, self-actualization, does not yield a basis for living? An old virtue must be relearned: humility. It is the realistic confession that we, in and of ourselves, do not provide our own compelling agenda for life ... I do not need to be isolated in a greenhouse so that I can find my own truth. I need brothers and sisters and fathers and mothers and teachers and books and theories and stories; with them I must negotiate what truth is and what truth demands ... Growing up and becoming old confirms the fact that we do not have much on our own with which to nourish ourselves. The hope that we can generate out of ourselves is too small. The courage that we can muster on our own is not enough. The dreams of our own hearts are too trite and temporary. We are beggars. We cannot nourish, comfort, and encourage ourselves all on our own.[11]

Not everything is worthy of being made public, so let me say, some of the changes we sought fainted and needed to be revived. Some have taken years to bear fruit. Denis became the most ardent supporter of my gifts, especially believing in my ability to write when I couldn't believe it myself. In every stage and phase of my pilgrimage, I have needed others. I haven't always listened or been changed, but I've been loved. In the smallness of who I am, I have been encouraged and made strong by the riches that flowed into my life through brothers and sisters and fathers and mothers and teachers and books and theories and stories. In the years to come, these riches fortified both Denis and I for the disappointments and tragedies that we faced. I have learned the joy of the small things of life—they are holy. With God any space can become sacred.

"I Wouldn't Take Nothin' For My Journey" was a song we used to sing back at His House. And it's true. Had I left for good that day when we were coming apart—and I almost did—I would have missed that God intended to make something more of us than we could imagine. I'm grateful.

EPILOGUE

Boxes stacked to the ceiling, the screech of packing tape, and the sharp scent of magic marker filled the air as I quietly packed up our son's bedroom. Only he could sleep so blissfully through the noise of his toys and clothing being sorted and packed, and his heavy sleep allowed me to check this room off my to-pack list. Plus, while he slept, he wouldn't be able to advise me on how many pounds of his collected rocks we should keep.

Six hours later I was shaken from a deep sleep. Howls of anguish rent the air. Leaping from bed, I ran to Jerem's room. Tears streamed down his face as he ran to my arms. "I thought you left me," he cried. He had awakened to a still house and a room he'd never seen before. Nothing familiar was in sight. He was certain we had left without him. Holding him tight, I rocked back and forth assuring him, "We would never leave you." But from then until the day we left for Minnesota, in the midst of the chaos, friends saying good-bye, and the truck being packed, he did not leave my side, worried we would forget we had a little five-year-old boy.

We were leaving New Mexico. It was no longer the alien desert we wandered, not knowing where we belonged or what we believed. But can we label any particular part or stage of life as "desert" and record the exact time we entered and then found our way out? Not likely. It seems most stages of life have some form of dry heat and thirst.

We had dropped out and were changed forever by a subculture we grew to love. We had three children. We loved the mountains, the beautiful Sandias. The turquoise sky, and the cross-pollination of Native American and Latino cultures. Even the Southwestern cuisine I first detested became a beloved part of our diet. More importantly, we were firmly grounded, knowing we belonged to a rich and ancient faith relevant to all human endeavors. We were hooked for life. But it was time to return to our roots.

There were two important reasons for leaving. We missed extended family. Our children were growing up without knowing their grandparents, their aunts, uncles, and cousins. We wanted to be closer and who knew? Perhaps there would be healing between us and my stepfather. Perhaps when Denis' parents retired from the mission field, they would get to know their grandchildren. Perhaps they would see us in a new light.

The second reason was L'Abri. Our mentor and spiritual guide, Francis Schaeffer had been diagnosed with lymphoma, and he and Edith were living in Rochester to be near the Mayo Clinic for his treatment. In spite of his illness, they were establishing another branch of L'Abri complete with additional workers. We were still eager to learn, and study with them. We were blessed to get to know them personally and sit with their teaching as long as Dr. Schaeffer lived and for the years after his death, when Mrs. Schaeffer remained a neighbor.

We were not drifting away like the hot air balloons that floated over our house each year during the International Balloon Fiesta. Living beneath their flight path as we did, when we heard the whoosh of their burners, we ran outside with the children to see the sky filled with dozens of giant brightly colored bubbles and to wave at pilots and their passengers as they silently floated past, some so low we could see the smiles on their faces. Their destiny was controlled by the whims of the wind. Ours was more certain. More substantial. We had been led by the steady hand of the Holy Spirit.

With Jayber Crow, we could say:

> Often I have not known where I was going until I was already
> there. I have had my share of desires and goals, but my life has
> come to me or I have gone to it mainly by way of mistakes and
> surprises. Often I have received better than I have deserved. Often
> my fairest hopes have rested on bad mistakes. I am an ignorant
> pilgrim, crossing a dark valley. And yet for a long time, looking
> back, I have been unable to shake off the feeling that I have been
> led—make of that what you will.[12]

We couldn't shake it off either, and yet it was more than a feeling, more than wishful thinking. We believed; we were led. Through all the stages of life, God continues to demonstrate his care for us, appearing in the unexpected joys of fireflies in summer and snowmen in winter, and in the human struggles so common to us all.

We christened our new place "Toad Hall."

Twelve years after we left Minnesota with Team Outreach—owning nothing but two sleeping bags and a few personal items—we pulled up to a house in Rochester, Minnesota, in a U-Haul truck packed with all our belongings. Even our Volkswagen camper van was stuffed full. As we looked up at that big American Gothic Foursquare house, so different from the flat-roofed adobe homes of New Mexico, Marsena was astonished. "This must be just like Toad Hall from *The Wind in the Willows!*"[13] We would settle into the home we named Toad Hall and live there for the next thirty-three years.

RECIPES

New Mex

The New Mexican way of preparing Mexican food is unique to the area. It's slightly different from Tex-Mex, although I would be the first to admit that when we first arrived in New Mexico, I had no idea. At first, I didn't like any of this cuisine, but it didn't take long for me to swallow it wholeheartedly. I learned that chile added to almost anything made it better. Throughout our years in New Mexico, I was blessed to have Latino neighbors who taught me some of the recipes included here. However, I never achieved the effortless way they made fresh flour tortillas for their family every day.

In New Mexico, the peppers of choice are the long green varieties and the dishes made from these are generally lighter when compared to Tex-Mex. In Texas, they like to use more jalapeños and drown the dishes in heavy gravies, sour cream, and lots of cheese. The most common spice is cumin, which is not an authentic Mexican spice, being from the Middle East. In New Mexico, there is more emphasis on oregano and cilantro for flavor.

Hatch, New Mexico, is an area famous for raising green chile. Authentic Hatch green chile comes only from this valley. Occasionally, I order my favorite variety, medium hot Anaheims. They arrive frozen directly from a farm. Anaheims are long, bright green when fresh and have a smoky, intense flavor when roasted. In flavor, there is no comparison. Green chile can be grown from seed elsewhere in the country, but they don't taste quite the same. Like grapes, chile peppers take on the unique properties of the soil they're grown in.

Hardly a week goes by when I don't prepare some New Mexican dish for ourselves. It now feels like part of my DNA and I love sharing it with family and friends.

This is one of my favorite ways to use whole green chile. Although I love the way chile rellenos are typically made (stuffed, battered, and fried), baking them preserves the intense flavor and is less complicated. When I serve this to guests, I find that, even if the casserole is a little hot, most guests can't resist going back for more.

Chile Relleno Casserole

Whole green chiles, canned or frozen *(8–12 depending on size)*
1 lb Monterey Jack cheese
1/4 lb mild cheddar cheese, grated
5 large eggs
1/3 cup milk
1/4 cup flour
1/2 tsp salt
Pepper
Paprika

Grease a 3–4 quart casserole dish.

Drain the chiles, if using canned. If using fresh chile, first blister the skins under the broiler. Keep turning them until they are uniformly blackened. Remove them from the oven and close them in a paper bag for about 10 minutes. Then run them under cool water and the skins will slip off easily. In both cases, fresh or canned, make a slit down the side and strip out the seeds.

Preheat oven to 350 degrees. Place a thick strip of Monterey Jack cheese inside each chile. Fold the edges over to encase the cheese and place them side by side in the baking dish. Some may be layered on top of one another.

In a mixing bowl, lightly whisk the eggs. Add milk and mix. Add flour, salt, and pepper. Whisk until most lumps are gone. Pour the batter over the chile. Sprinkle cheddar cheese and paprika on top.

Bake for 45 minutes or until top is puffed and golden.

Serves 4.

I learned to make flat enchiladas from a Latino neighbor. This dish is the New Mexican equivalent of the Minnesota hot dish. I was immediately on board. It's a little easier to make than rolled enchiladas and it comes together quickly. It is tasty, economical, and very forgiving in amounts *(all the amounts listed below can be adjusted according to taste or how much is on hand)*. Serve flat enchiladas with a shredded lettuce, chopped tomato, and cucumber salad, with a side dish of refried beans.

Flat Enchiladas

1 pkg corn tortillas *(1 dozen)*
3 tbsp oil
1 lb ground beef
Garlic salt
1 tsp red chile powder
Salt, pepper
1/2 onion, chopped
1 can green chile
1/2 lb grated Monterey Jack cheese or mild cheddar *(more, if you like cheese)*
1 can cream of chicken soup
1/2 cup milk

Preheat oven to 375 degrees. Heat oil in a small frying pan. Soften the tortillas by quickly dipping them in hot oil. Drain and set aside. *(This is how they are traditionally softened, but the same can be done in hot water to reduce calories. It's just not as authentic.)*

Brown the ground beef and season with salt, pepper, garlic salt, and chile powder.

Pour soup into a shallow bowl, add milk, and mix. Set aside the chopped onion and green chiles in small bowls. Grate cheese and set aside.

Grease a 9x13 baking dish. Layer the tortillas with the other ingredients. *(I usually manage to end up with 2 stacks of 4–6 tortillas each when placed side by side in the bottom)* First dip the tortilla in the soup mixture and place in the dish. Top with approximately 1–2 tbsp each of the ground beef, onion, green chile, and a sprinkle of cheese. *(Don't measure—use your hands and just go for it.)*

Repeat layers until you've used all the tortillas or until they reach the top of the dish. End the final layer with whatever remains. Pour the rest of the soup on top and generously add the rest of the cheese. Bake for 25 minutes or until bubbly.

Serves 4–6.

On a chilly fall day, this is such a welcoming dish. I often made this when we were low on groceries and cash. It is easy, economical, and comforting. Even if you reduce the amount of meat and increase the potatoes, you still have a tasty dish. I generally use canned green chile for this. Old El Paso brand has medium chopped green chile if you can find it. Medium gives more flavor than mild. Otherwise you can add a chopped jalapeño if you want to increase the heat. Served with flour tortillas or hot French bread, it's the perfect meal to serve a crowd.

Green Chile Stew

1 lb pork stew meat, cubed
2 tbsp olive oil
1/4 cup flour or cornstarch
1/2 tsp salt
3 medium potatoes, peeled and diced *(add more if you like)*
1 medium onion, diced
3–4 garlic cloves, minced
2 tsp salt
1/2 tsp pepper
2 cans of green chile or 6–7 fresh, chopped

Heat oil in a Dutch oven or other large skillet to medium hot.

Sauté onion, garlic, and green chile *(if using fresh)* in olive oil.

Combine pork with flour and salt in a Ziploc bag. Shake to coat. Add to the pan and sauté until browned.

Add enough water to cover the meat and simmer for 30 minutes until meat is tender *(longer if meat is tough)*. To boost flavor, chicken broth can be used in place of some of the water.

Add potatoes and canned green chile. Simmer until potatoes are done. Adjust salt. Serve with fresh flour tortillas.

NOTE: There are many variations to this recipe. Other vegetables like corn, tomato, or cabbage can be added. But this simple way is my favorite. It is captures the warm flavors of homemade New Mexican cooking. Leftovers taste even better the next day.

Makes 4–5 servings.

This was one of the first New Mexican recipes I learned to make. Avocados were cheap. Sometimes they were as little as 5 or 6 for a dollar. I learned to extend the recipe to save money by adding green chile, sour cream, and chopped tomato. It was delicious served as a salad or as an appetizer with tortilla chips.

Guacamole

5 large avocados
1 clove garlic, minced
2 1/2 tbsp lemon juice
1 tsp salt
1/2 cup sour cream
1 medium tomato, diced
1 can green chile

Peel and chop avocados into a bowl. Mash with a fork.

Add garlic, lemon juice, and sour cream. Keep mashing until smooth and creamy. Stir in remaining ingredients until thoroughly mixed.

To store leftovers in refrigerator, press plastic wrap onto surface of guacamole to prevent oxidation.

Serves 4–5 people.

I also economized by making my own tortilla chips. Homemade chips are unbelievably crisp and fresh-tasting—nothing like the packaged supermarket chips. It's difficult to stop eating them.

Homemade Tortilla Chips

1 pkg store-bought corn tortillas
Oil
Salt

Cut tortillas into strips or triangles. Heat a pan with oil at least 3–4 inches deep. Add a drop of water to the oil—if it sizzles, it's hot enough.

Adding tortillas a few at a time, begin frying. Drain each batch on paper towels and sprinkle generously with salt as they cool. *(The cooled oil can be jarred and saved for another time.)*

This recipe actually came from my mother's kitchen. Many years ago she learned it from a couple who lived with the Navajo Indians in New Mexico. It was modified for those who at the time didn't have access to authentic ingredients. Corn tortillas were made with corn meal and flour, not the traditional Masa Harina. Ketchup with a little Tabasco sauce had to make do for the salsa. Our children often requested it on special occasions. The only problem is that people tend to put too much filling on the tortilla. A little discretion is needed or you will never reach the end when you need to fold it in half.

Indian Tacos

CORN TORTILLAS

I cup cornmeal
I cup flour
1/4 tsp salt
I egg
1 1/2 cups cold water

Whisk all ingredients together in large mixing bowl. Add enough cold water to make a very thin batter. *(The consistency should be similar to crepe batter.)* Heat frying pan to medium hot. Add small amount of oil. Add 1/3 cup batter and roll pan to form a thin round tortilla. Turn when edges raise slightly and look a little dry. Fry only a few seconds on the other side. These may be used as they are—soft and pliable. Or they may be fried again with oil until a little crispy.

FILLING

I lb ground beef
1/2 cup onion, chopped
Garlic salt
Salt
Pepper
I can diced green chile
I can refried beans
1/2 lb Monterey Jack cheese, grated
4–5 cups iceburg lettuce, chopped
I tomato, diced
I cucumber, diced
Mayonnaise
Taco sauce or salsa

Brown and season the ground beef and onion with garlic salt, salt, and pepper. Add green chile. Set aside in a serving bowl.

Heat refried beans, adding enough water to make them spreadable. Set beans aside in another serving bowl.

Combine lettuce, tomato, and cucumber. Add enough mayonnaise to dress the salad. *(It's weird, but trust the recipe.)*

To serve: on a single tortilla, layer a spoonful each of refried beans, ground beef, cheese, and lettuce salad. *(Do not skip the salad. Promise me.)* Top with salsa. Fold in half and spoon more salsa on top if desired.

Serves 4–5.

It seems like every culture has its version of fried dough. Think of donuts and fritters. In New Mexico, it was sopapillas. We love these hot "pillows." I must get a grip on myself and not eat too many when I make them. Sopapillas are the perfect counterpoint to spicy, hot Mexican food.

Sopapillas

1 pkg active dry yeast
1/4 cup water, warmed
1 1/2 cups milk, warmed
3 tbsp lard *(if possible, otherwise use shortening)*
1 1/2 t salt
2 tbsp sugar
About 5 cups white flour
Oil for frying *(peanut oil is best, but canola will do)*

In a large mixing bowl, dissolve yeast in warm water and milk. Add salt, sugar, and lard, and stir to combine. Beat in 3 cups of the flour. Add the rest of the flour 1/2 cup at a time, mixing until you've formed a shaggy, stiff dough.

Turn out onto a floured surface and knead until dough is smooth and no longer sticky. Place in a greased bowl. Turn dough, cover, and let rest for 1 hour. *(Dough can be refrigerated overnight.)*

Punch down and knead out the air on a lightly floured surface. Divide dough in half and roll each one out until it's a little less than 1/8 inch thick. Cut into 2x5 rectangles. Place them on lightly floured wax paper. Cover with a damp paper towel to prevent drying out.

Heat oil *(3–5 inches deep)* to 350 degrees in a kettle or deep frying pan. *(It helps to have a thermometer to monitor the heat.)*

Fry sopapillas 2–3 at a time, pushing them down into the oil to help them puff more evenly. Turn several times and remove when lightly golden. Drain on paper towels. Sopapillas are eaten immediately, but you can place finished sopapillas in a warm oven until you've finished frying the dough. To eat, bite off a corner and drizzle honey inside.

NOTE: If at first they don't puff, you may need to roll the dough more thinly or raise the temperature of the oil. If they turn out flat, just call them Indian Fry Bread. No one will argue because they will still be very tasty when drizzled with honey.

Makes about 4 dozen small sopapillas.

A beautiful, sweet ending to a shared meal, this dessert is a delightful antithesis to spicy Mexican food. It is light, smooth, and cool. I serve it along with a small crisp cookie, like shortbread or a sugar cookie, and a cup of coffee. It can be made a day ahead of time (it will keep for several days in the refrigerator). I adapted it from *Simply Simpático,* a cookbook put out by the Albuquerque Junior League.

Flan Café

3 eggs, lightly whisked
6 tbsp sugar
1/4 tsp salt
1/4 cup espresso or very strong coffee *(or substitute 2 tbsp instant coffee or espresso and an extra 1/4 cup milk)*
1 tsp vanilla
2 3/4 cups milk *(heat in microwave until very warm but not boiling)*
6 tbsp Kahlua or other coffee liqueur
Whipped cream

Preheat oven to 375 degrees. In a large bowl, whisk together eggs, sugar, coffee, vanilla, and salt. Gradually add hot milk, whisking as you pour. Pour mixture into 6 custard cups. Place in a pan of hot water and bake for 25 minutes until firm. Chill. To serve, top with 1 tbsp Kahlua and a dollop of whipped cream.

Makes 6–8 servings (depending on the size of the custard cups)

ENDNOTES

BOOK I

1   As quoted by Wesley Hill in, "Jigs for Marriage and Celibacy," *Comment,* November 24, 2016, https://www.cardus.ca/comment/article/jigs-for-marriage-and-celibacy/.

2   *"I'm a Woman"* was a minor hit for Peggy Lee, from her album of the same name. It was written by Jerry Leiber and Mike Stoller, and reached #54 on the US pop charts in 1963.

3   A quote by Theodore Roszak from *Where the Wasteland Ends,* (New York: Doubleday, 1973, p. 449.) in *The Grave Digger File* by Os Guinness, InterVarsity Press, 1983. page 79.

BOOK II

1   C.T. Studd (December 2, 1860–July 16, 1931) was a British missionary to China, India, and Africa, where he established the Heart of Africa mission. He wrote several books, including *The Chocolate Soldier* (Fort Washington, PA: Christian Literature Crusade, 1912). He also wrote poetry, and his poem "Only One Life" is still well-known for containing the passage, "Only one life twill soon be past/ Only what's done for Christ will last." He inspired many to leave their homelands and become missionaries to peoples who had never heard the Gospel.

2   "Steps to Peace with God - Peace with God." 2015. Peacewithgod.Net. October 27, 2015. https://peacewithgod.net/steps-to-peace-with-god/.

3   Adelle Davis, *Let's Get Well: A Practical Guide to Renewed Health Through Nutrition* (United Kingdom: Harcourt, Brace & World, 1965). Although she was a help to me, later I learned, to my disappointment, that this book was met with criticism from the medical establishment and other professionals in the sciences. Many of the experts she referenced disliked the book because their views had been misquoted or taken out of context. Some of her claims had no factual basis and were even harmful.

4   La Leche League International, *The Womanly Art of Breastfeeding,* 8th ed. (New York: Ballantine Books, 2010).

5   Tasnim Nathoo and Aleck Ostry, *The One Best Way?: Breastfeeding History, Politics, and Policy in Canada* (Waterloo, Ontario: Wilfred Laurier University Press, 2009), 113. This text was from a vintage advertisement in a 1944 issue of *Life Magazine* for Carnation Evaporated Milk. The ad featured a depiction of an American soldier returning from WWII and holding his baby for the first time.

6   American Academy of Pediatrics, "Breastfeeding and the Use of Human Milk," *AAP News and Journals,* March 2012, https://pediatrics.aappublications.org/content/129/3/e827.

7   Randolph Blake and Robert Sekuler, *Perception,* 5th ed. (New York: McGraw-Hill, 2006).

8   Francis Schaeffer, *The God Who is There* (Downers Grove, IL: InterVarsity Press, 1968).

9   The Mamas & the Papas, "California Dreamin'," *If You Can Believe Your Eyes and Ears* (Dunhill Records: 1966).

BOOK III

1   Charles C. Mann, *1491: New Revelations of the Americas Before Columbus,* 2nd ed. (New York: Vintage Books, 2011).

2   Bob Dylan, "It's All Over Now, Baby Blue," *Bringing It All Back Home* (Columbia Records: 1965).

3   The Band, "The Weight," *Music from Big Pink* (Capitol Records: 1968). The Band first popularized this song. They produced their own music, but for a number of years in the 60s, they collaborated with Bob Dylan and were his backup musicians.

ENDNOTES

4 Buffalo Springfield, "For What It's Worth (Stop, Hey What's That Sound?)," *Buffalo Springfield* (ATCO Records: 1966).

5 Frederick Buechner, *Wishful Thinking: A Seeker's ABC* (New York: HarperOne, 1993), 118.

6 But it didn't compare to what I said after the birth of our third child. After an intense labor, and *no* anesthesia, I ripped from one end to the other when the doctor suddenly needed to do a forceps delivery. As I was being sewn up, Denis *says*—I don't remember this, so perhaps it is fiction—I rose on my elbow and, in front of a very amused medical staff, swore that if he didn't get himself *fixed* he would never touch me again.

7 Honest. This was a season of life, not a lifelong pattern!

BOOK IV

1 Belden Lane, "Interview—Discovering the Desert Paradox," *Christian History Magazine,* Issue 64, https://christianhistoryinstitute.org/magazine/article/interview-discovering-the-desert-paradox.

2 I'm sheepish about this now, but that's how I saw it. On second thought, remembering how naïve he was, maybe I was right to feel superior?

3 Wade Bradshaw, *by demonstration: God* (Manchester, UK: Piquant Editions Limited, 2005), 40.

4 Thomas C. Oden, *The Good Works Reader* (Grand Rapids, MI: Eerdman's Publishing, 2007), 115.

5 James M. Houston, *The Disciple: Following the True Mentor* (Colorado Springs, CO: David C. Cook, 2007), 50.

6 "Stairway to Heaven" by Led Zepplin is considered by some to be one of the most popular rock songs of all time. Every young guitarist we knew made a point of learning it. https://en.wikipedia.org/wiki/Stairway_to_Heaven.

7 The definition of philosophy is instructive. It is the study of the fundamental nature of knowledge, reality, and existence, especially when considered as an academic discipline. Paul's quarrel is not with academic philosophy *per se,* nor is it with anyone who drafts persuasive and learned arguments to advance the gospel truth. Paul himself was well educated in these matters: he often appeals to philosophical ideas and uses sophisticated arguments to explain the Gospel more effectively (see Acts 17:16–34). Rather, Paul opposes those whose learning is used to advance falsehoods as gospel truth. *The IVP New Testament Commentary Series* explains this in more detail.

8 *Abraham Kuyper: A Centennial Reader,* edited by James D. Bratt (Grand Rapids, MI: Eerdman's Publishing, 1998), 488.

9 If you would like to explore these questions and their implications in greater detail I recommend *The Universe Next Door,* 5th ed., by James W. Sire (Downers Grove, IL: InterVarsity Press, 2009) which has become a classic. Sire carefully explains "worldview" and asserts that every religion and every philosophy answers questions about the meaning of life.

10 *All Shall Be Well: Daily Readings from Julian of Norwich,* edited by Sheila Upjohn (United Kingdom: Morehouse Publishing, 1994), 44.

11 In 1981 when we moved to Rochester, Minnesota, the Schaeffers had also moved there so Dr. Schaeffer could be treated for lymphoma at the Mayo Clinic. As his health allowed, he continued the work of L'Abri. We lived just three blocks from them and Denis became one of the few students to be mentored by him until his death in 1984.

12 Her name is changed to protect her identity.

ENDNOTES

BOOK V

1   This title was inspired by *The Story of a Soul* by Thérèse of Lisieux, a Carmelite nun who sought to follow Christ's "little way," learning to be content with her rate of growth and whatever task was before her whether great or small. She is famous for having said, "Jesus does not demand great actions from us but simply surrender and gratitude" (TAN Books; 2010).

2   John White, *Eros Defiled: The Christian and Sexual Sin* (Downers Grove, IL: InterVarsity Press, 1977), 44.

3   Zack Eswine, *Sensing Jesus: Life and Ministry as a Human Being* (Wheaton, IL: Crossway, 2013).

BOOK VI

1   Renee Baron and Elizabeth Wagele, *The Enneagram Made Easy: Discover the 9 Different Types of People* (New York: HarperCollins, 1994).

2   Ranald Macauley and Jerram Barrs, *Being Human: The Nature of Spiritual Experience* (Downers Grove, IL: InterVarsity Press, 1998).

3   J.I. Packer, *Knowing God* (Downers Grove, IL: InterVarsity Press, 1973).

4   Barrs, *Being Human*, 16.

5   Barrs, 18.

6   Barrs, 118.

7   Barrs, 119.

8   Barrs, 122.

9   Packer, *Knowing God,* 37.

10 Charles E. Cotherman, *To Think Christianly: A History of L'Abri, Regent College, and the Christian Study Center Movement* (Downers Grove, IL: InterVarsity Press, 2020), 43.

11 *The Sound of Life's Unspeakable Beauty,* by Martin Schleske, (Erdman's Publishing Company; 2020) 24-25. Translated by Janet Gesme. The author is quoting from Fulbert Steffensky's book *Feier des Lebens: Spiritualität im Alltag* (Stuttgart, 2003).

12 Wendell Berry, *Jayber Crow* (Washington, DC: Counterpoint, 2000), 133.

13 Kenneth Graham, *The Wind in the Willows* (New York: Simon & Schuster, 1908).

About the Author

MARGIE HAACK is a writer living in Savage, MN, with her husband Denis, on a half-acre lot next to a wooded park where she tries to attract bumble bees and hummingbirds with marginal success. Nature and place connect her to the spiritual geography that has shaped her. She has a deep love for home and hospitality, art and culture, and an awareness of God's presence in everyday life. It has been her persistent quest to name what is holy, what is funny, and what is suffering in the ordinary and routine. She and her husband delight in three adult children, their spouses, nine grandchildren, and a great-grandson. Between 1983 and 2020 they worked as directors of Ransom Fellowship, a ministry encouraging Christians to learn to be discerning and to live faithfully in the midst of our culture. Besides the *Place* trilogy, Margie's writing has appeared in *Arthouse America, Comment Magazine* and other publications. You can find both Margie and Denis' writing at *Critique-Letters.com*.

Acknowledgments

Much of this book was written during 2020—the Summer of COVID. Denis, my partner of many years, stepped up to help with domestic chores and that allowed me to spend hours at my desk. Because this book was about both of us, I wanted to go over each chapter together to make certain the stories matched our memories of what happened. Or, as he jokes, "let's make sure this isn't fiction." As we bent our heads over the words, it prompted him to remember things long forgotten, and that helped craft the story I tell. I appreciated his patience and many helpful suggestions. He is still my greatest inspiration, and did jolly well with all the revelations about our marriage that places us in sharp relief.

Many thanks to Ned and Leslie Bustard of Square Halo Books. They helped bring this project to life. By the time *No Place* was being written *The Exact Place* and *God in the Sink* (now *This Place*) were out of print. Ned's creative vision was to revise and release all three as a trilogy, recognizing they were all about Place and how it shapes us. They were encouraging and patient each step of the way.

I'm deeply grateful to Marsena Adams-Dufresne who is a superb manuscript editor and who spent hours pouring over these pages. I felt confident in her hands, knowing it would be so much better for the work she did.

I thought marriage challenged my selfishness and invaded my space, but it was nothing compared to babies and children. They drank my milk, pressed slobbery kisses on my face, ate the frosting from my cake, filled my drinks with backwash, and demanded hours of time. They taught me what it meant to so love another person you could gladly tolerate all this and much more. Well, almost all. I thank each of them—Marsena, Jerem, and Sember—for gracing my life.

Thanks to my writing group at Church of the Cross, who kindly critiqued parts of it along the way, especially Barbara LaTondress, and Sue Awes who was taken by COVID. She was a beautiful person, ever thoughtful, encouraging and enthusiastic. Emily Awes Anderson had constructive and insightful suggestions. She also gave permission for her poem to appear at the beginning of the book.

Nancy Nordstrum plowed through an early draft and calmed my fears, declaring it was a worthy effort.

Lauri Reiter and Barbara Beck, who were among the young people who spent time at His House back in the day (and still live in Albuquerque) graciously made the drive over to the old His House and sent photos of this unusual log cabin. Lauri also took time to paint the front door, and then sent me an unexpected, exquisite work of art.

I am still grateful for the many friendships we made during our years in New Mexico. These people enriched our lives and became part of our story, some of it untold. The Fongs and the Swearengens, the Bolins, Butch and Mary Williams, Ron and Barbara Miller and many others all helped shape who we are today. There was not space to include all that happened so some stories have been left out.

the exact PLACE

[AN EXCERPT]

Dog Days

A lot of things died on our farm. In fact, death was the fate of most farm animals. At a certain point of growth, fatness, or maturity, they were harvested, butchered, or sold to keep us alive. It was the expected destination for pigs, chickens, steers, old milk cows, and sometimes sheep. We didn't need to learn to live with it. It was simply the way life was.

One of the exceptions to this pattern was dogs. Dogs were purely for pleasure. Our dogs didn't herd, guard, or hunt, as some might expect. They were simply companions for children. They followed us to the pasture, to the woods, to the fields, and to the ditch to play in the water and catch frogs. They ran beside us and playfully pulled at our clothes and wrists. They licked us with their soft tongues and loved us with their fetid breath. However, Dad required them to keep a few rules just like everyone else.

By the time I was nine I had five brothers and sisters and Dad had distilled law for children into one basic rule: "Don't do as I do, do as I say." In other words, obey me. There wasn't any arguing or defense when you were confronted. Forgetting to feed the chickens, leaving a gate open so the livestock escaped, going to bed when told—those weren't unreasonable expectations for children. It was the sudden enforcement of a rule and a temper that could melt iron that kept me jumpy, a little afraid and anxious. I was always vigilant trying to discern unspoken rules conveyed by a look or a sudden movement of his hand. Did he want me to move that chair? Pass the salt?

At the supper table I was especially alert, ducking my head, averting my eyes and making sure I held my fork properly not using the fingers of my other hand to push food onto my fork. He taught me not to do that by hitting me with the flat blade of a dinner knife. The first time I didn't see it coming, and when it hit, a flaming ball formed in my throat and hot tears dripped to my lap. I quickly placed my hand under the table hiding the red welt, too ashamed to continue eating. It didn't take long to break me of that habit. I watched warily as he ate. He had his own way of hunkering over his plate holding his fork in his palm like one might hold a small scoop shovel while his other forearm rested on the table encircling his plate, a relaxed fist holding it in place. He never had to ask for anything to be passed, he merely stared at it until someone noticed.

The rules for dogs made sense and anyone could see that keeping them would certainly prolong their lives and happiness.

Dog's Rules were:

> Stay home.
> Don't chase vehicles.
> Don't bite humans.
> Don't eat chickens or their eggs.
> Don't chase deer.

Especially, don't chase deer. That was a crime so felonious, a dog caught chasing deer or even known to have once chased a deer could be shot by anyone on sight. Anyone. That wasn't just Dad's rule, it was upheld by everyone in our county. Deer were loved and protected by all. For despite their shyness and graceful beauty, which were truly appreciated, venison was considered one of the major food groups along with dairy products, vegetables, and dessert. Deer were never resented for crop damage as they daintily stepped through fields of alfalfa and wheat, fattening themselves for the fall hunt.

My husband and a friend from Texas once witnessed this last rule in action, and marveled at the casual nature of the enforcement. During deer hunting season, they were with my brother, Rex, who stopped his pickup in the middle of the road and got out to talk with Jerry Khrone, who was going the other direction. Jerry had also stopped his pickup in the middle of the road and got out to talk. They stood beside their pickups and spoke of this and that: The effects of weather on the buck rut, some fool who was arrested by the game warden for firing at a deer decoy the night before the season opened. As they visited, Jerry spotted a white dog loping across the far field. He paused a moment: "There's that damn Bjork dog. Been chasin' deer. That's it then." He reached into his pickup, pulled out his rifle, fired once, and the dog flipped into the air and died in the plowed field 250 yards away. Rex and Jerry continued to talk about doe permits as though he had merely paused mid-sentence to hawk one.

There were no rules for dogs about eating horse biscuits, rolling in ripe manure, or chasing skunks. That was expected and left plenty of room for amusement.

We owned a series of dogs each memorable in his own way, but the death of one still stands out. This dog broke a lot of rules, and we kids worried. Corky was part Dalmatian and part black Lab and was born with the temper of an old crank and the resolve of a terrorist. For one, as soon as he could walk, he had gone to the neighbors to check out the local females. For another, he declared war on any vehicle that drove by our farm. He'd lay in wait in the tall grass along the edge of the road, and as a car neared, he would jump out snarling and running after the tires, his teeth bared and his hair standing on end. Any kid within hearing distance would run toward the road screaming "Corky! Get back here!" Not that he ever paid us any mind. He'd come back with defiance in his eye, tongue hanging out, and his tail up—no remorse at all. He was an addict who couldn't help himself. Dad warned again and again that Corky was going to get himself killed.

This had already happened to one of our dogs—getting herself killed by a car. She was a sweet Dalmatian named Spotty, and we tried desperately to stop her from chasing cars. We begged and reasoned with her. We beat her. We tied her up, but there was always someone who couldn't bear the sad look on her face and would set her free. Nothing worked. The next thing she'd be hiding in the tall grass along the road and jumping out after anything that dared to drive by. Then one day a fisherman from the Twin Cities whizzed by in a big Buick, and as she chased his tires, he swerved and got her with a dull popping sound. She lifted her head from the gravel, looked at us with sad, apologetic eyes, and tried to drag herself toward us on her front legs.

We ran to her and Randy picked her up, a heavy load for a seven-year-old. He staggered down the drive. Our younger sister, Jan, and I trailed along beside him crying, "Don't die, Spotty, please don't die." As we laid her on the back steps, blood trickled out her nose and ears. She gazed at us with her dark blue eyes that slowly turned a milky gauze. Her body stayed warm and limp for a while, as though she were just napping and could still wake if she chose.

So even though Corky was not going to win any personality prizes, we still didn't want him to die that way. Certainly not that way.

His fatal infraction was the violation of a more serious rule: biting people. He was always short tempered about his food and bones. If you happened near him while he was eating, he would stop and hang over his bowl in a protective stance. His body would rumble, his lips lifting in a snarl.

I guess it was the danger or the challenge that drew my five-year-old brother, Rex, into teasing him. It was like playing roulette in a way. Grab Corky's bone, dangle it in the air above him, and Corky would go ravening, leaping and snapping for it. The trick was to let go of the bone at just the right moment without making contact with Corky's teeth. One day Rex misjudged and got bit . . .

· · ·

This story continues (and the PLACE trilogy begins) in
The Exact Place, available from Square Halo Books.

A good PLACE to find some great books . . .

THE EXACT PLACE: A SEARCH FOR FATHER
—BOOK ONE OF THE *PLACE* TRILOGY

"Margie tells the story of her childhood and of the discovery of the kindness of God and the meaning of home. As I read the story of young Margie's life, I reflected on my own, and wondered at the goodness in the ordinary—land well-tended, food well-prepared, children sheltered and fed with sweat and tears—and at the unfolding of hope in the midst of hardship and heartbreak."
—Gideon Strauss, academic dean of the Institute for Christian Studies

THIS PLACE: A FEW NOTES FROM HOME
—BOOK THREE OF THE *PLACE* TRILOGY

"Margie Haack tries to accept life as it presents itself rather than bending it toward her preferences. In her trials, joys and blunders, we see ourselves. And this is Margie's humble gift to us."
—Zack Eswine, author of *Sensing Jesus: Life and Ministry as a Human Being*

GODLY CHARACTER(S): INSIGHTS FOR SPIRITUAL PASSION
FROM THE LIVES OF 8 WOMEN IN THE BIBLE

". . . these 'great eight' propel you towards habits of godliness—putting you in a place to receive grace and fall more deeply in love with your savior—and that in His love you might be re-shaped and re-formed."
—Robert William Alexander, author of *The Gospel-Centered Life at Work*

A BOOK FOR HEARTS & MINDS: WHAT YOU SHOULD READ AND WHY

I thank God for Byron and Beth Borger—they are such solid gold people, and friends as well . . . While Hearts & Minds exists, serious Christian books can live too.
—Os Guinness, author of *Impossible People: Christian Courage and the Struggle for the Soul of Civilization*

NAILED IT: 365 READINGS FOR ANGRY OR WORN-OUT PEOPLE

". . . if you, like me, long for a devotional that is sharpening, witty, and downright real, well then, you simply must read this book."
—Karen Swallow Prior, author of *On Reading Well: Finding the Good Life Through Great Books*

GOOD POSTURE: ENGAGING CURRENT CULTURE WITH ANCIENT FAITH

"I couldn't recommend this book more highly. Please read it cover to cover. Please share it. And please, for the love of God, start living it."
—Scott Sauls, pastor and author of *Jesus Outside the Lines*

SquareHaloBooks.com